The Pianist's Guide to Transcriptions, Arrangements, and Paraphrases

The Pianist's Guide to Transcriptions, Arrangements, and Paraphrases

Maurice Hinson

INDIANA UNIVERSITY PRESS
Bloomington and Indianapolis

Manufactured in the United States of America

The paper used in this publication meets the minimum requirements of American
National Standard for Information Sciences—Permanence of Paper for Printed Library
Materials, ANSI Z39.48-1984.   ⊗™

Library of Congress Cataloging-in-Publication Data

Hinson, Maurice.
The pianist's guide to transcriptions, arrangements, and
paraphrases / Maurice Hinson.
p.   cm.
Bibliography: p.
ISBN 0–253–32745–8
1. Piano music—Bibliography.   2. Piano music, Arranged—
Bibliography.   3. Piano music—Bibliography—Graded lists.
4. Piano music (4 hands)—Bibliography.   5. Piano music (Pianos
(2))—Bibliography.   I. Title
ML 128.P3H536   1)90
016.7862'138'026— ic20   89-45356
                                       CIP

1 2 3 4 5   94 93 92 91 90

This volume is dedicated to Fernando Laires, dear friend and superb colleague, who not only suggested the topic but who also encouraged and inspired me from the beginning to its completion.

Contents

Preface   ix

Using the Guide   xiii

Abbreviations   xv

American Agents or Parent Companies of Music Publishers   xvii

Addresses of Music Publishers   xix

The Pianist's Guide to Transcriptions, Arrangements, and Paraphrases   1

Bibliography   153

Index of Transcriptions for One Hand   159

Preface

It is impossible to know exactly when the first transcriptions were made; in a sense a prehistoric tune played on a primitive pipe was a transcription from the human voice. Transcriptions are a natural evolutionary process. As new instruments were invented and developed, composers naturally took advantage of their new colors and ranges, readapting their works and those of others. With the modern piano being the single most versatile instrument in Western European music, it is understandable that we probably have more transcriptions for it than for any other instrument.

Transcription is a time-honored art. Its tradition flourished under J. S. Bach, continued with Liszt, Busoni, and Ravel, and even lives today. There was never a recital by a great virtuoso that did not feature some transcriptions, especially of Bach, when this writer was a boy. In fact, earlier in this century, and especially in the nineteenth century, important artists performed transcriptions of all sorts on their programs, and critics and the public unquestioningly accepted the practice. The piano transcription contributed a great deal to the musical life of the Romantic era and has been a significant factor in developing the full potential of the piano.

In 1940, Egon Petri (1881–1962), one of the greatest performers of transcriptions, made known his view of transcriptions:

> I think that all transcriptions should be considered as the transcriber's additions or interpretation, rather than the faithful reproduction of the original into another medium. . . . It can all be reduced to the problem of whether the end justified the means, whether the psychological disruption of an entity is counter-balanced with a new vital expression. . . .[1]

And Earl Wild has declared:

> As long as there are creative musicians who can improvise and imagine backgrounds and settings, the art of transcription will remain timeless.[2]

Starting about forty years ago, the purist approach to music gained in popularity, and piano transcriptions, arrangements, and paraphrases gradually disappeared from view. Only in the last few years have they begun to make a comeback.

The New Harvard Dictionary of Music defines transcription as:

> The adaptation of a composition for a medium other than its original one, e.g., of vocal music for instruments or of a piano work for orchestra, a practice that began in Western music by the 14th century.[3]

The same book defines arrangement as:

> The adaptation of a composition for a medium different from that which it was originally composed, usually with the intention of preserving the essentials of the musical substance; also the result of such a process of adaptation.[4]

Paraphrase is defined as:

> In the 19th century, a solo work of great virtuosity in which popular melodies, usually from operas, were elaborated (as in Liszt's *Rigoletto: Paraphrase de Concert,* 1860); such pieces could also be called Fantasia or Reminiscences and were distinguished from works attempting to be faithful transcriptions.[5]

These three definitions show an overlapping of characteristics, in particular, between transcription and arrangement. Many composers used the terms interchangeably. Paraphrase is more clearly set apart from the other two.

C. Hubert Parry believes an arrangement is more literal than a transcription,[6] but Leonard B. Meyer believes a transcription is more literal than an arrangement.[7] According to Meyer a transcription uses means "different from those of the original work . . . to represent it as accurately as possible," whereas an arrangement "generally involves significant additions to, or deletions from, or changes of order in the original."[8]

It appears that the differences between these terms are a matter of the degree to which the original model is altered. With these definitions we can say that the transcription is the closest to being a literal treatment of the original, the paraphrase is the freest, and the arrangement is somewhere in between.

Transcriptions, arrangements, and paraphrases are becoming accepted again as we begin to realize that there is value in music that can be shifted from one medium of performance to another, utilizing the coloristic and technical potential of that new medium. We are also beginning to let our ears be the judge. The *raison d'être* of transcriptions, arrangements, and paraphrases should be their merit and beauty as independent compositions. Surely the nineteenth-century transcription for piano is above all an exercise in, and a search for, sonority.

Paul Hindemith said,"An arrangement is artistically justified only when the arranger's artistic effort is greater than the original composer's."[9] The performer and/or listener must make that decision. I have tried to keep this statement in mind while selecting material for this volume, but I am the first to admit that this criterion has not always been followed.

The field of piano transcriptions, arrangements, and paraphrases is enormous. The Library of Congress holds over 150,000 such items. Therefore it was necessary to set guidelines for the selection process. My criteria, in addition to the Hindemith statement, were:

1. Published works only
2. No pedagogically oriented pieces unless they are unusually musical and effective

3. In general, pieces by well-known composers only (because of lack of space and time to examine those by unknowns)
4. Works for solo piano, piano duet (one piano, four hands), two pianos, and a few outstanding transcriptions for one hand

I have asked the following questions about each piece examined for inclusion in this volume:

1. Is this arrangement, transcription, or paraphrase acceptable as a musical entity?
2. Is it a finer composition than the original?
3. Is it pianistic, that is, does it truly suit the piano?
4. Is it in good taste?

For each piece included in this volume, I examined at least ten. I feel that all the pieces listed here are effective and worthy of inclusion in the pianist's repertoire. A major effort has been made to include the most important contributions of the greatest transcribers: J. S. Bach, Beethoven, Brahms, Busoni, Liszt, Rachmaninoff, and Ravel.

One question I constantly grappled with was originally asked by Busoni: "Why are Variations considered worthy because they change the original, while Arrangements are considered unworthy *because they also change the original?*" [10] I still have not found a reasonable answer to that very valid question!

Many people have generously given me their help in preparation of this volume. I gratefully acknowledge the assistance of Martha Powell, Music Librarian of The Southern Baptist Theological Seminary; Elmer Booze and Rodney Mill of the Library of Congress; David Fenske, Music Librarian at Indiana University; Charles Timbrell of Howard University; my graduate assistant, Thomas Seel; Konrad Wolff of New York City; and The Southern Baptist Theological Seminary for making possible the typing of the manuscript and the aid of graduate assistants through the years.

Without the generous assistance of numerous publishers this volume would not be possible. Special appreciation goes to Donald Gillespie of C. F. Peters Corp.; George Hotton of Theodore Presser Co.; Corey Field of European American Music; and John Dowd of Music Obscura.

The longer I have worked in the medium of transcriptions, arrangements, and paraphrases, the more aware I have become of its immensity. I have developed a great appreciation for what Sir Isaac Newton said 300 years ago:

I do not know what I may appear to the world, but to myself I seem only to have been like a little boy playing on the seashore, and diverting myself in now and then finding a smoother pebble or a prettier shell than ordinary, whilst the great ocean of truth lay all undiscovered before me.

NOTES

1. From MCA Westminster record jacket 1414.

2. From Audioform record jacket 2008-2.

3. Bruno Nettl, *The New Harvard Dictionary of Music* (Cambridge, MA, 1986), p. 866.

4. Ibid., p. 53.

5. Ibid., p. 508.

6. C. Hubert Parry, "Arrangement," *Grove's Dictionary of Music and Musicians,* 5th ed., edited by Eric Blom (New York, 1956), I, 223.

7. Leonard B. Meyer, *Music, the Arts, and Ideas* (Chicago, 1967), p. 195.

8. Ibid.

9. Paul Hindemith, *A Composer's World* (Cambridge, MA, 1952), p. 141.

10. Alan Walker, "In Defense of Arrangements," *The Piano Quarterly* 143 (Fall 1988):26.

Using the Guide

Arrangement of entries. The Guide consists of one alphabetic list containing both composers and transcribers. A work is described under the name of the original composer and cross-referenced under the name of the transcriber (arranger, paraphraser): e.g., "Busoni. See Bach, J. S." This system will help the user find a suitable transcription of a particular piece as well as demonstrate what prolific transcribers some of the major composers have been. In the case of a few major transcribers (e.g., J. S. Bach and Liszt), in addition to the cross-references to original composers, collections containing transcriptions of works by a variety of composers are described. There are two other exceptions: the heading "Christmas Music" contains only cross-references to original composers; and under the heading "Songs," the (mainly anonymous) entries are arranged alphabetically by title according to country.

Compositions are listed under the original composer's name by opus number, or by title, or by a combination of the two. If no scoring is given the transcription is for solo piano. "Duet" indicates four hands at one keyboard; "2 pianos" indicates two pianos, four hands, unless otherwise stated ("for 8 hands," etc.). A few important transcriptions for one hand are also included; see "Index of Transcriptions for One Hand." In the main, the works surveyed here are written for piano(s) alone, but a considerable number, especially among the transcriptions by J. S. Bach, are scored for piano(s) and a small instrumental ensemble or full orchestra.

Descriptions have been limited to general style characteristics, form, unusual qualities, interpretative suggestions, and pianistic problems inherent in the music. Editorial and transcription procedures found in a particular edition are often mentioned. The term "large span" is used when a span larger than an octave is required. "Octotonic" refers to lines moving in the same direction one or more octaves apart.

Grading. Three broad categories are used: Intermediate (Int.), Moderately Difficult (M-D), and Difficult (D). The following standard solo works will serve as a guide to the grading:

Int.: Bach, *Twelve Little Preludes and Fugues*
Beethoven, *Ecossaises*
Mendelssohn, *Children's Pieces*, Op. 72
Bartók, *Rumanian Folk Dances* Nos. 1–5
M-D: Bach, *French Suites; English Suites*
Mozart, *Sonatas*
Brahms, *Rhapsody*, Op. 79/2
Debussy, *La Soirée dans Granade*

D: Bach, *Partitas*
      Beethoven, *Sonata, Op. 57*
      Chopin, *Etudes*
      Barber, *Sonata*

These categories must not be taken too strictly; they give only general indications of technical and interpretative difficulties.

Details of entries. When known, the date of composition is given after the title of the work. Then, in parentheses, are as many of the following as apply to the particular work: the editor, the publisher, the publisher's edition number, and the copyright date. When more than one edition is available, the editions are listed in order of preference, the most desirable first. The number of pages and the approximate performance time are frequently listed. The spelling of the composers' names and of the titles of the compositions appear as they do on the music being described. Specifically related books, dissertations or theses, and journal articles are listed following individual compositions or at the conclusion of the discussion of a composer's works (a more extended bibliography appears at the end of the book).

Sample Entries and Explanations

J. S. Bach (1685–1750) Germany
Beloved Jesu, We Are Here (Liebster Jesu, wir sind hier), arr. by Harriet Cohen
      (OUP 1928; LC) 2 pp. M-D.
      The original German title follows the English; Oxford University Press is the publisher; 1928 is the date of publication; there is a copy in the Library of Congress. The piece is two pages long. The work is graded Moderately Difficult.

Johannes Brahms (1833–1897) Germany
Academic Overture, Op. 80, originally for orchestra, trans. by the composer for
      duet (Simrock 1881; LC) 27 pp. M-D.
      Brahms transcribed this work for piano duet (4 hands); Simrock is the publisher; 1881 is the publication date; the Library of Congress has a copy. It is 27 pages in length and is graded Moderately Difficult.

Franz Liszt (1811–1886) Hungary
Mephisto Waltz No. 1, G. 514, trans. by Ferruccio Busoni 1904 (GS 1649) 10
      min. D.
      G.514 is the *New Grove Dictionary* number; 1904 is the date of the transcription; G. Schirmer is the publisher; 1649 is the edition number. The performance time is approximately 10 minutes; the work is graded Difficult.

Other assistance. See "Abbreviations" for terms, publishers, books, and periodicals referred to in the text; and the directories "American Agent or Parent Companies of Music Publishers" and "Addresses of Music Publishers" to locate publishers.

Abbreviations

ACA	American Composers Alliance	IU	Music Library, Indiana University
AMC	American Music Center	JALS	*Journal of the American Liszt Society*
AMP	Associated Music Publishers		
		JF	J. Ficher
AMT	*American Music Teacher*	JWC	J. W. Chester
		K	Kalmus
Anh.	Anhang (appendix)	K&S	Kistner & Siegel
arr.	arranged	LC	Library of Congress
Bk(s).	Book(s)	MA	*Musical America*
BMC	Boston Music Co.	MC	Mildly contemporary
Bo&Bo	Bote & Bock	MCA	M.C.A. Music (Music Corporation of America)
Bo&H	Boosey & Hawkes		
Br	Bärenreiter	M-D	Moderately Difficult
Br&H	Breitkopf & Härtel	Mer	Mercury Music Corp.
BrM	British Museum	ML	*Music and Letters*
c.	Copyright	M&M	*Music & Musicians*
Cen	Century Music Publishing Co.	MMR	*Monthly Musical Record*
CF	Carl Fischer	MO	*Musical Opinion*
CFP	C. F. Peters	MQ	*Musical Quarterly*
CM	*Current Musicology*	MR	*Music Review*
D	Difficult	MT	*Musical Times*
DM	Diletto Musicale. See Doblinger	MTP	Music Treasure Publications
Dob	Doblinger	NLA	New Liszt Edition (Ausgabe)
EBM	E. B. Marks		
ECS	E. C. Schirmer	Nov	Novello
EMB	Editio Musica Budapest	NYPL	New York Public Library
EMT	Editions Musicales Transatlantiques		
		OD	Oliver Ditson
ESC	Max Eschig	OMB	Conselho Federal da Ordem dos Músicos do Brazil
EV	Elkan-Vogel		
Fl	Edwin A. Fleisher		
GS	G. Schirmer	Op.	Opus
Hin	Hinrichsen	OUP	Oxford University Press
IMC	International Music Co.	para.	paraphrased
IMI	Israel Music Institute	Ph	Philharmonic Edition
Int.	Intermediate difficulty	PIC	Peer International Corporation

PQ	*Piano Quarterly*	TP	Theodore Presser
PWM	Polskie Wydawnictwo Muzyczne	trans.	transcribed
rev.	revised	UCLA	University of California, Los Angeles
Ric	Ricordi	UE	Universal Edition
Ric Amer	Ricordi Americana S.A.	UME	Union Musical Española
Ric BA	Ricordi Argentina	UMP	United Music Publishers
SA	Sonata-Allegro	USSR	Mezhdunarodnaya Kniga (Music Publishers of the USSR)
Sal	Salabert		
SB	Summy-Birchard		
S&B	Stainer & Bell	Var(s).	Variation(s)
SBTS	Southern Baptist Theological Seminary	vol(s).	volume(s)
		VU	Vienna Urtext Edition (UE)
SP	Shawnee Press		
SZ	Suvini Zerboni	WH	Wilhelm Hansen

American Agents or
Parent Companies of Music Publishers

1. Alfred Publishing Co., Inc., 16380 Roscoe Boulevard, Van Nuys, CA 91410-0003.
2. Associated Music Publishers, Inc., P. O. Box 13819, Milwaukee, WI 53213.
3. CPP-Belwin, 15800 Northwest 48 Avenue, Miami, FL 33014.
4. Boosey & Hawkes, Inc., 62 Cooper Square, New York, NY 10013.
5. Broude Bros., Ltd., 141 White Oaks Road, Williamstown, MA 01267.
6. Concordia Publishing House, 3558 South Jefferson Avenue, St. Louis, MO 62118.
7. Elkan-Vogel Inc. (see Theodore Presser), Presser Place, Bryn Mawr, PA 19010.
8. European American Retail Music, Inc., Dept. NT, P. O. Box 850, Valley Forge, PA 19482.
9. Carl Fischer, Inc., 62 Cooper Square, New York, NY 10003.
10. Foreign Music Distributors, 13 Elkay Drive, Chester, NY 10918.
11. Hinshaw Music, Inc., P. O. Box 470, Chapel Hill, NC 27514.
12. Hal Leonard Publishing Corp., 8112 West Blue Mound Road, Milwaukee, WI 53213.
13. MMB Music, Inc., 10370 Page Industrial Boulevard, St. Louis, MO 63132.
14. Oxford University Press, Inc., 200 Madison Avenue, New York, NY 10016.
15. C. F. Peters Corp., 373 Park Avenue South, New York, NY 10016.
16. Theodore Presser Co., Presser Place, Byrn Mawr, PA 19010.
17. E. C. Schirmer Music Co., 112 South Street, Boston, MA 02111.
18. G. Schirmer, Inc., P. O. Box 13819, Milwaukee, WI 53213.
19. Shawnee Press, Inc., Delaware Water Gap, PA 18327.
20. Southern Music Publishing Co., 1740 Broadway, New York, NY 10019.
21. Summy-Birchard Co., P. O. Box 2072, Princeton, NJ 08540.
22. Warner Brothers Publications, Inc., 9000 Sunset Boulevard, Penthouse, Los Angeles, CA 90069.
23. Location or American agent unverified.

Addresses of Music Publishers

A number following the name of a publisher corresponds to that of its American agent or parent company (see previous directory).

Ahn & Simrock
  Meinekestrasse 10
  1 Berlin 15, West Germany
Allans Music Australia
  165 Gladstone Street
  South Melbourne, Victoria,
  3205 Australia
Alsbach   18
American Composers Alliance
  170 West 74 Street
  New York, NY 10023
American Music Center
  250 West 54 Street
  Room 300
  New York, NY 10019
Johann André
  Frankfurterstr. 28
  Offenbach am Main
  West Germany
Arizona State University Library
  Tempe, AZ 85281
Artia   4, 8, 10, 13
Edwin Ashdown, Ltd.   4
Ashley Dealers Service
  263 Veterans Boulevard
  Carlstadt, NJ 07072
Augener   17
Axelrod   19
Bärenreiter Verlag   9, 10, 13
Barry & Cia. (Argentina)   4
Belwin-Mills   2
Gerald Billaudot, Editeur   16
Boccaccini & Spada   16
F. Bongiovanni
  Via Rizzoli 28c
  Bologna, Italy

Boston Music Co.
  116 Boylston Street
  Boston, MA 02116
Bote & Bock   2
Bourne Publishing Company
  437 Fifth Avenue
  New York, NY 10016
Breitkopf & Härtel
  Postfach 1707
  D-6200 Wiesbaden 1
  West Germany
Brodt Music Co.
  P. O. Box 1207
  Charlotte, NC 28201
Century Music Publishing Co.
  (see Ashley Dealers)
Chappell & Co.   16
J. W. Chester   13
Choudens   7, 15
Franco Colombo   3
Conselho Federal da Ordem
  dos Músicos do Brasil
  Av. Almte, Barroso, 72-7° Andar
  2000 Rio de Janeiro (RJ) Brazil
Converse College Library
  Spartanburg, SC 29301
Costallat   16
J. Curwen & Son (England)   18
Oliver Ditson   16
Ludwig Doblinger   10
Dover Publications, Inc.   1
Durand & Cie   7
Elkin & Co., Ltd.   17
Enoch & Cie   2
Max Eschig   2
Faber Music   18

J. Fisher & Bro.   3
H. T. FitzSimons
  615 North LaSalle Street
  Chicago, IL 60610
Harold Flammer   22
Edwin Fleisher Music Collection
  Free Library
  Philadelphia, PA 19107
Foetisch Frères, S.A. (Switzerland) 17
Charles Foley, Inc.   3
Forberg   15
A. Forlivesi & Co.
  Via Roma, 4
  Florence, Italy
Forsyth Brothers, Ltd. (see Brodt)
Foster Music Publishing Co.
  Chicago, IL
Sam Fox Music Sales Corp.
  Plymouth Music Co., Inc.
  170 Northeast 33 Street
  Fort Lauderdale, FL 33334
Fromont   23
Adolph Fürstner
  55 Iverna Court
  London W8, England
Galaxy Music Corp.   17
Galliard, Ltd. (England)   17
Gutheil   4
Hamelle & Co. (France)   7
Wilhelm Hansen   13
Harms   22
Frederick Harris Music Co., Ltd.   9
  529 Speers Road
  Oakville, Ontario
  Canada L6K 2G4
Heinrichshofen Edition   21
G. Henle Verlag
  2446 Centerline Industrial Drive
  St. Louis, MO 63043
Henn Editions
  8 rue de Hesse
  Geneva, Switzerland
Heugel & Cie   16

Friedrich Hofmeister (Germany)   15
Hug (Switzerland)   15
Bruce Humphries   23
  Boston, MA
International Music Corp. (see Bourne
  Publishing Co.)
Israel Music Institute   4
Jean Jobert   16
P. Jürgenson
  Moscow 200, USSR
Kistner & Siegel   7
Kjos (Kjos West) Music Co.
  4382 Jutland Drive
  San Diego, CA 92117
Lea Pocket Scores   8
Alphonse Leduc   7, 13
Lee Roberts   18
Leeds Music Corp. (see MCA Music)
Alfred Lengnick & Co., Ltd. (see
  Frederick Harris Music Co.)
Collection Litolff   18
Lyra Music Co.
  133 West 69 Street
  New York, NY 10023
E. B. Marks   12
MCA Music   12
Mercury Music Corp.   16
Mezhdunarodnaya Kniga   18
  (Music Publishers of the USSR)
Millikin University Library
  Decatur, IL 62522
Mills Music   3
Möseler Verlag   13
Music Treasure Publications
  620 Fort Washington Avenue
  New York, NY 10040
Editio Musica Budapest   4
Musica Obscura
  P. O. Box 2586
  Quincy, MA 02269
Musical Scope Publishers
  Box 125, Audubon Station
  New York, NY 08401

Myklas Press
  P. O. Box 929
  Boulder, CO 80302
Arthur Napoleão
  Music Imports
  2571 North Oakland Avenue
  Milwaukee, WI 53211
New World Music Corp.   22
Novello   7
Oberlin College Library
  Oberlin, OH 44074
Paragon Music Publishers
  57 Third Avenue
  New York, NY 10023
Peer International Corp.   20
Piwarski Verlag
  Cracow, Poland
Pro-Art   23
Rahter   16
G. Ricordi & Co. (International)   18
Ricordi BA (Argentina)   18
E. Rouart, Lerolle & Co. (see Salabert)
Rozsavölgi
  P. O. Box 149
  Budapest, Hungary
Editions Salabert   18
Schlesinger, Schemusikhandlung
  Lankwitzerstrasse 9
  Berlin-Lichterfeld-Ost, Germany
Arthur P. Schmidt Co.   21
Schott   8
Schott Frères   8

Schroeder & Gunther   2
Seesaw Music Corp.
  2067 Broadway
  New York, NY 10023
Maurice Senart (see Salabert)
Hans Sikorski   18
Methuen Simpson   3
N. Simrock   16
Southern Baptist Theological
  Seminary
    Music Library
    2825 Lexington Road
    Louisville, KY 40280
Stainer & Bell   17
Edizioni Suvini Zerboni
  Via M. F. Quintiliano, 40
  I-20138 Milan, Italy
Thames Music Publishing Co.
  14 Barlby Road
  London W. 10, England
Universal Edition   8
University of Kentucky Music Library
  Lexington, KY 40506
Wheaton College Library
  Wheaton, IL 60187
Willis Music Co.
  7380 Industrial Road
  Florence, KY 41042
Wright State University Library
  Dayton, OH 45435
Wilhelm Zimmermann   17
  Musikverlag

Publishers No Longer in Existence

Am-Rus Music Corp.
Delkas
Haslinger
Kunkel
Mackar & Noel

Mechetti
Richault
Shattinger
Troupenas

The Pianist's Guide to
Transcriptions, Arrangements,
and Paraphrases

A

Denes Agay (1911–   ) USA, born Hungary
See Handel; Songs, Hungarian; Songs, Israeli

Guido Agosti (1901–   ) Italy
See Stravinsky, I.

Julian Aguirre (1868–1924) Argentina
See Songs, Argentinian

Isaac Albéniz (1860–1909) Spain
Albéniz was a prolific composer for the piano and one of Spain's finest pianists. His works are a composite of Lisztian pianistic techniques and the idioms and rhythms of Spanish popular music.

Catalonia, originally for orchestra, trans. for duet by René de Castéra (Durand 1908; LC) in 3 parts. Part I, 19 pp. Strong rhythms, carefully laid out, some tremolos, strong waltz feeling in parts. M-D.

Spanish Rhapsody, Op. 70, originally composed for 2 pianos in 1886, trans. by Cristobal Halffter (UME 1962; IMC) 12 min. Transcription provides an effective complement and adds strength and a pedestal that shows off the work beautifully. Lisztian; concert-popularistic in tone. M-D.

Tango, Op. 165/2, originally for solo piano, trans. for duet by Ralph Berkowitz (EK 1941; LC) 5 pp. Very effective, lends itself to duet, easier than original. Int.

————. Trans. by Leopold Godowsky (CF; Schott). This transcription still appears in recitals and is generally preferred to the rather dull original. M-D.

Triana, from *Iberia* (CF 1938). Concert arrangement by Leopold Godowsky, dedicated to Arthur Rubinstein. Godowsky transformed this gypsy panache into a new piece—full of slithering chromaticism. D.

Eugen D'Albert (1864–1932) Germany, born Scotland
See Bach, J. S.

Alexander Aliabiev (1787–1851) Russia
Bohemian Song, song, 1842, trans. by Franz Liszt G.250 (Cranz). Canonic imitation is featured in the middle section, and the Allegro begins the development in florid, arabesque style, with a climax at the *ff* and a *pp* coda. The final four pages are the most effective. A complete virtuoso piece in miniature; an ideal closer for a recital. M-D.

1

The Nightingale, song, 1842, trans. by Franz Liszt G.250/1 (GS; UE). Also in collection *Twenty Piano Transcriptions by Franz Liszt* (A. Spanuth—OD 1903). This Russian song is generally not known, but the transcription is, and it makes a delightful piece. The accompaniment trill forms a useful study. This piece is a souvenir of Liszt's visit to St. Petersburg in 1842. M-D.

Charles Henri Valentin Alkan (1813–1888) France
Concerto da Camera I, Op. 10, trans. by the composer (Billaudot 2251) 23 pp. Allegro moderato; Adagio; Rondo:Allegro. Sonorous effects, virtuosic, like Liszt and Berlioz combined. D.
See also Bach, J. S.; Mozart; Weber

P. Humberto Allende (1885–1959) Chile
See Songs, Chilean

Anonymous
See Songs, French

George Anson (1903–1985) USA
See Raff

Thoinot Arbeau (1520–1595) France
Dance tunes from *Orchéographie* (1588). See Warlock.

Anton Arensky (1861–1906) Russia
Valse, from *Suite in Canon-Form* for 2 pianos, Op. 15, arr. by Carl Deis (GS 1925; LC) 12 pp. Retains the lilt and charm of the original but sonorities are overstretched in the *ff* parts. M-D.
————. Trans. freely by Vernon Warner (Bosworth 1935; LC) 8 pp. A little easier than the above but still about M-D.

Thomas Arne (1710–1778) Great Britain
Sonata for two pianos, arr. by Geoffrey Bush (Augener 1952; LC) 8 pp. Based on No. 5 of the *Sonatas* (or Lessons) for the harpsichord by Arne. Poco largo. Untitled second movement, just two lines: a short cadenza. Gavotta: interesting counterpoint. Int to M-D.

E. H. Mueller von Asow (1892–1964) Germany
See Mozart

Louis Aubert (1877–1968) France
Habanera, originally for orchestra, trans. for duet by the composer (Durand 1919; LC) 13 pp. *Langoureusement* opening, builds to big climax, strong rhythms, *ppp* closing. Requires numerous tempo subtleties. M-D.

George Auric (1899–1983) France
Les Fâcheux, originally a ballet, transcription de Concert by the composer (Rouart, Lerolle 1926; LC) 1. *Le Maître à dancer:* contrasting sections,

flowing, large ending. 2. *Nocturne:* bitonal, contando lines, *pp* ending. 3. *Les joueurs de boules:* chordal, *vivace e nettamente*. Eloquent melodies, strong rhythms. Fluent and attractive writing throughout. Int. to M-D.

Stanley R. Avery (–   )
See Haydn

B

Victor Babin (1908–1972) USA, born Russia

Three March Rhythms, arr. for 2 pianos (Br&H 1953; LC) 44 pp. *Military:* loosely based on "Taps" rhythm. *Funeral:* intense and expressive. *Processional:* scales, forceful, *maestoso* ending. M-D.

See also Bach, J. S.; Beethoven; Khachaturian; Milhaud; Rimsky-Korsakov; Stravinsky, I.; Telemann

C. P. E. Bach (1714–1788) Germany

Solfeggietto, from *Musikalisches Vielerley* (1770), trans. for 2 pianos by Richard McClanahan (Mills 1953; LC) 8 pp. First piano has the original piece, second piano adds a chordal accompaniment. Includes performance suggestions. Int.

————. With improvisation for second piano by Sylvia Rabinof (Belwin-Mills 1988) 6 pp. Thickens original textures considerably, but this is generally effective. Int.

————. Arr. for left hand by A. R. Parsons. In collection *Piano Music for One Hand,* edited by R. Lewenthal (GS 1971). Very effective. M-D.

Johann Christian Friedrich Bach (1732–1795) Germany

See Songs, French

Johann Sebastian Bach (1685–1750) Germany

Bach was greatly interested in arranging his own works as well as works by other composers. His keyboard transcriptions were part of a long and deeply rooted tradition. When Bach arranged orchestra concertos for keyboard instruments, he was simply following an old organist's custom of transcribing ensemble music for a solo instrument. This practice, known as intabulation, was widespread during the fifteenth and sixteenth centuries and forms the historical background for Bach's keyboard arrangements. See Theodor Göllner, "J. S. Bach and the Traditions of Keyboard Transcriptions," in *Studies in Eighteenth-Century Music,* edited by H. C. Robbins Landon (New York: Oxford University Press, 1970), pp. 253–260.

Adagio, from *Sonata* for piano and violin in f, trans. by Alexander Siloti (CF 1927; LC) 5 pp. Full chords over arpeggio and scalar left-hand figuration; requires excellent control of left hand. M-D.

Adagio, from *Organ Toccata* No. 1, in C, trans. by Myra Hess (OUP 1937; LC) 3 pp. Walking bass in octaves, beautiful treatment of melodic line. M-D.

Adagio in a, from *Concerto for Two Claviers* in C, BWV 1061, trans. for 2

pianos by Eric Steiner (Belwin-Mills 1962) 7 pp. Flowing, tranquil, lovely. Int. to M-D.

Adagio in G, BWV 968. In collection *At the Piano with J. S. Bach* (Hinson— Alfred 1987). A beautiful transcription by the composer of the first movement of the Sonata in C for unaccompanied violin, BWV 1005. Very effective. M-D.

Air in D (Air for the G String), from *Overture* in D, originally for orchestra, arr. for 2 pianos by Guy Maier (JF, 1940; LC) 7 pp. First piano part is easier than second. Teacher and student or two students of different grades can play this. Int. to M-D.

Allegro in g, from *Sonata* No. 3 for viola da gamba and harpsichord, set for 2 pianos by Ralph Berkowitz (EV 1937; LC) 15 pp. Octotonic, frequent use of octaves in both parts. M-D.

Andante, from *Sonata* for violin solo in a, trans. by Alexander Siloti (CF 1927; LC) 2 pp. Beautifully realized. M-D.

————. Trans. by Harold Bauer (TP 1950; LC) 2 pp. Slightly easier than the Siloti transcription and almost as effective. M-D.

Andante, from *Concerto* No. 3 in c, originally for 2 keyboards and orchestra, trans. for 2 pianos by Alexander Siloti (CF 1927; LC) 15 pp. Fingered, pedaled, and edited to bring out the most important part(s). M-D.

Andante, from *Brandenburg Concerto* No. 2, trans. by Siloti for 2 pianos (CF 1927; LC) 9 pp. Includes pedal markings and fingering. Phrases marked ⌐⌐ are to be brought out distinctly; contains some left-hand octaves near *fff* climax and end of the piece. Effective use of both instruments. M-D.

Andante in F, from *Clavier Sonata* in d, conceived for 2 pianos by Cyril Scott (Elkin 1928; LC) 7 pp. Expressive, very beautiful melodies, excellent version. M-D.

Aria, from *Suite* in D, trans. by Franco Mannino, Op. 213 (Boccaccini & Spada 1986) 2 pp. Left hand moves in slow octaves throughout; full harmonies, fingering and dynamics given. Int. to M-D.

Arioso (Largo), from *Harpsichord Concerto* in f, trans. by Alfred Cortot (Foetisch Frères 1947). Fingered; beautifully laid out. M-D.

Arioso, trans. by Max Pirani (GS 1917; LC) 3 pp. Some hand-crossings in accompaniment part, pedal indications. M-D.

"Awake Thou Wintry Earth," chorale from *Church Cantata* No. 129, arr. for 2 pianos by Leslie Russell (OUP 1950; LC) 6 pp. Animato. Includes words for chorale in the musical score. Somewhat thick texture but can be effective. M-D.

Bach Organ Preludes, trans. by Johana and Roy Harris (Mills 1946; LC) 7 pp. *Come God, Creator, Holy Ghost; Christ Lay in the Bonds of Death; The Old Year Has Passed Away; Dearest Jesus, We Are Here; In Sweet Jubilation.* "To insure perfect finger legato, students should study without pedal. Pedal at change of harmony may be added later for luminosity" (from the Preface). Performance suggestion given for each prelude. M-D.

Two Bach Works for Two Pianos (SP 1979; LC) 12 pp. *In Thee is Gladness,* trans. by Wallace Hornibrook. Moderato, octaves and eighths, allargando and crescendo ending. *Today Triumphs God's Son,* trans. by Charles Webb. *Maestoso,* chorale easily heard; omits all fermatas in original edition. M-D.

Be Contented, O My Soul, trans. for 2 pianos by Harriet Cohen (OUP 1950; LC) 8 pp. Adagio recitative. Allegretto aria: should be played with a lightly flowing easy rhythm and a bright, clear quality of tone. M-D.

Beloved Jesu, We are Here (Liebster Jesu, wir sind hier), arr. by Harriet Cohen (OUP 1928; LC) 2 pp. Florid melody accompanied by *legatissimo* bass and inner voices. M-D.

Blithe Bells, trans. by Percy Grainger, 1931 (GS). A "free ramble by P. Grainger on an Aria by Bach." One of Grainger's best transcriptions, but those expecting the familiar strains of "Sheep may safely grace" from Bach's *Cantata* No. 208 should be prepared for an extraordinary change of shape, color, and harmony! Beginning with Grainger's notion that Bach "may have aimed at giving a hint of the sound of sheep bells" and also conveying his belief that the three greatest composers were Bach, Delius, and Duke Ellington, there is nothing quite like this very sincere act of homage. Concert version: M-D. Easy version (no large stretches): Int.

————. Trans. for 2 pianos by Percy Grainger (GS).

Bourrée, from *Violin Partita* No. 2, arr. by Ignaz Friedman (Allans 1947; LC) 5 pp. Arpeggiated tenths, bass octaves, inner 16th-note voices, pedaled and fingered. M-D.

————. Arr. by Camille Saint-Saëns (CF 1909; LC) 4 pp. More difficult to bring off than the Friedman arrangement. M-D.

Brandenburg Concerto No. 3, trans. by Ignaz Friedman. In collection *Piano Arrangements of Popular Classics* (Allans 1225) 14 pp. Uses many octaves and full chords. Dynamics, articulation, and fingering by Friedman. Wide dynamic range, exploits the instrument. M-D.

Brandenburg Concertos, arr. for duet by Max Reger. Vol. I: Nos. 1–3; vol. II: Nos. 4–6 (K 03037, 03028; IMC). Reger has kept his arrangements as literal as possible and yet they are very much conceived in terms of the keyboard. He has resolved the problem with no fuss and without imposing his own personality. Highly effective. M-D.

Chaconne, originally for violin, BWV 1004, trans. by Arthur Briskier (CF); Ferruccio Busoni (GS 1579); and Alexander Siloti (CF). The Busoni and Siloti transcriptions are more like "free arrangements," while Briskier's version respects more of Bach's intentions as revealed in the autograph. But Busoni and Siloti managed by skillful use of all the piano's resources to give the work a wholly new personality without altering its thematic and rhythmic content. Busoni searched for a grandeur and richness that he felt the piano sonority could provide and gave us a work of monumental proportions. M-D to D.

————. Trans. for left hand alone by Johannes Brahms (Br&H; Dover; Ric; Simrock). Closer to the original than Busoni's setting. Effective. M-D.

————. Trans. for the left hand by Joachim Raff (Durand). Virtuosic. D.

————. Trans. for the left hand by Paul Wittgenstein, in *School for the Left Hand,* vol. 3: *Transcriptions* (UE 12329). This is a transcription of the Brahms transcription. Helpful fingering and pedaling. M-D to D.

————. Trans. for the left hand by Géza Zichy (Rahter). More efficient than the Raff version.

Chorale Preludes for Organ, trans. by Wilhelm Kempff (Bo&Bo). *Befiehl du diene Wege* (S. 727); *Es ist gewisslich an der Zeit* (S. 734); *Ich ruf zu dir, Herr Jesu Christ* (S. 639); *In dulci jubilo* (S. 751); *Nun komm' der Heiden Heiland* (S. 659); *Wachet auf! ruft uns die Stimme* (S. 645); *Wir danken dir, Gott, wir danken dir* (S. 29). These are similar and comparable to the transcriptions made by Ferruccio Busoni. Kempff makes clear distinctions between the various parts and uses ingenious fingering to create beautiful legato (without relying totally on the pedal). He also seems to enjoy the interplay of tone colors, finding the right register, and establishing the particular timbre of each part in polyphonic writing. M-D.

Chorale Preludes for Organ, trans. by Ferruccio Busoni, 2 vols. (Br&H; CF). *Komm, Gott, Schöpfer, Heilger Geist* (BWV 667); *Wachet Auf, ruft uns die Stimme* (BWV 645); *Nun komm' der Heiden Stimme* (BWV 659); *Nun freut euch, lieber christen* (BWV 734); *Ich ruf' zu dir, Herr Jesus Christ* (BWV 639); *Herr Gott, Nun Schleuss den Himmel auf!* (BWV 617); *Durch Adams Fall ist ganz verderbt* (BWV 637, 705; two versions); *In dir ist Freude* (BWV 615); *Jesus Christus unser Heiland* (BWV 665). Busoni refers to these transcriptions as written "in chamber music style," as opposed to "concert arrangements." He took some liberties, especially in changing melodic registers and in adding arbitrary repeats. But these arrangements make for marvelous piano music, which exists unashamedly on its own terms, with no serious attempt to imitate organ sonorities. They add immeasurably to the piano repertoire. Int. to M-D.

Chorale Preludes, Series I, arr. by Walter Rummel (JWC 1926; LC). Published separately. *Mortify Us By Thy Grace; Ah! How Ephemeral, How Transitory is Man's Life; Blessed Jesus Here We Stand; Our Father in Heaven; What God Hath Done, is Rightly Done; The Old Year Now Hath Passed; Jesus Christ the Son of God.* Handled very musically and fit the piano well. There are three more series, with seven pieces in each. M-D.

Two Chorale Preludes, originally for organ, arr. for 2 pianos by Christopher Le Fleming (JWC). *Mortify Us By Thy Grace; Jesus, Source of Our Desire.* Effective. Int. to M-D.

Eleven Chorale Preludes from the Little Organ Book, trans. for 2 pianos by C. H. Stuart Duncan (GS 1949; LC) 27 pp. Includes a broad variety of chorale preludes such as: *Christ lay in the bonds of death; In sweet jubilation; Dearest Jesus, we are here; Jesus, my joy.* Occasional doubling in octaves. M-D.

Thirty Chorales, arr. for duet by Louise R. Crosby (Schroeder & Gunther, 1931; LC) 35 pp. Delightfully effective. A wonderful way to introduce early grade pianists to this great body of literature. Easy to Int.

Cinq Chorales et un air, freely adopted by Isidor Philipp, Op. 81 (Heugel 1931; LC) 22 pp. *Herzlich thut mich verlangen; Freuet Euch, ihr Christen alle; Es ist vollbracht!; Seigneur Jesus, que ton aide; Christ, le seul fils de Dieu; Christen mussen auf der Erden.* Uses the full resources of the instrument in nineteenth-century fashion. M-D.

Christmas Pastoral (Pastoral Symphony from *Christmas Oratorio*), trans. by Clarence Lucas (OUP 1933; LC) 5 pp. Allegretto grazioso. Pedal with each change of harmony; pianistic. M-D.

————. Trans. for 2 pianos by Otto Vrieslander (Hin 1959; LC) 7 pp.

Pastoral Symphony, from *Christmas Oratorio,* trans. for 2 pianos by John Odum (Curwen 1955; LC) 8 pp. This piece lends itself naturally to two pianos. Excellent version. M-D.

Es ist gewisslich an der Zeit, BWV 734, chorale prelude, arr. by Wilhelm Kempff (Bo&Bo 1954; LC) 4 pp. Chorale is given at beginning. Kempff's arrangement has the chorale melody in the tenor voice, accompanied by fast-moving 16ths. M-D.

Four Etudes from the Cello Suites of Bach, trans. by Alexander Siloti, vol. II of *Transcriptions for the Young* (Gutheil 1925; LC) 15 pp. Prelude, from *Suite* No. 3; Bourrée, from *Suite* No. 3; Prelude, from *Suite* No. 1; Courante, from *Suite* No. 1. Mainly one line, frequently tossed between the hands. Clever and most effective for the less-advanced student. Int.

Quatre Etudes, trans. by Isidor Philipp for the left hand (Jobert 1963) 19 pp. Prelude in E; Bourrée in b; Presto in g; Chaconne in d. Remarkably effective. M-D to D.

Extended Chorale on "Jesu, Meine Freude," trans. by Willard Palmer (Alfred 1987) 2 pp. Originally a vocal chorale. New material has been added to the phrases of the chorale, mainly by use of seventh chords; flexible meters 4/4 to 2/4 and back again. Int.

Fantasy and Fugue on Bach, BWV 529 (Cortot—Sal 1949) 22 pp. Trans. by Franz Liszt in 1871 for piano from his organ version of 1855. As effective on the piano (if not more so) than on the organ. D.

Final Aria, from *Cantata* No. 36, *Schwingt freudig euch empor,* trans. by Harold Bauer (GS 1939) 8 pp. Flowing; use of *una corda* pedal; fingered; inner voices; eminently pianistic. M-D.

Thirty-Six Fugues, arr. for duet from the "Forty-Eight" by Charles Proctor (Lengnick: LC). Published separately. Includes from Vol. I: Nos. 1, 2, 4, 6, 7, 9, 10, 11, 12, 14, 15, 16, 17, 19, 20, 21, 24; from Vol. II: Nos. 1, 2, 4, 5, 6, 7, 9, 10, 11, 12, 14, 15, 16, 17, 19, 20, 21, 24. Effective and much easier to handle than the original. Int. to M-D.

Fugue in g (The Little), BWV 598, trans. by Arthur Briskier (CF 1954; LC) 9 pp., 4 min. Use of *sostenuto* pedal is clearly indicated. The organ-pedal notes are played by the left hand in octaves. "For clarity and smooth interpretation, some notes are played one octave higher or one octave lower, or are sometimes omitted" (from the Foreword). M-D.

————. Trans. for 2 pianos by Silvio Scionti (Ric 1940; LC) 12 pp. Gigantic conclusion. M-D.

————. Trans. by Olga Samaroff (EV 1931) 7 pp. One of the finest piano transcriptions of Bach. M-D.

Gavotte, from *Sonata* No. 2 for violin, trans. by Camille Saint-Saëns (GS 1912) 5 pp. Many bass octaves, texture thickened from original, numerous rolled chords of the tenth. M-D.

Gavotte in E, from *Sonata* No. 6 for unaccompanied violin, arr. by Ignaz Friedman (Allans 1948; LC) 7 pp. In spite of some "too full" textures the piece comes off well in this arrangement. M-D.

————. Trans. for the left hand by Raphael Joseffy. In collection *Piano Music for One Hand,* edited by R. Lowenthal (GS 1972). Joseffy's realization of the ornaments is debatable, but this transcription is a little gem. M-D.

"God Hath Filled the Hungry," aria from *Magnificat,* arr. for duet by Donald Waxman (Galaxy 1968) 9 pp. Originally scored for contralto, two flutes, and continuo. Primo plays the flute parts; Secondo plays the alto aria in the right hand and the continuo line in the left. In places a harmonic realization has been added to the Secondo part (in small notes). Beautifully realized. M-D.

"Gone is Sorrow, gone is Sadness," from *Cantata* No. 32, trans. for 2 pianos by Silvio Scionti (Ric 1940; LC) 10 pp. Fingered and pedaled; eloquent. M-D.

I Call Upon Thee, Lord (Ich ruf' zu dir, Herr Jesus Christ), chorale prelude, trans. for 2 pianos by Joan Lovell (OUP 1948; LC) 3 pp. The accompaniment must flow freely; the chords of the part with the melody must be played softly so that the tune can stand out clearly. M-D.

Italian Concerto, BWV 971, arr. in harpsichord style for 2 pianos by Harold Bauer (GS 1931; Converse College Library) 39 pp. Many doublings of pitch one or two octaves higher than written or one octave lower than written in an effort to reproduce 8', 4', and 2' pitches on the harpsichord. M-D.

————. Arr. by Alexander Siloti for solo piano with second accompanying piano as an orchestral part (CF 1930). Solo part is the original; accompanying part contains many additions that fit in most effectively. M-D.

Invention No. 8 in F, BWV 779, with improvisation for second piano by Sylvia Rabinof (Belwin-Mills 1987) 4 pp. Bach has not been changed; the written-out improvisation is in the second piano part, which adds interest and sparkle with substance and good taste. Int. to M-D.

I Step Before Thy Throne, O Lord, chorale prelude, arr. by Egon Petri (Bo&H 1945; LC) 4 pp. Each part starts with the diminution of the following chorale strophe, which is answered in the inversion and in stretto. Requires playing simply, sincerely, and beautifully. M-D.

"Jesu, Joy of Man's Desiring" (Jesus bleibt meine Freude), from *Cantata* No. 147, trans. by Harold Bauer (GS 1932; University of Kentucky Music Library) 7 pp. More octaves in the melody than in the Myra Hess version. Does not use triplets with chorale at all times; thicker textures than Hess version; builds to big climax *(ff)* before subsiding. M-D.

————. Trans. by Wilhelm Kempff (Bo&Bo). A free paraphrase. M-D.

————. *Chorale* from *Cantata* No. 147. Arr. for 2 pianos by Myra Hess from her piano solo transcription (OUP 1935; LC) 6 pp. Also available in duet form (OUP). One of the most famous transcriptions in the repertoire, and duly justified. M-D.

————. Trans. for 2 pianos by Victor Babin (Bruce Humphries, 1946; LC) 7 pp. Places more inner voices in first piano part than does the Hess edition. M-D.

Jig Fuge in G, conceived for 2 pianos by Cyril Scott (Elkin 1936; LC) 11 pp. Rolls along with clever additions by Scott; fast-moving chords. M-D.

"Komm, süsser Tod" (Come, sweet death), chorale, arr. by Harold Bauer (GS 1942) 3 pp. Full harmonies, all three pedals used. One of Bauer's most effective arrangements. Int. to M-D.

————. Trans. for 2 pianos by Mary Howe (Ric 1942; LC) 6 pp. Simple and effective version. Int. to M-D.

Kunst der Fuge (Art of Fugue), new version for 2 pianos by Walter Frey (Eulenburg GM 880 1980) 119 pp. Original instrumentation unknown. Concludes with chorale "Christ Lay in Death's Dark Prison," of which Frey says: "It is in the same key in which we have to end, and in all of its 16 bars and in all its main parts it bears a relationship to the main Theme of the *Art of Fugue.*" Also includes performance remarks and comments on the individual fugues. The work is well laid out for the two instruments. Frey makes this medium very appealing. Requires advanced pianistic equipment and much performing experience in the medium. D.

Largo, from *Keyboard Concerto* in f, BWV 1056, trans. by Wilhelm Kempff (Bo&Bo). A free paraphrase. M-D.

Six Little Pieces, trans. by Edward MacDowell (Musica Obscura) 13 pp. *Courante* in A; *Menuet* in G; *Gigue* in A; *Menuet* in F; *Menuet* in G; *Marche* in D. These are elaborations of the pieces in Bach's notebooks—for Anna Magdalena, etc. They are interesting for the view of Baroque music that MacDowell and others held around 1890, when they were arranged. Some textures are thickened; frequent use of octaves; highly edited. Stylistically out of character but contain some charming moments. M-D.

A Little Prelude in E Minor, from *Eight Short Preludes for Organ,* arr. freely by Harold Darke (OUP 1948; LP) 4 pp. Flows naturally; uses numerous left-hand octaves; grace notes. M-D.

Meditation, based on Prelude No. 1 from *WTC* I, as trans. by Charles Gounod, trans. for left hand by Paul Wittgenstein in *School for the Left Hand,* vol. 3: *Transcriptions* (UE 12329). Comes off well in this version. M-D.

O Mensch, Bewein' Dein Sunde Gross, chorale prelude, arr. by James Friskin (CF 1959; LC) 3 pp. Requires careful counting and bringing out of the melody in a singing and expressive manner. M-D.

Morning Song (Wachet auf, ruft uns die Stimme), second version, chorale from *Cantata* No. 162, arr. by Ignaz Friedman (Allans 1948; LC) 5 pp. Other than a few awkward, widely arpeggiated chords, this piece flows nicely. Left-hand octaves; chorale melody indicated in climax for voice leading. M-D.

––––––. *Sleepers Wake,* arr. by Christopher Le Fleming (JWC). Thinner sonorities than the Friedman arrangement. M-D.

"My Heart Ever Faithful," aria from *Pentecost Cantata,* trans. for 2 pianos by Nicolai Mednikoff (CF 1942; LC) 11 pp. Arpeggios, octave runs, full chords, quite elaborate. M-D.

––––––. Trans. by Ignaz Friedman, in collection *Piano Arrangements of Popular Classics* (Allans 1225) 6 pp. Fingered, pedaled, and articulated by Friedman. Some left-hand crossings over right hand; melody moves through various voices. Final statement of melody uses octaves and chords, *ff* closing. M-D.

"My Soul Doth Rest in Jesus Keeping," from *Cantata* No. 127, arr. by Harold Bauer (GS 1944; LC) 5 pp. Contains a most beautiful *molto tranquillo* section. M-D.

Now Comes the Gentle Saviour, chorale prelude, arr. for 2 pianos by Pierre Luboshutz (JF 1937; LC) 7 pp. Adagio, much octotonic usage, big ending. M-D.

Oeuvres d'Orgue de J. S. Bach, trans. for 2 pianos by Isidor Philipp (Ric; LC) 37 pp. Toccata; Adagio and Fugue. Facile transcription that uses the resources fully. M-D to D.

Orchestral Suites, arr. by Max Reger for duet (CFP; IMC; K). Reger's approach to these four arrangements is to suppress his own personality in the interest of Bach's music. Effective. M-D.

Three Organ Chorale Preludes, arr. by Max Reger (Br&H 5753; LC) 3 pp. *Es ist das Heil uns kommen her; Liebster Jesu, wir sind hier; Vom Himmel hoch, da komm ich her.* Contain numerous moving voices that arrive where they are supposed to, after much chromatic movement. M-D.

Three Organ Chorale Preludes, arr. for 2 pianos by Lee Hoiby (Bo&H 1965; LC) 15 pp. *Erst ander is der Heil' ge Christ; Meine Seele erhebt den Herrn; In dir ist Freude.* Much octotonic usage, chorale tunes clearly heard; fluent counterpoint. M-D.

Organ Fantasia and Fugue in g, BWV 542. Trans. by Franz Liszt (GS 25544 1915) 17 pp. Edited and fingered by August Fraencke. Contains numerous *ossias,* pedal marks, and long crescendos. Virtuosic ending. M-D to D.

––––––. Trans. by Arthur Briskier (CF 1957; LC) 15 pp. Faithful to the original, although in some instances notes are written an octave higher or lower in order to make them playable on one keyboard. Use of the *sostenuto* pedal is clearly indicated. Phrasing, dynamics, fingering, and metronome marks are editorial. Requires a round, full, and deeply felt singing tone. M-D to D.

Organ Prelude in E minor, trans. by Alexander Siloti (CF 1928; LC) 2 pp. Pedaled and fingered. Requires large hand span. M-D.

Organ Prelude in g, arr. by Alexander Siloti, after Th. Szanto's transcription (CF 1924; LC) 9 pp. *Adagio religioso;* contemplative; low bass cluster chords are depressed silently for pedal effects, scales, full chords; big ending. M-D.

Organ Toccata in d, trans. by Alfred Cortot (Foetisch Frères 1947).

Two Organ Toccatas: No. 1 in C, BWV 564; No. 2 in d, BWV 565, trans. by Ferruccio Busoni (BrH 1371, 1372 1900) 17 pp. Many octave transpositions or rearrangement of note order to suit the hand. Most of these alterations are legitimate in Busoni's style and were made in the name of good piano writing. Full harmonies, long pedals. Requires superb octave technique. M-D to D.

See: Busoni edition of Bach's *Well-Tempered Clavier,* vol. I (GS 1894), Appendix I, sec. 4: "On the Transcription of Bach's Organ-works for the Pianoforte."

Paraphrase on the Prelude in C sharp major, by Alexander Siloti (CF 1924; LC) 5 pp. Melodic line shifts between hands. Fingered and pedaled; very effective. M-D.

Partita No. 1, in B-flat, BWV 825, trans. by Harold Bauer (GS 1921; LS) 15 pp. Widely spread over the keyboard. An eye- (and ear-) opening experience! M-D.

Pastorale in F, trans. by Dinu Lipatti (Schott 1953; LC) 10 pp. Andantino tranquillo: flowing and smooth. Allegretto grazioso: cheerful and graceful. Andante cantabile: expressive and *legato.* Allegro deciso: quick and deliberate. Beautifully laid out for the instrument. M-D.

Passacaglia and Fugue in c, BWV 582, trans. by Arthur Briskier (CFP P2954). Originally composed for the pedal-cembalo and later transcribed for the organ, this masterpiece is well suited to the piano. M-D.

———. trans. by Eugen d'Albert (Bo&Bo). Eminently pianistic and very popular in the earlier part of this century. M-D.

——. Trans. for 2 pianos by Abram Chasins (JF 1935; LC) 19 pp. Omits the fugue except for the last six bars, which are used as a coda to the Passacaglia. Chasins claims that the Passacaglia is complete in itself while the Fugue, "when considered for the medium of two pianos, is deprived of the instrumental coloring possible of achievement on the organ or by the orchestra" (from the Preface). A masterly transcription. M-D to D.

———. Trans. for 2 pianos by Gino Tagliapetra (Ric 1956; LC) 24 pp. *Andante rigoroso;* stays closer to the original than the Chasins version. M-D.

Prelude, from *Cello Suite* in E-flat, trans. by Alexander Siloti (CF 1931) 8 pp. Some octaves are fingered with 4 and 5 used together on the outer note for emphasis. A note at the coda says, "Use the entire arm for the playing of all these octaves." Triple *forte* conclusion uses almost every resource of instrument and performer. M-D to D.

Prelude in g, originally for organ, trans. by Alexander Siloti (CF 1924) 9 pp., 3½ min. Siloti indicates that some keys are to be depressed silently to provide low bass pedal sonorities to support the active right-hand figuration. He dramatizes the conclusion by immensely increasing and thickening the textures, almost to the point where the work becomes a reconception, rather than a transcription. M-D to D.

Prelude, from the cantata *Wir danken Dir, Gott,* trans. by Alexander Siloti (Methuen Simpson 1909; LC) 9 pp. Hands work close together (interlocked) for some of the time, constant 16ths, melody frequently in the left hand. M-D.

Prelude in b from *Clavierbüchlein for W. F. Bach,* BWV 855a, trans. by Alexander Siloti (CF) 3 min. Originally *Prelude* No. 10 in E minor from the *Notebook of W. F. Bach.* It was one of Emil Gilels's favorite encores. The Siloti version is more elaborate than the original but retains its essence and spirit. M-D.

Prelude and Fugue in a, BWV 543, originally for organ, trans. by Franz Liszt (Hughes—GS 1475). 10½ min. Contains fingering, metronome marks, and pedaling. It is not possible to distinguish between Liszt's and Hughes's editing. Trans. by Arthur Briskier (CF 1965) suggests a continuous drive coupled with a constant legato touch from beginning to end. "For clarity and smoothness of interpretation, some notes are played one octave higher or one octave lower than originally written, while an occasional duplicated note is omitted" (from the Briskier Foreword). M-D.

Prelude and Fugue in a, for organ, trans. by Franz Liszt, edited by Edwin Hughes (GS 1475, 1923; LC) 19 pp. Low bass pedal notes, octaves, pedaled and fingered, builds to big climax. M-D.

Prelude and Fugue in b (The Great), originally for organ, trans. by Arthur Briskier (CF 1955; LC) 19 pp. Transcription and facsimile of the autograph manuscript appear on facing pages. Sustaining pedal used; organ-pedal notes are played by left hand in octaves. M-D to D.

Prelude and Fugue in D, originally for organ, trans. by Johana and Roy Harris (Mills 1949; LC) 14 pp. "As a concert instrument, the piano has overshadowed the organ in popularity to such an extent that piano transcriptions of the great Bach organ literature seem justified. [This piece] is a case in point. The romantic lyricism of the Prelude is heightened by the clear harmonic textures of the piano, while the massive structure of the Fugue, with all its swift moving contrapuntal web, is more clearly and dramatically articulated on the piano than can be possibly realized on the organ" (from the Preface). M-D.

Prelude and Fugue in D, BWV 532, trans. by Ferruccio Busoni (Br&H 3355 1902) 16 pp. Originally for organ, this transcription is full of octaves, thirds, and sixths. Pedal marks and constantly changing dynamics. Effective Busoni style. M-D to D.

Prelude and Fugue in E-flat, BWV 552, originally for organ, arr. for 2 pianos by Christopher Le Fleming (JWC 2933 1943) 36 pp., 15 min. Exploits both instruments, includes an ordinary and a "free concert ending"! Bravura nineteenth-century style. M-D to D.

————. Freely arr. by Ferruccio Busoni (Rahter 1914). Prelude skips 18 measures that are heard earlier. The triple fugue is one of the most successful works of its type. M-D to D.

Prelude and Fugue in e, trans. by Anis Fuleihan (GS 1946; LP) 6 pp. Many octaves and chordal tremolos; fugue builds to big climax. M-D.

Prelude, Fugue, Allegro in E-flat, originally for organ, trans. by Ferruccio Busoni (Br&H 4778, 1915; LC) 15 pp. Very few doublings, conservative transcribing. M-D.

Deux Preludes, Largo et Choral, trans. by Isidor Philipp (ESC) 18 pp. Allegro in G: many sixths in right hand, octotonic, many octaves for left hand. Allegro in a: melodic, big conclusion. Largo, from *Concerto* in f, BWV 1056: this is the famous slow movement in A-flat; melodious. Choral, "Dieu seul, dans les cieux, soit glorifie": very effective, *ppp* closing. M-D.

Due Preludii, from *Sonata* for solo violin in b, trans. by Riccardo Pick-Mangiagalli (Ric 1921) 9 pp. Adagio: bravura writing, improvisatory, big conclusion. Vivace: many octaves, toccata-like style, much alternation of figuration between hands, big conclusion. M-D to D.

Six Preludes and Fugues for Organ, arr. for piano by Franz Liszt. Bk. 1: BWV 542-44; Bk. 2: BWV 545-47 (CFP 7163, 7164). Some octave doublings in left hand (takes over the pedal part from the original), but generally remains very close to the original. M-D.

Presto, from *Sonata* in g for solo violin, arr. by Johannes Brahms 1879 (Br&H, separately; Ric; Simrock). Brahms made two arrangements of this movement. The first is "moto perpetuo" consisting of single notes for each hand; contrary motion and crossing of hands occur frequently. The second is an inversion of the first arrangement. M-D.

Rejoice, Beloved Christians, trans. for 2 pianos by Silvio Scionti (Ric 1942; LC) 11 pp. *Allegro scorrevole* throughout; requires fleet fingers. M-D to D.

Ricercar, from *The Musical Offering,* trans. by Karl Pillney (Br&H 6315, 1959; LC) 9 pp. This is the three-voice ricercar; very true to original. M-D.

School for the Left Hand, vol. 3: *Transcriptions,* by Paul Wittgenstein (UE 12329). Contains Prelude No. 1, from *WTC* I; Prelude No. 3, in c, from *Small Preludes for Beginners;* Gigue in B-flat, from *Partita* No. 1; Sicilienne in g, from *Sonata* No. 2 for flute and keyboard. Strange fingering but it does work for the left hand. Pedaling indicated. Effective. M-D.

Sheep May Safely Graze, from *Birthday Cantata,* No. 208, trans. by Egon Petri

(Br&H 1944; LC) 4 pp. Tranquil, many harmonic thirds and sixths; chorale sometimes in middle voice. M-D.

———. Arr. by Ignaz Friedman (Allans 1945; LC). More difficult than the Petri version.

———. Arr. for 2 pianos by Mary Howe (OUP) 7 pp. Includes recitative leading to the *Andante Pastorale*. The figure of the accompaniment is a fine example of Bach's amazing power of tone-painting, with its obvious suggestion of the sound of sheep bells. M-D.

Short Organ Preludes and Fugues, trans. by Dmitri Kabalevsky (Leeds 1946; LC) 16 pp. Bk. I: Nos. 1–4 in C, d, e, and F. Bk. II: Nos. 5–8 in G, g, a, and B-flat. Transcribed with skill and imagination. Int. to M-D.

Siciliano, from *Sonata* No. 2 for flute and harpsichord, BWV 1031b, trans. by Edwin Hughes (GS 1926; LP) 3 pp. Pedaled and fingered. A little tricky at spots. M-D.

———. Arr. by Ignaz Friedman (Allans 1948; LC) 3 pp. Flows a little easier than the Hughes version. M-D.

———. Trans. for 2 pianos by Guy Maier (JF 1924; LC) 6 pp. Effective. Int.

———. Trans. by Charles Alkan (Musica Obscura). Lovely and effective. M-D.

———. Trans. by Wilhelm Kempff (Bo&Bo). A free paraphrase. M-D.

First Sinfonia, from *Cantata* No. 35, arr. for 2 pianos by Walter Emery (Nov 1947; LC) 16 pp. *Allegro,* motoric rhythm that develops naturally. Fine version. M-D.

First Sonata, Trio Sonata for organ, arr. for 2 pianos by Victor Babin (Bo&H 1953; LC) 15 pp. Con spirito; Adagio; Allegro giocoso. Approximates the original medium. This is the first of a set of six completed by Bach in 1727. M-D.

Second Sonata, Trio Sonata for organ, arr. for 2 pianos by Victor Babin (Bo&H 1953; LC) 24 pp. Vivace; Largo; Allegro. Approximates the original medium. M-D.

Third Sonata in d, Trio Sonata for organ, arr. for 2 pianos by Victor Babin (Bo&H 1942; LC) 28 pp. Andante; Adagio e dolce; Vivace. Approximates the original medium. Important voices are easily heard. M-D.

Fourth Sonata, Trio Sonata for organ, arr. for 2 pianos by Victor Babin (Bo&H 1942; LC) 24 pp. Adagio; Andante; Un poco Allegro. Approximates the original medium. M-D.

Fifth Sonata in C, Trio Sonata for organ, arr. for 2 pianos by Victor Babin (Bo&H 1942; LC) 39 pp. Allegro; Largo; Allegro. Efficient and effective arrangement, very few dynamics. M-D to D.

Sixth Sonata, Trio Sonata for organ, arr. for 2 pianos by Victor Babin (Bo&H 1942; LC) 29 pp. Vivace; Lento; Allegro. Approximates the original medium. M-D.

Sonatina No. 5 (after J. S. Bach), trans. by Ferruccio Busoni 1919 (Br&H 5093; Ric). A very free transcription of Bach's *Little Fantasia and Fugue* in d, BWV 905. This piece gives Busoni a great opportunity to display his own

superb contrapuntal technique. M-D.
See: Larry Sitsky, "The 6 Sonatinas for Piano of Ferruccio Busoni," *Studies in Music* 2 (1968):66–85.

Toccata and Fugue in d, BWV 565, trans. by Alfred Cortot (Foetisch Frères 1947) 19 pp. In the Busoni tradition, gives a final ending in D major, which Cortot feels is justified. M-D to D.

————. Arr. for 2 pianos by Mario Braggiotti (GS 1952; LC) 23 pp. Virtuosic but useful. M-D to 'D.

————. Trans. by Carl Tausig (Musica Obscura). This virtuosic version is still popular and continues to turn up on recitals. M-D to D.

————. Trans. by Ignaz Friedman, in collection *Piano Arrangements of Popular Classics* (Allans 1225) 16 pp. Dedicated to Arthur Rubinstein. Many octave doublings; pedaling, fingering, dynamics, and articulation added. A large concert transcription with much display of the piano. M-D to D.

Toccata and Fugue in d (Dorian), for organ, trans. by Joseph Prostakoff (GS 1956; LC) 24 pp. Based on the Bach-Gesellschaft edition, whose directions for organ registration were used in transcribing the work for piano and in suggesting the manner of performance. Pedaled and fingered. M-D.

Variations on Weinen, Klagen (after J. S. Bach), trans. by Franz Liszt from *Cantata* No. 12, G.180 1862 (Cortot—Sal; Sauer—CFP). Cortot considered these variations to occupy "an exceptional place next to the Sonata in B minor" of Liszt. Emotional gamut ranges widely from fear, pain, and desperation to the reconciling chorale, in which the grief is overcome. Formally, it is among Liszt's most imposing works, largely because of its tightly controlled, carefully graded levels of tension. M-D to D.

Violin Partita No. 3 in E, by Bach, Preludio, Gavott, and Gigue, trans. by Sergei Rachmaninoff, in *A Commemorative Collection* (Belwin-Mills). Rachmaninoff added new melodic lines, giving this piece a greater contrapuntal texture and, by elaborating the implicit harmony with chords, built a richer sonority, which is available on the piano. M-D.

CONCERTOS:

Bach did not compose any original keyboard concertos, unless we designate the *Brandenburg* No. 5 as a harpsichord concerto. All his solo keyboard concertos are transcriptions for harpsichord of his own or other composers' concertos. He used them for convivial music making at the Leipzig Collegium Musicum, which he directed for a while in his spare time. Bach exercised considerable freedom with the originals, quite often changing the parts around, altering the basses, and even recomposing some of the melodies. They offer a unique opportunity to study Bach's incomparable art as a transcriber and arranger. See N. Carrell, *Bach the Borrower* (London, 1967), pp. 244ff.

Sixteen Concerti for Harpsichord (after Vivaldi and others), Bach-Gesellschaft edition (Lea 69).

Complete Keyboard Transcriptions of Concertos by Baroque Composers, BWV

922–987, reprinted from the Bach-Gesellschaft edition (Dover 1987) 128 pp. Early in his career, Bach transcribed for the keyboard a number of violin and other concertos, so that he could study the works of other composers while maintaining a supply of keyboard music for his own performances. This collection of sixteen of these celebrated transcriptions contains six transcriptions of violin concertos by Vivaldi; three based on concertos by Duke Johann Ernst; one each on violin concertos by Telemann, Alessandro Marcello, and Benedetto Marcello; and four from unknown sources. Tutti parts (reduced for keyboard) and solo parts indicated in some of the works. Bach's Vivaldi transcriptions became his own works through his own unique organizational and evocatory individuality. He would frequently add inner parts to them. M-D.

Concerto in d, BWV 1052 (CFP; Br&H; Schott; GS; Eulenburg; WH; Lea; CF) 23 min. Composed between 1730 and 1731. Allegro; Adagio; Allegro. The outside movements present challenges with respect to balance. The noble Adagio is similar in expressive content to the middle movement of the *Italian Concerto*. M-D.

Concerto in E, BWV 1053 (Sikorski; Br&H; CFP; WH; Lea; Fl; USSR) 18 min. Composed before 1731. Allegro; Sicilano; Allegro.

Concerto in D, BWV 1054 (CFP; Br&H; Lea; CF; Fl) 27 min. Composed between 1729 and 1736. (No tempo or character indication); Adagio e sempre piano; Allegro.

Concerto in A, BWV 1055 (CFP, Br&H; K; Lea; CF; WH) 16 min. Composed between 1729 and 1736. Allegro: strong first movement with musical interest tossed between strings and keyboard. Larghetto: has beautiful flowing keyboard solo. Allegro ma non tanto: florid figuration demands a moderato tempo, so less-brilliant effects than usual are obtained. M-D.

Concerto in f, BWV 1056 (CFP; Br&H; K; Schott; Lea; CF; IMC; Heugel; Eulenburg; SZ; Schott Freres; WH) 12 min. Composed ca. 1730. On a smaller scale than BWV 1052. (No tempo indication): echo effects. Largo: expressive; more familiar in its simpler version. Presto: a lively finale. M-D.

Concerto in F, BWV 1057 (Br&H; Moseler: Fl) 15 min. Transcribed after 1729. A transcription of *Brandenburg Concerto* No. 4, composed between 1717 and 1721. (No tempo indication); Andante; Allegro assai.

Concerto in g, BWV 1058 (Br&H; IMC; CF) 12 min. A transcription of *Concerto* in a, BWV 1041, for violin, composed between 1717 and 1723. Transcribed between 1729 and 1736. (No tempo indication); Andante; Allegro assai.

Concerto in d, BWV 1059 (Moseler). For keyboard, oboe, and strings. Composed around 1730. Reconstructed from BWV 35.

Concerto in c, BWV 1060 (CFP; Br&H; K; Eulenburg; IMC; CF; GS; Fl). For 2 keyboard instruments and orchestra. Composed between 1729 and 1736.

Allegro; Adagio; Allegro. The strings have more importance here than in BWV 1061. M-D.

Concerto in C, BWV 1061 (CFP; Br&H; IMC; Augener; CF; GS; Fl) 20 min. For 2 keyboard instruments and orchestra. Composed between 1727 and 1730. (No tempo indication); Adagio ovvero largo; Fuga. The strings are relegated to a minor role and are not used in the middle movement. The Finale is an exhilarating fugue. M-D.

Concerto in c, BWV 1062 (Br&H; CFP) 14 min. For 2 keyboard instruments and orchestra. Composed between 1729 and 1736. (No tempo indication); Andante; Allegro assai.

Concerto in d, BWV 1063 (Br&H; CFP; Eulenburg; K; Fl) 15 min. For 3 keyboard instruments and orchestra. Composed between 1730 and 1733. Allegro: ritornello, rondo; first piano is more brilliant and prominent than the others. Alla siciliano: opens with the three pianos in unison; then the first piano continues with a flowing figuration, dominated by its main theme. Allegro: light-hearted. M-D.

Concerto in C, BWV 1064 (Br&H; CFP; Eulenburg; K; Lea; CF; Fl). For 3 keyboard instruments and orchestra. Composed between 1730 and 1733 for performance by J. S., W. F., and C. P. E. Bach. Bach apparently adapted this work from a concerto for three violins, now lost, which may not have been his own. It is weightier than BWV 1063 and has a more elaborate slow movement. Both require much rehearsal to resolve the ensemble problems. M-D.

Concerto in a, BWV 1065 (Br&H; Eulenburg; K; Fl) 11 min. For 4 keyboard instruments and orchestra. After *Concerto* in b for four violins by Vivaldi, published ca. 1721. This is the grandest and most exciting of all J. S. Bach's Vivaldi transcriptions. Allegro: main theme is heard several times interspersed with episodes for the soloist. Largo: Bach wrote out in full what Vivaldi had only suggested in Baroque musical shorthand, especially in the arpeggio passages in the middle section. Allegro: gigue rhythm; Bach filled in Vivaldi's harmonies and achieved the richest possible effect. M-D.

All the multiple keyboard concertos require ensemble experience, careful balance of sonority, and strict performance discipline.

Concerto in a, BWV 1044 (Br&H; CFP; Eulenburg; CF). For keyboard, violin, and flute, accompanied by strings and flute. This is not a true triple concerto but a sort of companion piece to *Brandenburg Concerto* No. 5. Its origin goes back to a keyboard Prelude and Fugue in a, BWV 894 (a manuscript from 1725). It is an austere work filled with intricate writing and a monolithic web of triplets. Allegro: highly pianistic; continuous brilliant passagework and arpeggios. Adagio ma non tanto e dolce (taken from *Sonata* No. 3 in d, BWV 527, for organ): allotted entirely to the three soloists; equal treatment of the three melodic parts, at times in strict canon, question and answer. Alla breve: fugal relationship in the strong rhythmic motion of thematic material; broad melodic outlines; piano explores lower register (bar 85 onward); free cadenza introduced near the end of the movement is left to the imagination of the performer, with only the transition to the final tutti written out. The technical difficulties of the outer movements make us marvel at the extraordinary command of the keyboard Bach must have possessed. M-D.

Brandenburg Concerto No. 5 in D, BWV 1050 (Br; Eulenburg; CFP; Ph; Lea). For keyboard, flute, violin, and orchestra. Allegro; Affettuoso; Allegro. Could be considered Bach's first original harpsichord concerto. The three concertino instruments—keyboard, solo violin, and transverse flute—do not function as a group, and generally the keyboard predominates. Bravura writing including chain trills and a 65-bar cadenza in the first movement. A unique work. M-D to D.

Works for Three and Four Harpsichords (R. Eller, K. Heller—Br 5045). New complete edition, Series VII, vol. 6. Includes BWV 1063, 1064, 1065.

See also Duke Johann Ernst of Saxe-Weimar; Marcello, Alessandro; Marcello, Benedetto; Telemann; Vivaldi

Wilhelm Friedemann Bach (1710–1784) Germany

Andante, from *Concerto* in E-flat for 2 harpsichords and orchestra, trans. by Celius Dougherty and Vincenz Ruzicka (AMP 1945; LC) 5 pp. Flowing melody, equal division of players. M-D.

Concerto pour orgue (attributed to Vivaldi), trans. by Isidor Philipp (Durand 1922; LC) 14 pp. Moderato tranquillo. Moderato, Fuga. Largo e spiccato: especially beautiful. Allegro non troppo. Treated in nineteenth-century approach with full exploitation of the keyboard. M-D.

Phantasie und Fuge in a, for the organ, trans. by August Stradal (Br&H 1907; LC) 23 pp. Follows the Tausig-Busoni transcribing tradition. M-D to D.

Paul Badura-Skoda (1927–   ) Austria
See Mozart

Mili Balakirev (1837–1910) Russia
See Glinka

Samuel Barber (1910–1981) USA

Adagio for Strings, Op. 11, arr. by Lawrence Rosen (GS 1987; LC) 6 pp. Lovely and effective. Int.

Souvenirs, Op. 28 1952, arr. for 2 pianos by Arthur Gold and Robert Fizdale (GS) 20 min. Originally for piano duet. These six pieces are a satirical evocation of once-popular social dances—Waltz, Schottische, Pas de deux, Two-step, Hesitation-Tango, and Galop. Lightweight, clever, wide audience appeal. Sustained pedal points. Displays expert craft, fine melodic invention, much rhythmic charm. M-D.

Ethel Bartlett (1906–1978) Great Britain
See Franck; Granados; Grieg; Liszt; Mendelssohn

Béla Bartók (1881–1945) Hungary

Bartók for Two, trans. for duet by Benjamin Suchoff (EBM 1960; LC) 12 pp. Includes *Slovakian Folk Tune; Boatman! Boatman!; Tortuous Struggle; Two Hungarian Folk Tunes; Hungarian Folk Song.* These transcriptions are based on the suggestions Bartók made in the Preface to his *Mikrokosmos,* Vol. I, i.e., doubling the melody at the octave in the Primo part. Except for some fingerings and divisions of the accompaniment between the hands in the Secondo part, nothing has been added or deleted from the original piano solos. Int.

Dance Suite, originally for orchestra, 1923, trans. by the composer 1924, (UE) 18 min. Six movements containing some of Bartók's most arresting and invigorating writing. M-D to D.

Seven Pieces from Mikrokosmos, arr. for 2 pianos by the composer (Bo&H 1947; LC) 34 pp. *Bulgarian Rhythm; Chord and Trill Study; Perpetuum Mobile; Short Canon and Its Inversion; New Hungarian Folk Song; Chromatic Invention; Ostinato.* Super arrangements in every way. M-D.

Petite Suite, from *44 Duos for Two Violins,* arr. by the composer (UE 1938; LC) 11 pp., 6 min. *Lassu; Forgatós; Pengetos; Oroszbs; Dudás.* Highly effective, with Bartók "sound" throughout. Int. to M-D.

Pieces and Suites, originally for solo piano, trans. for piano duet by Benjamin Suchoff (Sam Fox 1962) 31 pp. *Hungarian Folk Suite:* three movements, all from *For Children. Evening in the Country,* from *Ten Easy Piano Pieces. Dirge* No. 3, from *Four Dirges. Slovakian Folk Suite,* three movements, all from *For Children.* Includes explanation of symbols and terms. A charming collection excellently done. Int.

See also Della Ciaia; Frescobaldi; Marcello, B.; Rossi; Scarlatti; Zipoli

Harold Bauer (1873–1951) Great Britain

Great Composers of the Past. Ten adaptations for the pianoforte, with an introduction and historical notes by Richard Aldrich (BMC, 1918) 49 pp. J. J. Froberger, *Toccata* in d: many octaves, virtuoso transcription. C. Merulo, *Toccata* in G: large and full rolled chords, virtuosic. G. Frescobaldi, *Capriccio on the Cuckoo's Call:* contrapuntal, sectional, quiet closing. J. C. Kittel, *Nachspiel* (Postlude): full, big, virtuosic *allegro con brio.* J. Mattheson, *Air varie:* three variations on a charming theme with arpeggiated chords; and *Minuet* in C: variation technique; builds to large climax. G. Muffat, *Sarabande* in g: tenths in left hand; builds to climax, then subsides; and *Fughetta* in G: trills and many 16ths makes this more difficult than it looks. J. Schobert, *Minuet* in E-flat: sectionalized; sixths, octaves, and octaves and thirds filled in. *Capriccio:* charming, not as full sounding as some of the others in this collection. M-D.

See also Bach, J. S.; Beethoven; Boyce; Brahms; Franck; Haydn; Kuhnau; Mussorgsky; Raff; Schubert; Schumann, R.; Songs, French

Arthur Baynor (–   )

See Scarlatti

Ludwig van Beethoven (1770–1827) Germany

Beethoven did a good deal of arranging, and his piano transcriptions include examples from his ballets, German dances, ecossaises, marches, chamber music, concertos, symphonies, overtures, and vocal works. He also made numerous chamber-music arrangements with and without piano, as well as a few orchestral and vocal arrangements.

Adelaide, Op. 46, trans. by Franz Liszt, G.466 1840 (Friedman—UE 11505; Sauer—CFP 606; Br&H 11641) 8½ min. To speak of a vocalise for the piano may seem a contradiction in terms, but just as the pianist is called upon to characterize the voice of the tenor in the *Waltz* from Gounod's *Faust,* so here the player must simulate the singer of the famous poem by Matthisson. It is thus, in a very real sense, an essay in the very thing a piano is not supposed to possess—*cantabile,* or singing tone. But given suitably resourceful hands (and feet), it can be done. M-D.

Capriccio alla Turca sur des Motifs de Beethoven (Ruines d'Athènes), by Franz Liszt, G.388 1846, in Series II, vol. 7 of NLA (c. 1988) 14 pp. A free arrangement of No. 4, "Marcia alla turca," and No. 3, "Chor de Dervische," from Beethoven's incidental music to the play *The Ruins of Athens,* Op. 113. (Liszt later used the same themes for two versions of his *Fantasy on Themes from Beethoven's "Ruins of Athens."* See below.) D.

Concerto in D, Op. 61A 1806, trans. for piano and orchestra by the composer from his *Violin Concerto* Op. 61 (W. Hess—Br&H 6565 1970) 43 min. Allegro ma non troppo; Larghetto; Rondo—Allegro. Transcription made after the suggestion of Muzio Clementi. The essential character of the work is not changed, even though the left-hand parts are not equal in invention to the original. The violin part, with slight modification, is given to the right hand. Piano cadenzas were composed specifically for this version. The cadenza for the first movement is over 130 bars, with repeats, and calls for a kettle-drum obbligato. All three Beethoven cadenzas are rather wild and fully pianistic. M-D to D.

Ecossaises, concert arrangement by Ferruccio Busoni (Br&H 2550). Structurally, Busoni cut out a few bars of Beethoven's conventional introduction, but he also wrote a coda that brings back the first *Ecossaise.* By this means he tied the piece together very successfully and provided an effective and brilliant conclusion. Busoni's ingenious and most successful editing gives a different character to each episode and a varied turn to each refrain. Int. to M-D.

Fantasy on Themes from Beethoven's "Ruins of Athens" for piano and orchestra, by Franz Liszt, G.122 1848–52 (Joseffy—GS) 11 min. Dedicated to Nicholas Rubinstein. Beethoven composed his incidental music to Kotzebue's festival play *The Ruins of Athens,* Op. 113, in the summer of 1811. The Overture and "Turkish March" are the only parts of the score that are performed with any frequency today. The "Turkish March" was actually adapted by Beethoven from a set of variations for solo piano, Op. 76 1809. (Liszt also composed his *Capriccio alla Turca,* a completely different work, on themes from *The Ruins of Athens*. See above.) The *Fantasy* is a short, brilliant work and one of the most effective Liszt ever arranged. The orchestration is well meshed with a masterful solo piano part. M-D. Also arr. by Liszt for piano alone, G.389.

————. Trans. for 2 pianos by Franz Liszt, G.649 1848–52 (Joseffy—GS 1915) 39 pp. This transcription is one of the most effective Liszt ever arranged for two pianos, with the two parts interlocked masterfully. For sheer charm, he never surpassed what he achieved in this brilliant and altogether lovable piece. M-D.

Gavotte in F, originally for duet, arr. by Harold Bauer (GS 1929; LC) 6 pp. This charming piece, which dates from Beethoven's earlier period (about 1786), came to light around 1920. It was first performed in its original form by Bauer and Olga Samaroff at a concert given by the Beethoven Association on January 13, 1920, in New York City. Int.

Sechs Geistliche Lieder, Op. 48 (Gellert), arr. by Franz Liszt, G.467 1840 (Schuberth). *Gottes Macht und Versehung:* In JALS IV (December 1978):74–75. *Bitten:* In JALS II (December 1977):52. *Busslied. Vom Tode:* In JALS V (June 1979):101–102. *Die Liebe des Nächsten:* In JALS I (June 1977):33. *Die Ehre Gottes aus der Natur:* In JALS VI (December 1979):72–75. Straightforward arrangements of the original songs without much addition by Liszt. Int. to M-D.

Grande Sonate für Klavier, Op. 3 1792 (Eugene Hartzell—Dob DM 326 1968) 30 pp. An arrangement of five of the six movements of the string *Trio,* Op. 3. It is questionable whether Beethoven transcribed all or part of it, but most of the work is expertly pianistic. M-D.
See: Ates Orga, "An Authentic Beethoven Transcription," M & M (December 1968): 30–33.

Great Fugue, Op. 134, originally for string quartet, trans. by the composer for duet (Henle). This is the only Beethoven transcription with an opus number. The work is cumbersome, surprisingly so in view of Beethoven's genius for the piano. The duet slavishly follows the quartet version. It is a kind of "eye music," in which the voice-leading as indicated on the printed page is considered more important than the comfort of the two performers. M-D to D.

Grosse Fuge, Op. 133, edited and trans. for 2 pianos by Harold Bauer (GS 1927) 51 pp. Based on Beethoven's arrangement for piano duet, Op. 134. Beethoven's string *Quartet* in B-flat, Op. 130, of which the *Grosse Fuge* is the Finale, was first performed in Vienna on March 21, 1826. Its success was such that the second and fourth movements ("Presto" and "Danza alla tedesca"), had to be repeated, but the fugue was not appreciated by the public or the critics. Beethoven's friends urged him to write another movement to replace it, and the publisher Mathias Artaria, who had purchased the quartet, offered to publish the fugue separately, provided the composer furnished an arrangement for piano, four hands, and write a new Finale for the quartet. Beethoven finally and reluctantly consented to do so, and at his request the pianist Anton Halm was commissioned to make the transcription. The result proved unsatisfactory, and Beethoven wrote a piano arrangement himself, which was published by Artaria on March 10, 1827, as Op. 134, simultaneously with the original score for the string quartet, which was published as Op. 133. Beethoven's friend and biographer Anton Schindler erroneously states that it was Halm's arrangement that was published by Artaria; Thayer, however, has reestablished the facts of the case. Unfortunately the publisher's hopes that a pianoforte arrangement would contribute to the popularity of the fugue did not materialize. The work remains, today as then, a stumbling block to quartet players; and the piano version, if anything, more difficult than the original for strings, is long out of print and has become very scarce. A collection of Beethoven's works for piano, including this arrangement of the *Grosse Fuge,* was published in Leipzig by Wolfenbüttel, under the editorship of Franz Liszt, who corrected some of the mistakes of the first Vienna edition; but this has also failed to survive. Bauer's transcription for two pianos was made to alleviate the difficulty of performance. Although it is based on the composer's arrangement for four hands, in some instances the greater freedom afforded by the two instruments permits the introduction of the more effective passage-work written for the strings. M-D to D.

Grosse Messe in D, Op. 123, arr. for duet by Gustav Nottebohm (Schott 185?; LC) 97 pp. One of the finest arrangements of a large work this author has seen. Text included in the score. D.

Marcia Turca, from the *Ruins of Athens,* arr. for 2 pianos by Silvio Omizzolo (Ric 1955; LC) 6 pp. Strong rhythms emphasized by 16th triplets in Piano II. Effective and fun for all. M-D.

Sonatina in C, originally for mandolin and cembalo 1796, trans. by Felix Van Dyck (GS 1962; LC) 6 pp. Much use of arpeggio figuration, some octaves. Dynamics are editorial. Int.

Septet, Op. 20, trans. by Franz Liszt for duet, G.465 (Br&H). Beethoven always seemed to bring out the best in Liszt, and this transcription is no exception—a beautiful and highly successful transcription. M-D. (Beethoven himself arranged this Septet for piano trio, as Op. 38.)

Nine Symphonies, trans. by Franz Liszt G.464 (Belwin-Mills). Vol. I: Symphonies 1–5; Vol II: Symphonies 6–9. "The name of Beethoven is sacred in art. His symphonies are at present universally acknowledged to be masterpieces; whoever seriously wishes to extend his knowledge or to produce new works can never devote too much reflection and study upon them. For this reason every way or manner of making them accessible and popular has a certain merit. Such has been my aim in the work I have undertaken and now lay before the musical world. I confess that I should have to consider it a rather useless employment of my time, if I had but added one more to the numerous hitherto published piano-arrangements, following in their rut; but I consider my time well employed if I have succeeded in transferring to the piano not only the grand outlines of Beethoven's compositions but also all those numerous fine details, and smaller traits that so powerfully contribute to the completion of the ensemble. My aim has been attained if I stand on a level with the intelligent engraver, the conscientious translator, who comprehend the spirit of a work and thus contribute to the knowledge of the great masters and to the reformation of the sense for the beautiful. Rome, 1865—F. Liszt" (from the Preface).

Liszt's transcriptions of the Beethoven symphonies are probably his most remarkable ones—the most extensive and outstanding accomplishment ever at translating music from one medium to another, on the keyboard.

In an interview published on September 25, 1988 in the *New York Times,* Vladimir Horowitz was asked if, looking back on his life, he had any regrets. He admitted to one—that he had never played these transcriptions in public. " 'These are the greatest works for the piano, tremendous works. But they are "sound works," ' he explained, meaning works that draw on the piano's vast coloristic possibilities. 'For me, the piano is the orchestra—the oboe, the clarinet, the violin, and of course, the voice. Every note of those symphonies is in these Liszt works. . . . I played them all the time for myself. But I thought people would not understand this music. We are such snobs.' " M-D to D.

Turkish March from *The Ruins of Athens,* arr. by Anton Rubinstein, revised and fingered by Carl Deis (GS) 7 pp. Many thirds have been turned into octave chords including a third; large left-hand skips; chords of tenths. Builds to big climax, ends *ppp.* M-D.

Variations and Fugue on a Theme by Beethoven (Op. 77), arr. for 2 pianos by George A. Schumann, Op. 32 (Simrock 1903; LC) 39 pp. This work uses the Saint-Saëns *Variations,* Op. 35, as its model. M-D.

Variations on a Theme by Count von Waldstein, arr. for 2 pianos by Victor Babin (EV 1946; LC) 22 pp. Theme and eight variations; final variation is the most extensive and serves as coda. Beethoven style throughout. Excellent set. M-D.

Franz Behr (1837–1898) Germany

Polka de W. R., trans. by Sergei Rachmaninoff 1911 (Bo&H) 9 pp. The original polka was a favorite of Rachmaninoff's father. Its origin is to be found in Behr's *Lachtaübchen—Scherzpolka* (La rieuse—Polka badine), Op. 303. There the tempo is Allegretto grazioso and the key is F. M-D.

Vincenzo Bellini (1801–1835) Italy

Capriccio sull' opera "La Straniera," arr. for left hand by Ferdinando Bonamici (Ric). Extremely effective, beautiful voicing. M-D.

Fantaisie on Themes from the Opera I Puritani of Bellini, trans. by Sigismond Thalberg, Op. 57/1 (Br&H; SBTS) 18 pp. Themes follow each other without much development. M-D to D.

Fantaisie on Themes from the Opera Norma by Bellini, trans. by Sigismond Thalberg, Op. 57/4 (Br&H; SBTS) 11 pp. Contrasting themes, extensive chromatic figuration, bravura ending. M-D to D.

Grand Caprice on Themes from La Sonnambula of Bellini, trans. by Sigismond Thalberg, Op. 46 (Schott; SBTS) 17 pp. Requires dash and power plus a fine *cantabile* style. D.

Grand Concert Fantasy from Sonnambula, trans. by Franz Liszt, G.393, in collection *Franz Liszt—Piano Transcriptions from French and Italian Operas* (Dover) 23 pp. Themes from Acts I and II are worked out in this demanding and bravura fantasy. D.

Grand Concert Fantasy on Sonnambula by Bellini, arr. by Franz Liszt for duet, G.627 1852 (USSR), for solo piano G.393 (Dover) 13 1/2 min. A dazzling display of technical and contrapuntal fireworks—themes are combined with embellishments, trills, cadenzas, arpeggios, fiendishly difficult alternating chords, octaves, and tremolos. Collisions of the four hands pose a major problem. One of the most brilliant compositions ever conceived for piano duet. D.

Grande Fantaisie et Variations on the Opera I Capuleti ed I Montecchi of Bellini, trans. for duet by Sigismond Thalberg, Op. 10 (Schlesinger; LC) 35 pp. A "tour de force" with all kinds of cadenzas, virtuoso runs, and written-out tremolos. Four variations plus a finale. M-D to D.

Grosse Fantasie und Variationen über Themas aus der Oper "Norma" von Bellini, arr. by Sigismond Thalberg for 2 pianos, Op. 12 (André; LC) 11 pp. Themes worked out with much fluent figuration and octaves. M-D to D.

————. Arr. by Sigismond Thalberg for solo piano (Haslinger). May have been composed before the 2-piano arrangement. This piece prompted Robert Schumann to say in the *Neue Zeitschrift für Musik* of 1835 that Thalberg "speaks more profoundly than is permitted in higher circles." Uses two themes from the opera, saving the more lyric one until near the end of the work. Three variations appear in measures 97–165. Fugato passages are also included. D.

Hexameron Variations on the March from Bellini's I Puritani, 1837 (K). Franz Liszt, Sigismond Thalberg, Johann Peter Pixis, Henri Herz, Carl Czerny, and Frédéric Chopin each wrote one variation, Liszt also wrote the Introduction, several interludes, and the Finale. One of the grandest of the grand Romantic extravaganzas. It mostly dazzles, but also pleases (e.g., Chopin's nocturne-like variation) and even at times entices us with its poetic potions. D.

Réminiscences de "Norma," trans. by Franz Liszt, G.394 1841 (Schott). Also in collection *Franz Liszt—Piano Transcriptions from French and Italian Operas* (Dover). This concert paraphrase attempts to tell the story of the whole opera and dramatizes Norma's psychological struggle between her duty as high priestess of the Druids and her thwarted passion for Pollione, a Roman soldier. The introduction is based on Norma's entrance theme from Act I. It is followed by a long section elaborating all the themes from the opera's opening scene, in which the assembled Druids seek aid for their gods in their struggles with the Romans and call upon Norma for guidance. Norma's entrance theme interrupts and leads into an expressive recitative

(Liszt's own material), followed by an elaborate treatment of the climactic finale of the opera. Here Norma reveals her betrayal of her sacred vows and her love affair with Pollione, and offers herself to the Gauls as a victim, in place of Pollione. Although this section and the next one reach an incredible emotional fury, they are dwarfed by the even greater climax in the following section, a combination of themes from the opening and closing of the opera. This contrapuntal section provides both a colossal pianistic climax and a psychological one, as it brings together themes relating to Norma as high priestess and as rejected, but forgiving, lover. A most successful transformation of a two-hour opera into a sixteen-minute piano piece. D.

Reminiscences of I Puritani, trans. Franz Liszt, G.390 1836 (Schott). Uses selected themes from the first act. Includes virtuosic broken octaves all over the keyboard. The Finale glitters. D.

Rondiono brilliante on a Theme from Bellini's "I Montecchi ed i Capuleti," trans. by Mikhail Glinka, in Vol. 6: *Complete Piano Works* of *Complete Edition* (N. Zagornie—USSR 1958). In Mendelssohn style, brilliant, glittering, showy. M-D.

Julius Benedict (1804–1885) England, born Germany

Divertissement on a Theme from the Opera The Gipsy's Warning by Jules Benedict, trans. by Sigismond Thalberg, Op. 34 (Schott; SBTS) 12 pp. Developed somewhat like variations, skillfully and effectively written. M-D to D.

A. Benfeld (–   )
See Debussy

Alban Berg (1885–1935) Austria
See Mahler

Ralph Berkowitz (1910–   ) USA
See Albeniz; Bach, J. S.; Gilbert and Sullivan; Levitzki; Ravel; Saint-Saëns; Tchaikowsky

Hector Berlioz (1803–1869) France

Danse des Sylphes, from *La Damnation de Faust,* Berlioz-Liszt, arr. for 2 pianos by Mark Hambourg (OUP 1939; LC) 12 pp. Elfin-like, colorful, and effective. M-D.

———. Trans. for 2 pianos by Isidor Philipp (Costallat 1903; LC) 7 pp. Less involved than the Hambourg version. M-D.

Menuet des Follets, from *La Damnation de Faust,* trans. for 2 pianos by Isidor Philipp (Costallat 1903; LC) 13 pp. Pedaled; fluent writing for both players; colorful and unusual ending. M-D.

Overture de la Flute en Egypte, trans. by Isidor Philipp for 2 pianos (Costallat 1903: LC) 8 pp. Flowing, gentle, and charming. M-D.

Overture to King Lear by Berlioz, trans. by Franz Liszt (Liszt Society Publications ["32 Chivelston," 78 Wimbledon Park Side, London SW19 5LH,

England] Vol. 8 1987) 32 pp. Berlioz wrote the *King Lear* overture in 1831, but it was not published until 1840, as his Op. 4. Liszt's transcription is a faithful recasting of the orchestral score as a piano piece, rather like his transcriptions of the Beethoven symphonies. D.

Rakoczy March, arr. for 2 pianos by Ernest Hutcheson (JF 1928; LC) 22 pp. Occasional free use of the Berlioz and Liszt versions. Virtuosic, glissando, brilliant closing. M-D to D.

La Reine Mab ou la Fée des Songes (Scherzo), from *Romeo et Juliette*, Op. 17, trans. for 2 pianos by Zoltan Kocsis (EMB 1981) 36 pp. Excellent version; requires two pianists with well-developed *leggiero* technique. M-D.

Toccata, arr. by Raymond Songayllo (Musica Obscura 1983) 4 pp. Most of the arrangement involves turning left-hand moving single-line eighths into moving eighth-note thirds. A few octaves have been added to the right hand. M-D.

Leonard Bernstein (1918–) USA

Four Movements, from *West Side Story,* arr. by Leo Smit (GS 1957) 20 pp. Jets; Jump; Cha-cha; Cool. Contrasting moods, clever, effective, strong syncopations; all have much audience appeal. M-D.

See also Copland

Helen Bidder (1891–) Great Britian
See Songs, English

Sir Henry Rowley Bishop (1786–1855) Great Britian

Variations on Home! Sweet Home!, Op. 72, trans. by Sigismond Thalberg. (GS 1857; LC; Musica Obscura) 14 pp. This fantasia was very popular in its day. It helped to bring to the art of piano playing the same kind of emotional feeling that the great singers aroused. D.

Georges Bizet (1838–1875) France

Carmen, arr. by the composer (Choudens). This entire score has much to recommend it to the pianist. The Preludio, 4 pp. would make a superb program opener; even the final chord, a diminished seventh, would be an ear-opener! The three Intermezzos have much charm and beauty. All are eminently pianistic. But then we should remember that Liszt, Berlioz, and Saint-Saëns all admired Bizet's remarkable piano playing. M-D.

Carmen Fantasy 1906, trans. by Moritz Moszkowski (Musica Obscura) 6½ min. Moszkowski has produced a notable and brilliant act of homage to the famous opera in this noble transcription. M-D to D.

Jeux d'Enfants, originally for duet, trans. by Lucien Garban (Durand 1952; LC) 44 pp. 12 pieces. Very effective, but some like No. 2, "La Toupie," are considerably more difficult than the original version. M-D.

Menuet, from *L'Arlesienne,* trans. by Leopold Godowsky (Musica Obscura) 6 pp. Flowing, attractive. M-D.

———. Trans. by Sergei Rachmaninoff. In collection *Rachmaninoff—A Commemorative Collection* (Belwin-Mills) 3 min. Falls easily on the ear. M-D.

Sonatina No. 6, Fantasy on themes from Bizet's *Carmen,* trans. by Ferruccio Busoni 1920 (Br&H). Written in the tradition of the Liszt fantasies (especially related to Liszt's *Don Juan* fantasy) but subtler than Vladimir Horowitz's treatment of the same themes. Five sections. Ends quietly, much as the opera does. M-D to D.

Frederick Block (–   ) USA
See Mussorgsky; Rimsky-Korsakov; Shostakovich

Léon Boëllman (1862–1897) France
Suite Gothique, originally for organ, trans. by Jacques Durand (Durand 1895; LC) 18 pp. Introduction—Choral; Menuet Gothique; Prière à Notre-Dame (available separately); Toccata. The Prière à Notre-Dame is the most successful movement on piano. M-D.

Carl Bohm (1844–1920) Germany
Calm as the Night, song, trans. by Leopold Godowsky (CF 11921). A sublimely beautiful work made even more beautiful in this version. M-D.

Ferdinando Bonamici (1827–1905) Italy
See Bellini

Alexander Borodin (1833–1887) Russia
Borodin, the illegitimate son of a Georgian prince, became one of Russia's greatest chemists. Music for Borodin was an avocation, as it was for many of the great Russian composers. He left only about twenty works.
Scherzo in A-flat, originally for orchestra, trans. by the composer (Br&H; IMC; Leduc; in collection *Encores of Great Pianists*—GS). Kind of a Polovtsian dance tamed down for the drawing room. Rachmaninoff made a wonderful recording of it. Effective. M-D.

Leonard Borwick (1868–1925) Great Britain
See Debussy

Louis Bourgeois (ca. 1510–ca.1561) France
Psaume, from *Church at Geneva,* trans. by Franz Liszt G.156/6, in collection *At the Piano with Liszt* (Alfred). This transcription dates from about 1840 and is an arrangement of the setting of Psalm 42 (King James version) found in the French Psalter of 1562. Liszt has provided a simple harmonization to the melody throughout, with some embellishment as the piece progresses. M-D.

William Boyce (1711–1779) Great Britain
Ye Sweet Retreat, based on a melody from Boyce's cantata *Solomon,* 1748, arr. for 2 pianos by Harold Bauer (GS 1923; LC) 7 pp. *Allegretto espressivo,* siciliano rhythm; thoroughly pianistic for both players. M-D.

Mario Braggiotti (1909–   ) USA, born Italy
See Bach, J. S.; Falla

Johannes Brahms (1833–1897) Germany

Brahms shows us in his transcription of his own works that he was consistently interested in recreating the orchestral sonority on his favorite instrument, the piano. See Robert Komaiko, "The Four-Hand Arrangements of Brahms and Their Role in the Nineteenth Century," diss., Northwestern University, 1975. Discusses the four-hand versions of Opp. 11, 16, 18, 25, 26, 36, 51/1,2, 60, 67, 88, and 111 and of *A German Requiem*.

Academic Overture, Op. 80, originally for orchestra, trans. by the composer for duet (Simrock 1881; LC) 27 pp. Also works extremely well on two pianos. M-D.

The Brahms Arrangements for Piano Four Hands of His String Quartets (E. Derr—Dover 1985) 145 pp. No. 1, Op. 51/1; No. 2, Op. 54/2; No. 3, Op. 67. In "Note to Performers," the editor says that these works "are not simply accommodations to the piano of the notes of ensemble pieces. They are *translations* from one performance medium to another. . . . ensemble pieces were transformed into 'real' piano pieces which for their projection call on the full range of that instrument's resources, making them a delight as much for the two performers as the listeners." Includes no pedal marks but provides a few fingerings. M-D.

Six Chorale Preludes for Organ, Op. 122 1897, trans. by Ferruccio Busoni 1897 (Simrock). *Herzlich thut mich erfreuen* (My inmost heart rejoices); *Schmücke dich, o liebe Seele* (Deck thyself out, o my soul); *Es ist ein "Ros" entsprungen* (A rose breaks into bloom); two settings of *Herzlich thut mich verlangen* (My inmost heart doth yearn); *O Welt, ich muss dich lassen* (O world, I e'en must leave thee). Some of these chorale preludes sound better on the piano than on the organ. In some of the eleven organ originals it is difficult to achieve a satisfactory *legato* because of the slightly uncomfortable way the music lies under the hands; in others there is a problem of bringing out the inner voices. Brahms was, after all, primarily a pianist. Busoni arranged some of the most pianistic of the set. They are attractive and idiomatic, complete recreations in nineteenth-century esthetic terms. M-D.

Eleven Chorale Preludes, Op. 122, originally for organ, arr. for piano by Paul Juon. Vol. I: Nos. 1–5; vol. II: Nos. 6–11 (Simrock 1785, 1786, 1902). Very musical and not overblown. No pedal indications or fingering. Well-controlled polyphonic technique required. Int. to M-D.

Cradle Song, Op. 49/4, freely arr. by Percy Grainger (GS 1923). Simple and lovely setting. M-D.

Hungarian Dances, originally for duet, arr. by the composer for solo piano (Henle; Schott; Ric; CFP; Heinrichshofen; WH; Br&H; GS; UE). Brahms made the solo piano arrangement after the dances became so popular. They are among the happiest products of his flair for folk music. Int. to M-D.

————. *Favorite Brahms Hungarian Dances,* adapted in playable versions for piano solo from the original piano duets by Henry Levine (Alfred) 32 pp. These adaptations of Brahms's solo arrangements of the first seven Hungarian Dances are based on the original piano duets. They are rendered somewhat easier than the original duets by deleting octaves, especially in the left hand, and by frequently moving the right hand down one octave. Int. to M-D.

————. No. 3, in collection *At the Piano With Brahms* (Alfred 1988).

Liebeslieder Waltzes, Op. 52a, originally for four singers and piano duet, trans. by the composer for duet (Simrock). Originally composed in 1858 as a direct consequence of Brahms's first visit to Vienna. Concerning these eighteen waltzes, the critic Eduard Hanslick wrote, "Brahms and the Waltz! One is stupefied by the elegance of the page on which these two words are written together. Brahms the serious, the taciturn, the true younger Brother of Schumann, writing waltzes! And yet, he is so northern, so protestant, so unworldy. . . . Some of these appear to be melodic Viennese waltzes, but many more possess the spontaneous equilibrium of the ländler. In these we find the distant echo of Schubert and Schumann." M-D.

My Faithful Heart Rejoices, originally for organ, trans. by Harold Bauer (GS 1942; LC) 2 pp. Some large skips in the left hand are awkward. M-D.

My Heart Is Filled with Longing, originally for organ, trans. by Harold Bauer (GS 1942; LC) 2 pp. Many low repeated octaves, but effective. M-D.

Organ Prelude and Fugue in a trans. by Vincent Persichetti (EV 1940; LC) 7 pp. Very little "padding." Large span required; some octaves and double sixths at conclusion. M-D.

O World I Now Must Leave Thee, originally for organ, trans. by Harold Bauer (GS 1942; LC) 2 pp. Many chords filled in from original. M-D.

Piano Quartets, Op. 25 in g, Op. 26 in A, arr. for piano duet by the composer (Simrock). As an outstanding pianist, Brahms felt very positive about writing for this combination. Adler refers to these piano quartets as the worthiest of all Mozart's successors in chamber music with piano. Op. 25 lends itself exceedingly well to performance in this duet version. Op. 26 is quite lyrical. These arrangements are as difficult to perform as the originals. D.

See: Guido Adler, "Johannes Brahms," MQ XIV (1933):132.

Piano Quartet in c, Op. 60, arr. for piano duet by Robert Keller 1877 (Simrock). Brahms evidently approved of this arrangement since he and his friends used it. He wrote to his publisher, Simrock, in December 1876: "We'll leave *Opus 60* to Mr. Keller [for four-hand arrangement] . . . he should have something to do. I only ask him not to be reticent . . . easy, smooth, and to leave out as much as possible" (Johannes Brahms, *Briefwechsel mit Simrock* [Berlin, 1907–1922], vol. X, p. 21). But Keller did not leave out as much as possible; the textures are dense, and faulty balance is sometimes a problem. D.

Requiem, arr. for duet by the composer, edited by Leonard Van Camp (GS 1968; LC) 110 pp. Includes performance suggestions. The editor feels this arrangement works well with two pianos. Brahms's sensitivity to the contrapuntal sections is especially effective in this version, which highlights the voices. They are thrown into sharp relief against the transparent lines of the piano. English text appears between the piano parts. M-D to D.

Rondo alla Zingarese, arr. by Ernst von Dohnányi (EMB Z.3583, 1961; LC) 13 pp. *Presto,* strong rhythms, left hand crossing over right hand (large skips); cadenza, brilliant coda. M-D.

A Rose Breaks into Bloom, Op. 122/8, originally for organ, arr. for 2 pianos by Lilias Mackinnon (GS 1949; LC) 5 pp. Effective and usable. M-D.

————. Trans. by Harold Bauer (GS 1942; LC) 2 pp. Fingered and pedaled. Uses a little filler with added notes, but effective. M-D.

Serenades, Op. 11 in D (Br&H), Op. 16 in A (Simrock), originally for orchestra, arr. by the composer for piano duet. These four-hand arrangements were published with the original publications. Both are extremely pianistic. Brahms wrote to Joachim: "These days I have arranged my second Serenade for four hands. Don't laugh! It gives me extreme pleasure. I have seldom written music with greater delight; it seemed to sound so beautiful that I was overjoyed. I can honestly say that my happiness was not increased by the knowledge that I was the composer. But it was amusing, all the same" (Johannes Brahms, *Briefwechsel mit Joachim* [Berlin, 1907–1922] vol. V, p. 267). A new edition of Op. 11 was published by Simrock in 1906. Both works give the Secondo more accompanying figures than seem necessary. The slow movement of Op. 16 is a quasi-passacaglia; Brahms distributes the counterpoint so that the Secondo gets the passacaglia figure as well as other interesting voices. M-D to D.

Sextet in B-flat, Op. 18 1860, trans. by the composer for duet (Simrock). Very few notes in the entire work are changed from the string sextet version, and though many large chords must be broken on the piano, the result is very similar to Brahms's own keyboard style. Joseph Joachim wrote to Brahms on October 15, 1861: "The piano arrangement [of Op. 18] is very playable and sounds well. The work gave me the same pleasure as before" (Johannes Brahms, *Briefwechsel mit Joachim* [Berlin, 1907–1922], vol. V, p. 305). M-D.

Sextet in G, Op. 36 1864, trans. by the composer for duet (Simrock). Brahms was studying counterpoint intensely at the time this work was composed and it shows this aspect of his writing. He kept the texture clear while including most of the original material, although durations of some bass notes were changed. M-D.

String Quintets, Op. 88 in F 1882, Op. 111 in G 1890, arr. for duet by the composer (Simrock). These four-hand arrangements were published at the same time as the score to help ensure as wide a circulation as possible. Kalbeck says Op. 111 is the work "in which German humor and Slavic melancholy, Italian temperament and Hungarian pride are all to be found" (Max Kalbeck, *Johannes Brahms,* 8 vols. [Berlin, 1908], vol. 4, p. 210). Op. 88 requires much lyric playing and *sforzandos* that are not overly accented. M-D.

Symphony No. 1, Op. 68, trans. by the composer for duet (Simrock 1877; LC) 67 pp. It is most revealing to see what Brahms leaves out in his remarkable transcribing process. M-D.

Symphony No. 2, Op. 73, arr. by the composer for duet (Simrock). Brahms enjoyed playing this arrangement with his friends. It was made very close to the time of the original work. M-D.

Symphony No. 3, Op. 90, arr. by the composer for 2 pianos (Simrock). Perhaps Clara Schumann did not know of this arrangement when she wrote to Brahms on December 2, 1884: "I was furious when I heard that your F major symphony is now really going to appear arranged by [Robert] Keller. I think it very heartless of you, for no one can arrange your things half as well as you can yourself, and what a pleasure we shall all lose in consequence" (Berthold Litzman, ed., *Letters of Clara Schumann and Johannes Brahms,* trans. by A. M. Ludovici, 2 vols. [London: Edward Arnold, 1927], vol. II, p. 96). Keller made arrangements of this work for piano duet, for solo piano, and for two pianos, eight hands (1884), all published by Simrock. M-D to D.

Symphony No. 4, Op. 98, arr. for 2 pianos by the composer (Simrock 8667 1886; IU) 83 pp. The arrangements of Symphonies Nos. 3 and 4 came into being simultaneously with the orchestral scores, probably as a means of hearing the symphonies immediately. M-D to D.

————. Arr. by the composer for duet (Simrock). Brahms was just as careful and meticulous when making his arrangements as when he was composing. All his arrangements show that he carefully rethought the new medium. He was an extraordinary pianist who knew the limitations and possibilities of his instrument. M-D.

See: Herbert F. Peyser, "Johannes Brahms—The Master as Teacher," MA 67 (February 1947):3, 224, 357.

Variations, Op. 18 1860, trans. by the composer from his String Sextet, Op. 18 (Alfred, in collection *At the Piano With Brahms;* CFP; Dover) 6 pp. This transcription was intended for concert performance. It was written as a birthday present for Clara Schumann. The six variations exploit numerous characteristics of the composer. In Var. 3 the numerous scale passages for the left hand support the syncopated chordal right-hand melody. Theme returns at conclusion. Ends quietly in D. A beautiful set that deserves more performance. M-D.

Violin Concerto in D, Op. 77, arr. for piano and violin by Arthur Schnabel 1905, copyright renewed 1933 (Simrock, Sole American Issue AMP 1933). Although Schnabel's name does not appear, Konrad Wolff assures me that Schnabel told him he was the arranger and that "he was still proud of his achievement" (letter to the author from Konrad Wolff, December 25, 1988). This edition surprisingly lists Brahms and Joachim as the composers!

Six Waltzes, from *Liebeslieder,* Op. 52, trans. for 2 pianos by Guy Maier. Set 1 (JF 1924) 21 pp. Set 2 (JF 1928) 15 pp. Originally for vocal quartet and piano duet. Charming, delightfully appealing. Int. to M-D.

Five Waltzes, Op. 39, arr. for 2 pianos by the composer (CFP; Hughes—GS L

1530). Nos. 1, 2, 11, 14, and 15 from the original cycle for piano duet. Brahms made the 2-piano arrangement for Carl Tausig and his wife. Each waltz is a study in rich harmony, full texture and tone, and rhythmic complexity. Of special note are the consecutive octaves in No. 14 and the consecutive sixths in No. 15. Most are Viennese waltzes, but there is a Ländler influence, with the emphasis rhythmically changed. M-D.

Wiegenlied, Op. 49/4, trans. by Alfred Cortot (Foetisch Frères 1947) 3 pp. Melody in middle voice for first verse, top voice for second verse; coda uses some arpeggios. Effective and charming. M-D.

See also Bach, J. S.; Chopin; Gluck; Handel; Haydn; Joachim; Paganini; Schubert; Schumann, R.; Weber

Roger Branga (–) France
See Ravel

John Branson (–)
See Clementi

Arthur Briskier (–) USA
See Bach, J. S.

Benjamin Britten (1913–1979) Great Britain
Playful Pizzicato, from *Simple Symphony,* trans, for duet by Howard Ferguson (OUP 1972; LC) 12 pp. Displays some delightful imitation between the players. Much fun for all. Int. to M-D.

Peter Grimes Fantasy on Themes from Benjamin Britten's Opera, 1945, by Ronald Stevenson (Bo&H 1972) 12 pp., 6½ min. This powerful transcription follows in miniature form the design of the opera. Full sonorities, bravura octaves, and arpeggio passages; some Impressionistic effects; eclectic style. Free recitativo middle section, stricter outer sections. Effective calm ending. Requires virtuoso technique. D.

Dave Brubeck (1920–) USA
See Songs, American

Anton Bruckner (1824–1896) Austria
Nine Symphonies, arr. for 2 pianos, 8 hands by Karl Grunsky (CFP). These arrangements are fairly literal but they make these little-known works available to pianists. M-D to D.

Henri Buesser (1872–1973) France
See Debussy

Hans von Bülow (1830–1894) Germany
Dante's Sonett "Tanto gentile e tanto onesta," trans. by Franz Liszt G.479 (in JALS 8 [December 1980]:108–111). A six-bar introduction leads to the song. The text appears over the melodic line. Fingered and pedaled by Liszt. Beautifully elegant. M-D.
See also Liszt

Geoffrey Bush (1920–   ) Great Britian
See Arne

Ferruccio Busoni (1866–1924) Italy
Emil Gilels said of Busoni: "At the end of the nineteenth century and the beginning of the twentieth, the piano becomes an orchestral, organ-like instrument due to the virtuosity of Franz Liszt. Busoni was a virtuoso who (with his transcriptions) prolonged the tradition of Liszt—for Liszt had made many transcriptions which in their way served to educate the audiences in the music of Tchaikowsky, Wagner, Meyerbeer, etc. Busoni found the sound of the organ in the piano; developed the technique of the three pedal system—the piano becoming not so much a 'hammer' instrument as a 'sound' instrument. The tone of the piano can be a long, singing line; singing as in the slow episode of this transcription." (Record jacket of Bach-Busoni *Prelude and Fugue* in D, BWV 532, Melodya-Angel SRBO-4110.)

Busoni's transcriptions number over 100 and comprise works by 23 composers (Chopin, Cornelius, Cramer, Gade, Goldmark, Schubert, Schumann, Wagner, and Weber, in addition to those listed below). Everyone knows Busoni as a transcriber of Bach; few know him as a transcriber of Mozart, although he made 30 transcriptions of his works alone! Busoni's enormous output of transcriptions constitutes a giant school for pianists. His transcriptions are usually faithful to the original, his changes being governed by the sonorities and techniques of the medium. Nevertheless, small musical alterations occur from time to time.

See Bach, J. S.; Beethoven; Bizet; Brahms; Gounod; Liszt; Mendelssohn; Meyerbeer; Mozart; Ochs; Offenbach; Paganini; Schoenberg; Songs, English; Songs, Finnish

Dietrich Buxtehude (1637–1707) Denmark
Nun bitten wir den heil'gen Geist, chorale prelude for organ, trans. by Egon Petri (Bo&H 1944; LC) 4 pp. Florid melody. *Ossias* for large hands; use of sostenuto pedal. M-D.
Organ Prelude and Fugue in d, trans. by Sergei Prokofiev (Leeds 1948; LC) 5 pp. Faithful to the original, except that the fugue has been abbreviated considerably. A fine recital opener. M-D.
Prelude and Fugue in g, originally for organ, arr. for 2 pianos by Celius Dougherty (GS 1944). A fine example of the way contrapuntal and dialogue effects, inherent in the organ idiom, may be realized successfully on two pianos. M-D.

William Byrd (1543–1623) Great Britain
The Bells, arr. for 2 pianos by Martin Penny (OUP 1948; LC) 15 pp. Generally requires a non-*legato* touch except in the melodic passages of the middle section. Big sonorities, brilliant scalar passages. M-D.

C

E. C. Cabiati (–   )
See Lecuona

Charles Wakefield Cadman (1881–1946) USA
Dancers of the Mardi Gras, arr. for 2 pianos from the orchestral score by the
Composer (FitzSimons 1934; LC) 22 pp. The work takes its name from the
Negro side of the Mardi Gras, although no Negro themes have been used. It
reflects the fantastic, the grotesque, and the bizarre spirit of the carnival.
This sectionalized fantasy has much color even in the two-piano arrange-
ment. M-D.

John Cage (1912–   ) USA
See Satie

André Caplet (1878–1925) France
See Debussy

Henry Carey (ca. 1687–1743) Great Britain
There is still a question whether Carey composed the tune "God Save the King"
("My Country 'tis of Thee"), but he is generally accepted as its composer. See
Ives.

Geoffrey Carroll (–   ) USA
See Mozart

Mario Carta (–   )
See Lecuona

Grace Castagnetta (–   ) USA
See Gershwin

Mario Castelnuova-Tedesco (1895–1968) Italy
Alt Wien (Viennese Rhapsody) 1923, originally for solo piano, trans. for 2
pianos by the composer (Forlivesi; Arizona State University Library) 50 pp.
Alt Wien (Walzer); Nachtmusik (Notturno); "Memento mori" (Fox-trot
tragico). Chromatic, nostalgic, effective. Carefully exploits both instruments and requires much "give and take" between the performers. M-D.
See also Khachaturian; Ravel; Tchaikowsky

René de Castéra (1873–1955) France
See Albéniz

Ignacio Cervantes (1847–1905) Cuba

Cuban Rhapsody, a concert paraphrase of Cervantes' *Potpouri of National Airs*
by José Echaniz (Foster Music Publishing Co.; LC) 13 pp. Cadenza-like
opening, tunes tossed between the hands, virtuoso ending. M-D to D.

Emmanuel Chabrier (1841–1894) France

Cortège Burlesque, op. posth., originally for orchestra, trans. for duet by the
composer (Costallat 1923; LC) 15 pp. A delightful romp, well distributed
between the players. M-D.

Trois Valses Romantiques, originally for 2 pianos, trans. by Gustave Samazeuilh
(Enoch 1920; LC) 27 pp. These pieces come off well in this transcription,
but the solo pianist must work harder than the two performers in the original
version. M-D.

Cécile Chaminade (1857–1944) France

Le Matin, Op. 79/1; *Le Soir,* Op. 79/2, originally for orchestra, arr. for 2 pianos
by the composer (Enoch 1895; Bo&H; LC; SBTS). Contrasting sections,
facile and flowing; cool and colorful endings in both pieces. Int. to M-D.

Jacques Charlot (–   ) France

See Debussy; Ravel

Abram Chasins (1903–1987) USA

See Bach, J. S.; Bizet; Gluck; Rimsky-Korsakov; Strauss, Johann Jr.; Strauss,
R.; Weinberger

George Chavchavadze (–   )

See Falla

Gaston Choisnel (–   )

See Debussy

Frédéric Chopin (1810–1849) France, born Poland

Arrangement de Concert, of *Rondo,* Op. 16, by Leopold Godowsky (A. P.
Schmidt 1899; LC) 19 pp. Much crossing of hands, virtuosic. D.

Six Chants Polonais, Op. 74, trans. by Franz Liszt G.480 (Galaxy; Durand;
Schlesinger). No other composer has ever achieved the caliber of art and
craftsmanship that Liszt did in his transcriptions of the song literature. In the
entire nineteenth century, no one had as much impact on contemporary
composers and performers as he. *Six Chants Polonais* make a beautiful set,
with little dramas contained in each song. No. 2 is in the collection *At the
Piano with Liszt* (Alfred). M-D.

————. "My Delights," Op. 74/5, trans. by Franz Liszt, revised and edited by
Leopold Godowsky (Musica Obscura). A study edition. Godowsky has
added fingering, pedaling, extra phrasing, and interpretative suggestions.
M-D.

Concert Etude, after *Waltz,* Op. 64/1 ("Minute"), featuring double notes, trans.
by Isidor Philipp (GS 1941); LC) 7 pp. Mainly double thirds and sixths;

cadenza-like passages. Much more difficult than the original. M-D to D.
————, after *Waltz*, Op. 64/1 ("Minuet"), featuring the left hand, trans. by Isidor Philipp (GS 1941; LC) 7 pp. Glittering! M-D to D.
————. Arr. by Leopold Godowsky (Musica Obscura) 12 pp. Sparkles. D.

Etude in f, Op. 25/2, arr. by Johannes Brahms 1869. In *Five Studies Arranged from the Works of Others* (Dover; Ric; Simrock); available separately (Br&H). Arranged with thirds and sixths in the right hand; Chopin's bass remains intact. M-D.

Etude de Concert, after *Etude*, Op. 10/2, by Isidor Philipp (Hamelle) 7 pp. Right hand consists of octaves and full chords; left hand has a chord on each first beat followed by single notes. A real "tour de force." M-D to D.

Etude de Concert, after *Etude*, Op. 10/5 ("Black Key"), by Isidor Philipp (Hamelle; Musica Obscura) 7 pp. Right hand has sixths, fifths, and some single notes. This version is acrobatic and much more difficult than the original. D.

Etude de Concert, after *Etude*, Op. 25/6, by Isidor Philipp (Hamelle) 5 pp. Left hand has the original right-hand part. Right hand has new melody. D.

Deux Etudes after *Etude*, Op. 25/6, trans. by Isidor Philipp (Leduc) 13 pp. Two versions: 1. Right hand is in chromatic sixths. 2. Left hand is in chromatic thirds. D.

Etude de Concert, after *Etude*, Op. 25/2, by Isidor Philipp (Hamelle) 4 pp. This octave study divides the octaves between the hands. D.

Introduction et Polonaise Brillante, Op. 3, for cello and piano, arr. by Charles Czerny (Mechetti 183?; LC) 18 pp. Pedaled, effective treatment, contains lots of fire. M-D to D.

Largo, from *Sonata* for cello and piano, Op. 65, trans. by Alfred Cortot (Foetisch Frères, 1953; LC) 2 pp. Fingered, a beautiful movement beautifully transcribed. M-D.

Paraphrase de Concert, of *Valse*, Op. 18, trans. by Leopold Godowsky (A. P. Schmidt 1899; LC) 11 pp. *Con bravura*, glissando in sixths; chromatic glissando to be played with the second finger on the black keys and the fourth finger on the white keys! D.

53 Studies Based on Chopin Etudes, trans. by Leopold Godowsky, 5 vols. (CFP). These pieces push piano technique beyond the frontiers established by Liszt. Godowsky explained his transcriptions of these etudes as follows: "The fifty-three studies based upon twenty-six Etudes of Chopin have manifold purposes. Their aim is to develop the mechanical, technical and musical possibilities of pianoforte playing, to expand the peculiarly adapted nature of the instrument to polyphonic, polyrhythmic and polydynamic work, and to widen the range of possibilities in tone colouring. The unusual mental and physical demands made upon the performer by the above mentioned work must invariably lead to a much higher proficiency in the command of the instrument, while the composer for the piano will find a number of suggestions regarding the treatment of the instrument, and its musical utterance in general. Special attention must be drawn to the fact, that owing to innumerable contrapuntal devices, which frequently encompass almost the whole range of the keyboard, the fingering and pedalling are often of a revolutionary character, particularly in the twenty-two studies for the left hand alone. The preparatory exercises included in a number of the studies will be found helpful in developing a mechanical mastery over the pianoforte by applying them to the original Chopin studies as well as to the above mentioned versions. The fifty-three studies are to be considered in an equal degree suitable for concert purposes and private study." Twenty-two of these transcriptions are for the left hand alone. Harold Schonberg says: "And despite the enormous difficulties, the *Paraphrases* (Studies) were not intended to be played as bravura stunts. Godowsky had musical aims in mind . . . they . . . represent a philosophy where the piano itself was the be-all and the end-all, less a musical instrument than a way of life, and the paraphrases end up not music for the sake of music but music for the sake of the piano" (*The Great Pianists,* p. 323).

> See: James McKeever, "Godowsky Studies on the Chopin Etudes," *Clavier* 19 (March 1980):21–29. Includes Godowsky's study on Op. 25/4.

Sonata, in b-flat, Op. 35, trans. for 2 pianos by Camille Saint-Saëns (Durand 1907; LC) 44 pp. Looks very different from the original; easier but is remarkably effective. M-D to D.

13 Transcriptions for Piano Solo of Chopin's Minute Waltz, Op. 64/1 (Garvelmann—MTP 1969) 106 pp. Transcriptions by Giuseppe Ferrata (2 versions), Joe Furst, Rafael Joseffy, Max Laistner, Aleksander Michalowski, Moritz Moszkowski, Isidor Philipp (2 versions), Max Reger, Moriz Rosenthal, Keikhosru Shapurji Sorabji, and Michael Zadora. Appendix contains information about various manuscripts and first editions. Virtuoso transcriptions, lavish edition. M-D to D.

Waltz in A-flat, Op. 64/3, concert arr. by Leopold Godowsky (Musica Obscura) 11 pp. Many chromatic inner voices added to the original. Accelerando to the end. M-D.

Waltz in A-flat, Op. 69/1, concert arr. by Leopold Godowsky (Musica Obscura) 13 pp. Many octaves and much filler. Big sweep to the end, then suddenly the final two bars are quiet and slower. M-D.

Waltz in D-flat, Op. 64 ("Minute Waltz"), second piano part by Leonard Pennario (Mills 1949; LC) 8 pp. Most of the added part is in thirds or sixths with the original. Clever, useful. M-D.

Waltz in f, Op. 70/2, concert arr. by Leopold Godowsky (Musica Obscura) 9 pp. Melody has many filled-in chords for support. A graceful setting. M-D.

Six Famous Waltzes, arr. for duet by William Scher (GS 1965; LC) 57 pp. Opp. 34/2; 64/2; 64/1; 69/2; 69/1; 70/2. Primo is usually one octave higher than originally written. Int. to M-D.

Wiosna (Spring), Op. 74/2 1846, trans. by the composer. In collection *At the Piano with Chopin* (Alfred). One of Chopin's most plaintive songs. He

arranged it for friends several times between 1838 and 1848. It was transcribed by Franz Liszt for the second of his *Chants Polonais*. Int.
See also Bellini; Moore; Mozart

Christmas Music
See Dello Joio; Schroeder; Songs, Hungarian

Jeremiah Clarke (1673–1707) Great Britain
The Prince of Denmark's March, trans. by Willard Palmer and Amanda Lethco (Alfred 1987) 2 pp. Main text is in dark print. Simple realizations of each ornament written out in light print, to be used on repeats. Choose your own dynamics! Int.

Muzio Clementi (1752–1832) Italy
Six Sonatines, Op. 36, arr. for duet by Renaud de Vilbac (Litolff; LC) 39 pp. Charming and very effective arrangements. Division between players is logical and musical. Int.
Sonatina, Op. 36/5, with second piano part by Camil Van Hulse (Willis 1978; LC) 19 pp. Very usable. Int.
Sonatina, Op. 36/6, with second piano part by Camil Van Hulse (Willis 1978; LC) 15 pp. Very usable. Int.
Sonatina, Op. 37/1, with second piano part by John Branson (Myklas 1975; LC) 20 pp. Very usable. Includes pedaling and fingering. Int.
Sonatina, Op. 38/1, with second piano part by John Branson (Myklas 1975; LC) 15 pp. Extensive editing. Very usable. Int.
See also Songs, French

Harriet Cohen (1895–1967) Great Britain
See Bach, J. S.

Samuel Coleridge-Taylor (1875–1912) Great Britain
Ethiopia Saluting the Colours, Op. 51, concert march for orchestra, arr. by the composer for duet (Augener 1902; LC) 19 pp. Colorful and moderately effective. M-D.
Incidental Music to Herod, Op. 47, suite for orchestra, trans. for duet by the composer (Augener 1901; LC). Published in four separate movements: Processional; Breeze Scene; Dance; Finale. A fine transcription. M-D.

Will Marion Cook (1869–1944) USA
Cook was very active in composing musical comedies. He helped open a golden era for black musical theater.
In Dahomey, "*Cakewalk Smasher*," trans. by Percy Grainger (R. Stevenson— (CFP 1988) 6 min. A startling concert rag full of swooping glissandos and virtuoso technical tricks. Grainger borrowed one of Cook's tunes from the black musical *In Dahomey* (1902) and one from Arthur Pryor's cakewalk "A Coon Band Contest" (1899). D.

Aaron Copland (1900–   ) USA

Leonard Bernstein has summed up Copland's influence on music: "Aaron is Moses." This says it all about the composer who has been so commanding, so vital, and so essential a figure on the American musical scene.

Billy the Kid, excerpts from the ballet, arr. by the composer for 2 pianos (Bo&H 1946; LC) 34 pp. "The Open Prairie"; "In a Frontier Town: (a) Cowboys with Lassos, (b) Mexican Dance and Finale"; "Billy and His Sweetheart"; "Celebration after Billy's Capture"; "Billy's Demise"; "The Open Prairie Again." Very effective throughout. Requires strong rhythmic control. M-D to D.

Dance of the Adolescent, trans. for 2 pianos by the composer (Bo&H 1968) 24 pp., 6 min. A movement from the ballet *Grogh* (1922–24), about a magician who could revive the dead and make them dance. In 1930 this movement was reworked and became the first movement of the *Dance Symphony.* This version is exuberant, invigorating, rhythmically inventive, and angular. With accomplished players it makes a fine effect. M-D.

Danza de Jalisco, originally a chamber-orchestra work composed for the Spoleto Festival of Two Worlds; trans. for 2 pianos by the composer in 1963 (Bo&H 1968) 4 min. Energetic, engaging, percussive; varied meters. Full of cross-rhythms and hand-slaps. Requires a vivid performance. M-D.

El Salón México, trans. for 2 pianos by Leonard Bernstein (Bo&H 1943). Bernstein is reported to have said that he "grew tired of hearing American pianists end their programs with Hungarian rhapsodies!" This transcription was to be the showpiece to take their place. Dazzling and full of complex rhythms. Sophisticated handling of popular music elements. Many changing meters. "The rhythmic intricacies may be greatly simplified if the performer remembers that the approach to these rhythms should be in terms of eighth-notes, rather than quarters" (from the score). M-D.
   See: A. Brown, "Copland: El Salón México," *Music Teacher* 55 (June 1976):17–18, for an analysis of this work.

Rodeo. "Hoe Down," "Saturday Night Waltz," arr. for 2 pianos by Arthur Gold and Robert Fizdale (Bo&H 1950; LC) 16 pp. Excellent arrangements, very effective. M-D.

Variations on a Shaker Melody, from *Appalachian Spring,* arr. for duet by Bennett Lerner (Bo&H 1985) 12 pp., 6 min. The melody is "Simple Gifts." The words reflect the general philosophy of the Shakers, whose search for simplicity in all things, together with a form of ritual dancing, constituted a major part of their worship. Introduction, followed by six contrasting variations, including a "moderato, like a prayer." Ends on simple C-major triad. M-D.

See: H. Cole, "Popular Elements in Copland's Music," *Tempo* 95 (Winter 1970–71):6–10.

Archangelo Corelli (1653–1713) Italy

Sarabanda and *Giga,* from *Concerto Grosso,* Op. 6/11, arr. for 2 pianos by Joan Last (Galliard 1962; LC) 8 pp. Charming, very usable. Int.

Tempo di Gavotta, from *Trio Sonata,* Op. 4/9, arr. for 2 pianos by Joan Last (Galliard 1964; LC) 4 pp. Cheerful, effective. Int.

Alfred Cortot (1877–1962) France
See Bach, J. S.; Brahms; Chopin; Schubert

Fred Coulter (1934–   ) USA
See Songs, French

François Couperin (1668–1733) France
La Tendre Fanchon, trans. by Ignaz Friedman. In collection *Transcriptions of Ignaz Friedman* (UE 5416; Musica Obscura). With its sweeping arpeggio figures, this transcription is dedicated to the pianist Elly Ney. M-D.

Johann B. Cramer (1771–1858) Germany
See Mozart

Louise R. Crosby (–   ) USA
See Bach, J. S.

César Cui (1855–1918) Russia
Oriental, arr. for 2 pianos by Pierre Luboschutz (JF 1937; LC) 7 pp. Charming and effective. Int. to M-D.
Tarantella, Op. 12, trans. freely by Franz Liszt, G.482 1885 (Durand). The original work (for orchestra) consists of 310 measures; the Liszt version contains 630. Dark and obsessive. Liszt wrote to the Countess Marcy-Arganteau, who requested this transcription, on October 24, 1885: "I hope that Cui will not be angry about the changes and additions I have made to bring the pianist more to the fore. In transcriptions of this kind, one must be able to take liberties" (quoted in Vladimir Stasov, *Selected Essays on Music,* translated by Florence Jonas [New York, 1968], p. 190). M-D.

Carl Czerny (1791–1857) Austria
See Bellini; Chopin; Mozart; Schubert; Strauss, Johann Jr.

D

Ingolf Dahl (1912–1970) USA, born Switzerland

Quodlibet on American Folk Tunes ("The Fancy Blue Devil's Breakdown") (CFP 1957) 5½ min. Arr. for 2 pianos, 8 hands. Four old-fiddler tunes, one hillbilly song, and one cowboy tune combined in the style of a quodlibet. Tunes are easily recognizable but much new material is added. Much use of pentatonic scale. Tart, lean, and contrapuntal in a rhythmic as well as a linear sense. Full of bounce. M-D.

Nicolas Dalayrac (1753–1809) France

Romance, from the opera *La Pazza per Amore,* trans. by Ignaz Friedman, in collection *Transcriptions of Ignaz Friedman,* vol. 1 (UE 17825) 4 pp. Contains a richly romantic melody in D-flat; highly decorated. M-D.

William Daly (–) USA
See Gershwin

José Vianna Da Motta (1868–1948) Portugal
See Alkan

Jean François Dandrieu (1684–1740) France

Les Fifres, trans. by Ignaz Friedman. In collection *Transcriptions of Ignaz Friedman,* vol. 2 (UE 17826). Marchlike; brilliant optional glissandos on final page. M-D.

Le Caquet, trans. by Ignaz Friedman. In collection *Transcriptions of Ignaz Friedman,* vol. 1 (UE 17825) 3 pp. Repeated staccato octaves and thirds require a delicate light touch. M-D.

Jean-Henri D'Anglebert (1635–1691) France
See Lully

Alexander S. Dargomizhsky (1813–1869) Russia

Tarantella, trans. by Franz Liszt, G.483 1879 (Rahter; USSR). This work was originally for piano, three-hands (the Secondo part consisted of a basso ostinato) and was transcribed and enhanced ("transcrité et amplifée") by Liszt. M-D.

Harold Darke (1888–1976) Great Britain
See Bach, J. S.

Claude Debussy (1862–1918) France

Debussy's piano works have been very popular with transcribers, himself and Ravel, in particular. Both lavished a great deal of care on their transcriptions. Debussy left fewer than twenty pedal marks in his entire piano music, and none appear in his transcriptions. But he did notate additional indications via long notes or long notes plus slurs. Debussy studied with a pupil of Chopin's, and he was imbued with the spirit of Chopin, who was his early inspiration. In many cases, Chopin's pedal marks may lead directly to Debussy, i.e., a subtle, fluctuating, but considerable use of the damper and *una corda* pedals, often together. None of Debussy's pianos—a Pleyel, a Gaveau, a Bluethner, and a Bechstein—had a sostenuto pedal. However, many places in these transcriptions can benefit greatly from its use.

Clair de Lune, arr. for 2 pianos by Henri Dutilleux (Jobert 1947; LC) 8 pp. Usable M-D.

———. Arr. for 2 pianos by Godfrey Schroth (JF 1953; LC) 13 pp. Usable. M-D.

———. Arr. for 2 pianos by Phyllis Gunther (Belwin-Mills 1979; LC) 11 pp. Easier than the Dutielleux and Schroth arrangements. Int. to M-D.

Cortège et Air de Danse, from cantata *L'Enfant Prodigue,* arr. for duet by the composer (Durand 1905; LC) 9 pp. Laid out nicely; fits the fingers. Requires firm rhythmic control. M-D.

Danses 1903, originally for harp or piano with string orchestra, arr. for 2 pianos by the composer (Durand) 22 pp., 9 min. Danse Sacrée; Danse Profane. M-D.

———. Trans. for duet by A. Benfeld (Durand 1904; LC) 25 pp. Danse Sacrée; Danse Profane. An efficient transcription that works well. Requires subtle dynamic control. M-D.

Doctor Gradus ad Parnassum, from *Children's Corner,* arr. for 2 pianos by Léon Roques (Durand 1912; LC) 8 pp. Clever arrangement. Int. to M-D.

L'Enfant Prodigue, "Scene lyrique," "Prélude, Cortège et Air de Danse," trans. for 2 pianos by Gaston Choisnel (Durand 1906–1909; LC) 12 pp. A graceful and charming transcription. M-D.

Six Epigraphes Antiques 1914, originally for duet, Debussy made this solo version in 1915 (Durand; CFP) 23 pp., 14½ min. *Pour Invoquer Pan, dieu du vent d'éte* (For invoking Pan, God of the summer wind): ABCBA; idyllic; themes capture the spirits of the two personages of the poem languishing in the torpor of a summer day. *Pour un tombeau sans nom* (For a tomb without a name): elegy, formalized grief, highly refined, whole-tone, chromatic embroidery, parallel diminished chords. *Pour que la nuit soit propice* (So that the night may be propitious): a nocturne suspending murmuring voices above the sounds of the night; one musical idea; binary form with statement and development; whole-tone; ostinato unifies the piece. *Pour la danseuse aux crotales* (For the dancer with rattles): thrusts of groups of notes depict the dancer's rattles; harplike scoring; pentatonic;

quiet closing. *Pour l'Egyptienne* (For the Egyptian): oriental element, improvisation, long drone pedal, exotic figuration, parallel tone clusters, varied levels of timbre sounding simultaneously in various keyboard registers. *Pour remercier la pluie au matin* (For thanking the morning rain): Impressionistic tone paining; loose formal design; opening figure permeates the texture and generates the drive for the entire piece; numerous thematic materials. M-D.

Golliwogg's Cake-Walk, from *Children's Corner,* arr. for 2 pianos by Léon Roques (Durand 1912; LC) 7 pp. Effective. Int. to M-D.

Images, originally for orchestra, trans. for duet by André Caplet (Durand 1912; LC). *Gigues,* 15 pp. *Iberia,* 41 pp. *Rondes de Printemps,* 21 pp. There are awkward spots in this transcription, and much of the original color is lost. Serviceable. M-D to D.

Jeux (Poeme Danse), originally for orchestra, trans. for duet by Léon Roques (Durand 1914; LC) 42 pp. Terribly "busy." Requires superb pianists to get effective sonorities from it. D.

Khamma, Légende Dansée, reduction by the composer (Durand 1912) 32 pp. This colorful piece, with an Egyptian subject, contains some highly interesting music. It was sketched out by Debussy in 1911, then turned over to Charles Koechlin for instrumentation. It was never danced, but after Debussy's death it was performed as concert music. This reduction relies heavily on tremolo. Four staves are used at some places, and two pianos might be more appropriate for a successful performance. M-D to D.

Lindaraja, originally for 2 pianos, trans. by Jean Jules Roger-Ducasse (Jobert 1926; LC) 7 pp. Effective, colorful; highly recommended. Large span required. M-D.

Le Martyre de Saint Sébastien 1911, Prelude to Act I, originally for soloists, chorus, and orchestra; trans. for duet by Jacques Charlot (Durand 1912; LC) 7 pp. Charming and effective. Requires careful pedaling. M-D.

La Mer 1903–1905, arr. for duet by the composer (Durand 6606 1905) 57 pp. Fairly literal arrangement. The absence of orchestral color leaves clearly visible—as might a black-and-white photograph of an oil painting—the complexity of the counterpoint and the structure of the discourse; the intensity of these partially compensate for the lack of color. Some tremolo usage. D.

————. Arr. for 2 pianos by the composer (Durand).

————. Trans. for 2 pianos by André Caplet (Durand 1905–1909; LC) 61 pp. Uses much tremolo but some interesting effects are created. D.

————. Trans. for 2 pianos by Lucien Garban (Durand 1919; LC) 28 pp. Symphonic fragments. Four movements. Effective. M-D.

Nocturnes. Nuages, trans. by Gustave Samazeuilh for duet (Jobert 1923) 14 pp. Much tremolo use, written on three staves. *Fêtes,* trans. by Leonard Borwick (Jobert). *Sirènes,* trans. by Gustave Samazeuilh (Jobert). D.

————. Trans. for 2 pianos by Maurice Ravel (Durand 1908; LC), 49 pp.
Nuages; Fêtes; Sirènes (each available separately). This orchestral work has been translated into the two-piano idiom with independent artistry. *Fêtes* is unique in its realization of the fullest potential of the two-piano sonority. For all its Impressionistic feeling, the music is classically precise, firm, and well knit. This transcription ranks with the best original writing in the two-piano medium. D.

Pelléas et Melisande. "Duo à la Fontaine" (Act II), 15 pp; "Les Cheveux" (Act III), 13 pp; "La Mort de Pelléas" (Act IV), 19 pp., arr. for duet by Léon Roques (each available separately, Durand 1906; LC). These arrangements are well carried out and effective. They require pianists with an excellent "feel" for the style. M-D.

Petite Pièce, originally for clarinet, trans. by Jacques Charlot (Durand 1911; LC) 2 pp. A lovely piece that has much to offer in this version. Int. to M-D.

Petite Suite, trans. by Jacques Durand (Durand 6679 1906) 23 pp. Four popular pieces that are more difficult in this version than in the original duet. M-D.

————. Trans. for 2 pianos by Henri Buesser (Durand 1904, 1908; LC) 31 pp. Very close to the original. M-D.

Prelude à l'après-midi d'un faune 1894, reduction for 2 pianos by the composer, prepared at the same time as the orchestral score (Durand—Costallat; Fromont; GS) 10 min. This version has surprising depth and subtleness for a work that depends so much on orchestral color. It has lovely sonorities, but does not lend itself to one of the most characteristic features of two-piano writing, dialoguing and antiphonal treatment. Debussy maintains a discursive, linear quality throughout, only occasionally dividing a repeated passage or a bass line between the instruments. This arrangement needs some thinning of the low-register tremolos and the addition of the original harp arpeggios. Requires experienced ensemble players to bring off the subtleties. M-D to D.

————. Trans. by Maurice Ravel for duet (Fromont 1910; LC) 15 pp. Awkward at one piano; would be easier to handle on two. May not be pure Ravel, for the American pianist George Copeland made a solo-piano version and may have helped Ravel with the duet. M-D to D.

————. Trans. by Leonard Borwick (Fromont 1914). Pianistically adept and convincing. M-D to D.

Prélude, from *La Damoiselle Élue*, trans. by Léon Roques for duet (Durand 1906–1909; LC) 7 pp. Very beautiful and effective. M-D.

Prélude de L'Enfant Prodigue, originally a cantata, trans. for duet by the composer (Durand 1907; LC) 5 pp. Beautifully effective. M-D.

Printemps—Suite symphonique 1887, trans. for duet by Henri Busser (Durand 8551 1904) 33 pp. Très modéré; Moderato. Works well; sonorities are generally spread over the keyboard; some tremolo. M-D.

1er Quatuor, Op. 10, originally for string quartet, trans. by Harry Loevy (Durand

1909; LC) 31 pp. Some places are very awkward for the pianist. Double thirds, much tremolo usage. Third movement *(Andantino doucement expressif)* is the most effective on the piano. M-D to D.

Rapsodie, originally for orchestra and saxophone 1903, trans. for duet by Lucien Garban (Durand 1919; LC) 23 pp. Works rather well; some simultaneous tremolos in the two parts; much "give and take" between players required. M-D to D.

Serenade for the Doll, from *Children's Corner,* arr. for 2 pianos by Léon Roques (Durand 1912; LC) 8 pp. Much easier than the original. Int. to M-D.

Le Triomphe de Bacchus (The Triumph of Baccus), originally for orchestra, trans. by Marius Gaillard (Durand 1928; LC) 7 pp. Some tremolo use. Works well and sounds well. M-D.

See also Saint-Saëns; Schumann, R.

Carl Deis (1883–1960) USA
See Arensky

Leo Delibes (1836–1891) France
Three Concert Transcriptions on Themes of Schubert, J. Strauss and Delibes, trans. by Ernst von Dohnányi (Rosavölgyi). Concert versions that were typical though outstanding products of the period—when love of the piano and its sound was an esthetic tradition. M-D to D.
Available separately: *Nalia Waltz* 1927 (Allans). This is the lightest of Dohnányi's waltz transcriptions.

Pizzicato Polka, from ballet *Sylvia,* trans. by Rafael Joseffy, in collection *Encores of Great Pianists* (Lowenthal—GS). This piece absolutely bubbles throughout. Many famous pianists from the past played this celebrated transcription. M-D.

Scarf Dance (La Source), arr. for duet by Henry Geehl (Ashdown 1956; LC) 9 pp. Attractive tunes and rhythms. Requires good staccato touch and firm grasp of rhythms. M-D.

Frederick Delius (1862–1934) Great Britain
Brigg Fair—An English Rhapsody 1907, originally for orchestra, trans. for duet by the composer (UE 1911) 19 pp. This colorful transcription has much to recommend it; the layout is excellent and lends itself to this medium. M-D.

"La Calinda," dance from the opera *Koanga,* arr. for 2 pianos by Joan Trimble (Bo&H 1947; LC) 12 pp. Effective. No major performance problems. M-D.

A Dance Rhapsody 1908, arr. for 2 pianos by Percy Grainger (UE 7142 1923) 23 pp. Idiomatic, faithful to original, effective. Highly recommended. M-D.

On Hearing the First Cuckoo in Spring, arr. for 2 pianos by Rudolf Schmidt-Wunstorf (OUP 1952; LC) 8 pp. In an easy-flowing motion. A charming cuckoo! M-D.

On Hearing the First Cuckoo in Spring, Summer Night on the River, two pieces for small orchestra, arr. for duet by Peter Warlock (OUP 1931; LC) 15 pp.

These lovely pieces work well in this version. Impressionistic sonorities. M-D.

A Song before Sunrise 1918, trans. for duet by Philip Heseltine (Augener 1922; LC) 11 pp. Fresh and charming. M-D.

Four Works Transcribed for Piano Solo (Thames 1982) 44 pp. *A Song before Sunrise,* arr. by Eric Fenby. *On Hearing the First Cuckoo in Spring,* arr. by Philip Heseltine. *In a Summer Garden,* arr. by Philip Heseltine. *Late Swallows* (from the *String Quartet*), arr. by Eric Fenby. Colorful and useful versions. Wide span required. M-D.

Bernardino Azzolino Della Ciaia (1671–1755) Italy

Sonata in G, originally for harpsichord, trans. by Béla Bartók (CF 1930; LC). Each movement published separately. Toccata in a: improvisatory opening, contrasting sections, fast octaves, virtuoso scale passages, 7 pp. Canzone: a fugue in C; fast double thirds, big conclusion, 10 pp. Primo Tempo: *Allegro molto,* constant 16ths, 4 pp. Secondo Tempo: *Andantino pastorale,* a flowing 12/8, *pp* closing. M-D.

Norman Dello Joio (1913–   ) USA

Christmas Music, trans. for duet by the composer (EBM 1968; LC) 31 pp. "A Christmas Carol"; "Brighter Star" (Light of the World); "God Rest Ye Merry, Gentlemen"; "Hark! The Herald Angels Sing"; "O, Come All Ye Faithful"; "Silent Night"; "The Holy Infant's Lullaby." A lovely collection, eminently duetable! Int.

Claude Delvincourt (1888–1954) France

Val Venitien, originally for orchestra, reduced for 2 pianos by the composer (Durand 1936; LC) 66 pp. Forlane; Passamezzo; Burlesca; Moresca; Tarentella. A big splashing work with many colorful and exciting moments. M-D.

R. Nathaniel Dett (1882–1943) USA

Juba Dance, from the suite *In the Bottoms,* trans. for 2 pianos by Edouard Hesselberg (SB 1926; LC) 9 pp. A very effective transcription that has even more flair than the original. M-D.

Anton Diabelli (1781–1858) Austria

Variation on a Waltz by Diabelli, trans. by Franz Liszt G.147, in collections *Liszt* (G. Green—OUP 1973) and *The Young Liszt* (Alfred 1990). This variation was written when Liszt was eleven years old. Diabelli invited fifty musicians prominent in Vienna to write one variation each on a waltz theme of his own composition. Beethoven composed his *33 Variations on a Waltz of A. Diabelli,* Op. 120, and made Diabelli's name immortal. Liszt's variation is in the style of Beethoven. Int. to M-D.

Grigoras Dinicu (1889–1949) Rumania

Hora staccato, arr. for 2 pianos by the composer (CF 1942; LC) 13 pp. Requires fine left-hand broken-octave technique; tremolo chords; long trills. M-D.

J Doebber (–   )
See Rameau

Ernst von Dohnányi (1877–1960) Hungary
Dohnányi's first fame came as the result of being an international virtuoso
pianist. His music follows the Brahms tradition. It is pianistic and effective but
not always very original.
See Brahms; Delibes; Schubert; Songs, French; Strauss, Johann Jr.

A. Doloukhanian (–   ) Armenia
See Khachaturian

Gaetano Donizetti (1797–1848) Italy
Fantasy on "Don Pasquale," Op. 67, trans. from the opera by Sigismond
    Thalberg (MTP). Thalberg was nicknamed "Old Arpeggio" by his con-
    temporaries because he specialized in arpeggio passage-work. This fantasy
    is a good example of the three-hand illusion he frequently produced. This
    device (achieved by dividing a third voice between the hands) had come to
    be considered his private property, as he used it so much. Thalberg was
    among the new order of pianists, who loved special effects and *misterioso*
    suggestion. He purposely avoided transparent textures, which formerly
    were deemed a prerequisite for good piano playing. M-D to D.
Fantaisie on the Opera "Lucrezia Borgia," trans. by Sigismond Thalberg, Op.
    50 (Br&H; SBTS) 19 pp. Requires a brilliant technique and a singing style;
    sparkling passage-work. D.
Funeral March and Cavatina from "Lucia di Lammermoor," trans. by Franz
    Liszt G.398, 1835–36. In collection *Liszt* (G. Green—OUP 1973). The
    "Funeral March" and "Cavatina" occur at the end of Act III. The material in
    measures 96-209 is taken from the final number of Act II, and the conclud-
    ing chord sequence (measure 254) is derived from the orchestral accompani-
    ment to the Sextet. But an aria by the hero, Edgardo, dominates from its
    first appearance to the end of the work. There are two versions for some
    sections. Many deviations from the basic tempo which players must handle
    in accordance with their own musical feelings. M-D to D.
Réminiscences de "Lucia di Lammermoor," trans. by Franz Liszt G.397, 1835–
    36 (UE). Based on the Sextet. Improvisatory introduction followed by a
    sparkling transcription of the broad, attention-demanding subject. Tempos
    gradually increase, and a truly virtuoso coda closes the piece, with an
    impetus that takes it a long way from the original, in both form and content.
    M-D to D.
Réminscences de Lucrezia Borgia, trans. by Franz Liszt G.400 (Cranz). This
    large-scale work has a strange mixture of themes and displays a bravura
    style throughout. Numerous scales in octaves, thirds, and sixths; melody
    often in lower registers. In four sections, each more brilliant than the last.
    D.
Andante Finale de "Lucia di Lammermoor," trans. for left hand alone by

Theodor Leschetizky, Op. 13 (GS; Cen). Laid out very beautifully for the left hand. Many arpeggios. Relies on the thumb for playing the melody. M-D.

Valse de concert sur deux motifs de Lucia et Parisina, G.401 1850, second version of G.214/3 (rev. ed.), trans. by Franz Liszt (Schlesinger; in collection *Piano Transcriptions from French and Italian Operas,* Dover; in collection *Dances for Piano,* Liszt Society Publication, vol. 4, Schott). Donizetti's *Parisina* was first produced in Florence in 1833, and his *Lucia di Lammermoor* in Naples in 1835; Liszt's original transcription of the waltz was written in 1842. Ten years later Liszt revised it and produced this version. It appeared together with the second versions of the *Grande Valse di Bravura* and the *Valse mélancolique* as *Trois Caprices-Valses.* Both themes are combined at the climax of the waltz. Here Liszt has combined innocent little tunes from two Donizetti operas to produce what became not just a virtuoso warhorse but a convincing and original character piece that greatly elevates the basic material into a waltz-poem. M-D to D.

Variations de Concert sur le motif de l'Opera L'Elisire d'amore de Donizetti "Io son ricco e tu sei belle," Op. 1, trans. by Adolf Henselt (Br&H ca. 1838). Schumann called this a work of "German genius." These variations were very popular for their originality. A 50-measure introduction mingles fragments of the themes with varied types of figuration. A ritornello appears between all the variations except after the last one, which is followed by a brilliant finale that features interlocking octaves. The form blends variation with fantasy. D.

Variations on a Theme from Donizetti's "Anna Bolena," trans. by Mikhail Glinka 1831. In *Complete Piano Works,* vol. 6 of *Complete Edition* (N. Zagornie—USSR 1958). Theme and four variations. Var. 3 is in two parts: *Un poco più vivo* and *Andante.* M-D.

Celius Dougherty (1902–1986) USA
See Bach, J. S.; Bach, W. F.; Buxtehude; Falla; Lanner; Tchaikowsky

Madeleine Dring (1923–1977) Great Britain
See Purcell

Maurice Dumesnil (1886–1974) France
See Ravel

C. H. Stuart Duncan (–   )
See Bach, J. S.

Thomas F. Dunhill (1877–1946) Great Britain
See Purcell

Jacques Durand (–   ) France
See Boëllman; Debussy

Henri Dutilleux (1916–   ) France
See Debussy

Jean Baptiste Duvernoy (1802–1880) France
See Rossini

Antonin Dvořák (1841–1904) Czechoslovakia
Slavonic Dances, Op. 72, trans. by Robert Keller (Simrock 217). Vol. I: No. 1
in B; No. 2 in e; No. 3 in F; No. 4 in D-flat. Vol. II: No. 5 in b-flat; No. 6 in
B-flat; No. 7 in C; No. 8 in A-flat. Pianistic, tricky in spots, effective.
M-D.

E

Brian Easdale (1909–   ) Great Britain
See Handel

José Echaniz (1905–1969) Cuba
See Cervantes

Hermene Eichhorn (1906–   ) USA
See Kreisler

Jan Ekier (1913–   ) Poland
See Chopin

Edward Elgar (1857–1934) Great Britain
Enigma Variations on an Original Theme, Op. 36, originally for orchestra, arr.
by the composer (Nov 1899) 42 pp. One of Elgar's most famous works. The
arrangement is highly effective and makes for an exciting piece. These
variations owe their nickname to the heading "Enigma" Elgar placed over
his theme, which he remarked "went with" some other melody; the puzzle
has never been satisfactorily resolved. The theme and fourteen variations, in
the manner of Brahms's *St. Antony Variations,* form something like a
condensed symphony. M-D to D.

Walter Emery (1909–1974) Great Britain
See Bach, J. S.

Andrei Eshpay (1925–   ) USSR
See Glinka

Stepán Esipoff (–   ) Russia
See Tchaikowsky

Heinrich Esser (1818–1872) Germany
See Wagner

F

Manuel de Falla (1876–1946) Spain

7 Canciones Populares Españolas, trans. by E. Halffter (ESC). Effective transcriptions by one of Falla's students. M-D.

Dance of the Miller's Wife (Fandango) from *The Three Cornered Hat,* trans. for 2 pianos by C. Dougherty (JWC).

Danza ritual del fuego (Ritual fire dance) from *El Amor Brujo,* arr. for 2 pianos by Mario Braggiotti (JWC 2932 1921) 13 pp. Strong rhythmic drive even more effective in this arrangement than in the original for solo piano. Trills, fast octaves in alternating hands, glissandi. M-D.

Pantomine from *El Amor Brujo,* trans. for 2 pianos by C. Dougherty (JWC).

Suite on Themes from El Amor Brujo, arr. by George Chavchavadze (JWC 9747 1950) 34 pp., 19½ min. Includes the best-known themes; some pedal instructions. Builds to thundering climax, pianistic. M-D to D.

Gabriel Fauré (1845–1925) France

Deuxième Quintette, Op. 115, *Andante,* trans. by Gustave Samazeuilh (Durand 11316 1927) 8 pp. Originally for strings. Effective and beautiful; pianistic. M-D.

See also Saint-Saëns

Eric Fenby (1906–   ) Great Britain
See Delius

Howard Ferguson (1908–   ) Great Britain
See Britten

Giuseppe Ferrata (1865–1928) Italy
See Chopin

John Field (1782–1837) Ireland

Rondo, from *Sonata,* Op. 1/1 in E-flat, arr. for 2 pianos by Martin Penny (OUP 1945; LC) 19 pp. Contains much filler when compared with the original but is still effective. M-D.

Robert Fizdale (1920–   ) USA
See Barber; Copland; Thomson

Andor Foldes (1913–   ) Hungary
See Kodály

Hubert Foss (1899–1953) Great Britain
See Vaughan Williams

Stephen Foster (1826–1864) USA

Oh, Susanna, trans. for 2 pianos by Morton Gould (H. Flammer 1937; LC) 12 pp. Fast, spirited, delightful, and brightly effective. M-D.

Swanee River, trans. for 2 pianos by Gregory Stone (EBM 1937; LC) 22 pp. Fantasia di Bravura on "Old Folks at Home." Virtuosic handling throughout. D.

See also Gottschalk

César Franck (1922–1890) France

Prelude, Fugue and Variation, Op. 18, originally for organ, trans. for 2 pianos by Ethel Bartlett and Rae Robertson (OUP 1951; LC) 13 pp. Stays close to the version for piano and organ made by the composer. The two parts have equal interest. This "work should be played in a devotional manner, 'religoso,' avoiding over-sentimentality" (from the score). M-D.

———. Trans. for 2 pianos by Rudolph Gruen (AMP 1936; LP) 19 pp. Pedaled, thicker sonorities than in the Bartlett-Robertson version. M-D.

———. Trans. by Ignaz Friedman in collection *Piano Arrangements of Popular Classics* (Allans 1225) 13 pp. Fingering, pedaling, and some dynamics added by Friedman. This version is so pianistic and sounds so fine on the piano that one might think it was originally conceived for the instrument. Beautifully effective throughout; highly recommended. M-D.

Oeuvres d'Orge, trans. by Blanche Selva (Durand 1910; LC).

1re Fantaisie, Op. 16, trans. by Jacques Durand (Durand; 1910; LC) 10 pp.

2e Fantaisie, trans. by Blanche Selva (Durand 1912; LC) 11 pp.

Prière, Op. 20, trans. by Blanche Selva (Durand 1912; LC) 11 pp.

Pastorale, trans. by Harold Bauer (Durand).

Prelude, Fugue et Variation, trans. by Harold Bauer (Durand).

These six transcriptions are remarkably effective on the piano, in spite of their being originally conceived for the organ. The Bauer versions are eminently pianistic. M-D. Much of this music is also available for 2 pianos (Durand).

Morceau Symphonique de Redemption, reduced for duet by the composer (Heugel; LC) 12 pp. Requires expert ensemble experience. M-D.

Symphonie in d, trans. for duet by the composer (Hamelle; LC) 73 pp. This remarkable version fits the medium superbly. D.

Robert Franz (1815–1892) Germany

Franz was one of the finest masters of the German lied.

The Messenger (Die Bote), Op. 8/1,3, trans. by Franz Liszt G.489/2. In collection *Twenty Transcriptions by Franz Liszt* (OD). Liszt combines two songs in this transcription: "Passing through the Moonlit Woods" and "The Messenger." The middle section is based on the first song. Contains brief cadenza-like passages. Liszt's settings are convincingly characteristic of the words. M-D.

Arnold Freed (1926–   ) USA

Win, Place or Show, originally for orchestra, trans. by the composer (Belwin-Mills 1981; LC) 21 pp. Simulates a horse race; clever. M-D.

Girolamo Frescobaldi (1583–1643) Italy

Capriccio on the Cuckoo's Call. See Bauer.

Fuga in g, originally for organ or harpsichord, trans. by Béla Bartók (CF 1930; LC) 6 pp. Octaves; written-out trills. Final statement of subject ends *fff*. M-D.

Toccata in G, originally for organ or harpsichord, trans. by Béla Bartók (CF 1930; LC) 9 pp. Contrasting sections; filled-in octave chords; final section requires four staves for notation; *fff* ending. M-D.

Walter Frey (1898–   ) Switzerland
See Bach, J. S.

Ignaz Friedman (1882–1948) Poland
Friedman, a pupil of Leschetizky, left some unique recordings that prove he was one of the twentieth century's greatest pianists. He composed about 100 piano pieces of startling keyboard originality.

The Friedman Collection—Piano Arrangements of Popular Classics (Allans 1225) 88 pp. Contains: J. S. Bach: *Morning Song; Toccata and Fugue* in d, BWV 565; *Sheep May Safely Graze; Brandenburg Concerto* No. 3; *Gavotte* (Rondeau) from the *Violin Sonata* No. 6; *Siciliano* from *Sonata for Flute and Piano* No. 2; *My Heart Ever Faithful; Bourrée* from *Violin Partita* No. 2. Mendelssohn: *Scherzo* from *String Quartet,* Op. 44/3. Franck: *Prelude, Fugue and Variation,* Op. 18/3. Gluck: Flute solo from the ballet *Orpheus.* See original composers for more-detailed entries. M-D to D.

See also Bach, J. S.; Couperin; Dalayrac; Dandrieu; Franck; Gärtner; Gluck; Grazioli; Mendelssohn; Moniuszko; Rameau; Scarlatti; Schubert; Strauss, Johann Jr.

James Friskin (1886–1967) USA, born Scotland
See Bach, J. S.

Johann Jakob Froberger (1616–1667) Germany
See Bauer

Anis Fuleihan (1900–1970) USA, born Cyprus
Fuleihan was strongly influenced by his recollections of and eventual research into Mediterranean music.

Epithalamium, originally for piano and string orchestra, trans. by the composer for 2 pianos (GS 1942; LC) 40 pp., 12½ min. The theme is a traditional Lebanese wedding song, to be "played expressively, with a very even rhythmic flow" (from the score). Piano II is basically a reduction of the original string orchestra part. M-D.

See also Bach, J. S.; Songs, English

Joe Furst (–   ) USA
See Chopin

G

Marius Gaillard (1900–1973) France
See Debussy

Paolo Gallico (1868–1955) USA, born Italy
See Rimsky-Korsakov

Lucien Garban (–   ) France
See Bizet; Debussy; Ibert; Ravel; Saint-Saëns

Percival Garratt (1877–1953) Great Britain
See Handel

Eduard Gärtner (–   ) Austria
Gärtner was a prominent baritone.
Six Viennese Dances on Motifs by Gärtner, trans. by Ignaz Friedman 1916–29
   (UE 8585). In G-flat, G, D-flat, F, A-flat, C. No. 2 is dedicated to Isidor
   Philipp. Dense textures, thoroughly charming. Richard Strauss's influence
   is felt—especially post-*Rosenkavalier*. M-D to D.
Viennese Dance No. II, arr. by Ignaz Friedman after motives by Gärtner, arr. for
   2 pianos by Otto Schlaaf and Robert Riotte (UE 1936; LC) 10 pp. This
   arrangement of an arrangement is very effective. M-D to D.

Henry Geehl (1881-1961) Great Britain
See Delibes

George Gershwin (1898–1937) USA
An American in Paris, originally an orchestral tone poem, trans. by William
   Daly (New World Music 1929) 35 pp. Includes all the sights and sounds of
   Paris for an American visitor. Well written for the piano but loses much
   color and effect as compared to the orchestral version. M-D to D. Also
   trans. for 2 pianos by Gregory Stone (New World Music).
Concerto in F, 1925, trans. by Grace Castagnetta (New World Music) 30 min.
   One of the most popular works of the twentieth century. This transcription
   loses some of its effectiveness, especially in vitality. It requires a fine
   technique with strong rhythmic projection. M-D to D.
Cuban Overture 1932, originally for orchestra, trans. for duet and for 2 pianos
   by Gregory Stone (New World Music in two separate publications). Attractive tunes separated by filler material. Full of blue notes, especially flat-
   tened thirds and sevenths, plus syncopations of all kinds. M-D to D.

Embraceable You, trans. for piano duet by Percy Grainger (GS 1951). Fluent. M-D.

———. Trans. for 2 pianos by Gregory Stone (New World Music 1955; LC) 12 pp. Excellent. M-D.

Fascinating Rhythm, trans. for 2 pianos by Gregory Stone (New World Music 1955; LC) 12 pp. Extremely effective. M-D.

———. Concert paraphrase by Gregory Stone (Harms 1951; LC) 6 pp. Very effective section entitled "alla viennoise" done in excellent taste. Many skips of tenths in left hand; large span required. M-D.

Gershwin's Improvisations for Solo Piano (A. Wodehouse—New World Music 1987). Transcriptions Gershwin recorded between 1926 and 1928: "Clap yo' hands"; "Looking for a boy"; "Maybe"; "My one and only"; "Someone to watch over me"; "Sweet and lowdown"; " 'S Wonderful/Funny face"; "That certain feeling." Contains the editor's performance notes on tempo, dynamics, touch, articulation, and pedaling. Delightful; has an appealing breezy charm. M-D.

"Gershwin's keyboard style in these improvisations has several distinct characteristics. The first is the close relationship they have to the dance music of the 20's and their frequent references to ragtime-stride. Another is their thick and complex textures, which conjure up the rich sonority of a dance band. In the variations contained within each improvisation Gershwin wove styles taken from the wealth and variety of musical contexts familiar to the music-loving public of the 20's. These included the spicy and dream-like harmonies of the Impressionists, jazz, the dizzying cross-rhythms of the novelty ragtime pianists, interpenetration of dance styles (a waltz within a foxtrot, for instance), Yiddish theater music, and even sly quotes from the classical masters. Gershwin's improvisations have virtuoso flair, craftsmanship and whimsical invention—enough to hold the interest of even the most discriminating music lover" (from a letter to the author from Artis Wodehouse, August 21, 1987).

See: Artis Wodehouse, "Gershwin's Solo Piano Disc Improvisations," *Clavier* 27/8 (October 1988):22–30. Includes Gershwin's transcription of "Someone to Watch Over Me."

Gershwin at the Keyboard (New World Music), eighteen song hits arranged by the composer. First-rate transcriptions that are full of fun and fancy. M-D.

Love Walked In, trans. by Percy Grainger (Chappell 1946). Gershwin called this tune "Brahmsian" because of certain harmonic resemblances to many pieces by Brahms that he liked. Grainger evokes musical glasses by two-note treble tremolos, containing the tune and a descant—the tremolos are called "woggles." Remarkable writing. M-D.

The Man I Love, concert adaptation of Gershwin's own piano transcription by Percy Grainger (GS 1944).

———. Trans. for 2 pianos by Gregory Stone (Harms 1951; LC) 12 pp. First-rate. M-D.

Oh, I Can't Sit Down, trans. by Percy Grainger, for one piano, 6 hands (GS 1950).

Oh, Lady Be Good, paraphrase by Maurice Whitney (Harms 1948; LC) 4 pp. Slow free section contrasts with a bright rhythmic section. Effective. M-D.

————. Trans. for 2 pianos by Henry Levine (Harms 9149; LC) 8 pp. Effective. M-D.

Preludes 1934, trans. by Gregory Stone for duet and for 2 pianos (separate publications, New World Music). The two-piano version is the more effective one. The first and third Preludes are almost more exciting on two pianos than in the original solo version. M-D.

Porgy and Bess, fantasy for 2 pianos by Percy Grainger (GS 1951). Weaves together a number of the best tunes from the opera. M-D.

Soon, paraphrase by Maurice Whitney from *Strike Up the Band* (New World Music 1947; LC) 5 pp. Contrasting sections, *pp* ending, good "feel" for Gershwin style. M-D.

Strike Up the Band, trans. for 2 pianos by Gregory Stone (New World Music 1956; LC) 12 pp. Wonderfully effective. M-D.

Rhapsody in Blue, trans. for duet by Henry Levine (New World Music), and for 2 pianos by the composer (New World Music) 16 min. Requires a strong sense of rhythm. M-D.

Variations on "I Got Rhythm" 1934, originally for piano and orchestra, trans. for 2 pianos by the composer (Warner Brothers) 8½ min.

Elizabeth Gest (–   ) USA
See Songs, American; Gottschalk

Walter Gieseking (1895–1956) Germany, born France
See Strauss, R.

Alberto Ginastera (1916–1983) Argentina
Ginastera's style combines nationalistic traits with advanced contemporary techniques.

Pequeña danza, trans. by the composer from the ballet *Estancia* 1941 (Barry 1955) 4 pp. Fast bitonal waltz punctuated with glissandos and strong syncopation, *pp* ending. M-D.
See also Zipoli

William Gilbert (1836–1911) and **Arthur Sullivan** (1842–1900) Great Britain
Dialogue on Gilbert and Sullivan Themes, for 2 pianos by Ralph Berkowitz (EV 1944; LC) 20 pp. Fun for all, clever. Touches on some of the most popular tunes. M-D.

Alexander Glazounoff (1865–1936) Russia
Dance, from the ballet *Raymonda,* trans. by Alexander Siloti (CF 1927; LC) 3 pp. The middle section, *molto espressivo,* is especially effective. M-D.

Reinhold Gliere (1875–1957) Russia

Dance, from *Red Poppy,* originally for orchestra, trans. for duet by Leo Kraft (Cen 1950; LC) 7 pp. Dry, snappy, and effective. A choice transcription. Int. to M-D.

Russian Sailor's Dance, trans. for 2 pianos by Rudolph Gruen (AMP 1938; LC) 15 pp. Bright, colorful, effective. M-D.

Mikhail Glinka (1804–1857) Russia

The Lark (L'Alouette), trans. by Mily Balakirev (E. MacDowell—Br&H 1895) 7 pp. No. 10 of a group of twelve songs Glinka wrote in 1840 and entitled *Farewell to St. Petersburg.* Flowing figuration; exceptionally beautiful melody; moves through numerous keys; glissandos. M-D to D.

―――. Arr. for 2 pianos by Pierre Luboshutz (JF 1951; LC) 12 pp. Effective but tricky. M-D.

Réminiscences de l'Opera "Le vie pour le Czar," trans. by Mily Balakirev (Zimmermann). Written in 1855, when Balakirev was 18, but not published until 1899. A long virtuoso work built mainly on one theme with each variation becoming more brilliant and complex. M-D to D.

Tscherkessenmarsch (March of Chernomor), from *Russlan and Ludmilla,* trans. by Franz Liszt for duet, G.406 1843 (USSR) 6½ min. Liszt was so impressed with Glinka's opera that he composed this brilliant four-hand version only one year after its premiere. The March accompanies the movements of the sorcerer, Chernomor, and his group of wicked magicians in Act IV. Liszt also published versions of the March for solo piano (USSR), piano 8-hands, and full orchestra. M-D.

11 Variations on a Theme by Glinka (AMP). Variations by leading Soviet composers on "Vanya's Song," from the opera *Ivan Susanin.* One variation each by Dmitri Kabalevsky, Eugen Kapp, Andrei Eshpay, Rodion Shchedrin, Georgi Svirodiv, and Yuri Levitin; two by Vassarion Shebalin; and three by Dmitri Shostakovitch. Brilliant and highly interesting writing. M-D.

See also Bellini; Donizetti

Christoph Willibald Gluck (1714–1787) Germany

Ballet, flute solo from *Orpheus,* trans. by Ignaz Friedman, in collection *Piano Arrangements of Popular Classics* (Allans 1225) 3 pp. *Lento,* arpeggiated tenths, melody rides on broken-chord figuration, some hand-crossing. Eminently pianistic, flowing. Would make a wonderful encore. M-D.

Melodie d'Orfée (Dance of the Blessed Spirits), trans. by Giovanni Sgambati (Schott) 4 min. This transcription represents a perfection of style rarely encountered. Rachmaninoff was very fond of this work. M-D.

Gavotte, from the ballet *Don Juan,* trans. by Ignaz Friedman, in collection *Transcriptions of Ignaz Friedman,* vol. 2 (UE 17826). Much filigree work in right hand necessary to pinpoint melodic detail. M-D.

Gavotte after Gluck 1871, from *Iphigenia in Aulis,* trans. by Johannes Brahms

(CPF; Dover; Ric; Schott). Frequent use of three staves makes the middle part easier to read. Requires a good technique, especially a "singing" power by the weaker fingers. M-D.

Melody (Second Ballet), from *Orpheus*, trans. by Abram Chasins (CF 1938; LC) 4 pp. Chasins requests that "The tenths throughout should not be broken unless it is absolutely necessary to do so" (from the score). M-D.

―――. Trans. for 2 pianos by Pierre Luboschutz (JF 1954; LC) 7 pp. A lovely version. M-D.

―――. Trans. by Ignaz Friedman, in collection *Transcriptions of Ignaz Friedman*, vol. 2 (UE 17826). Harmonious and lovely. M-D.

Variations on a theme from "Armide" by C. W. Gluck, by Johann Nepomuk Hummel, trans. by Alexander Siloti (CF 1928; LC). Theme and six charming variations; in the series Transcriptions and Revisions for Piano Students by Alexander Siloti. Wonderfully pianistic and effective; fluent and naive writing. Int. to M-D.

Benjamin Godard (1849–1895) France

Canzonetta, from *Concerto Romantique*, freely trans. from the violin by Leopold Godowsky (CF 1927). Dedicated to Jerome Kern. Flowing melodies. M-D.

Leopold Godowsky (1870–1938) Poland

Godowsky is considered by many authorities to have possessed one of the best pianistic mechanisms of all time. His piano compositions are unique in many ways, and their contrapuntal complexities and elaborate detail make many of them very difficult. Godowsky used to say: "There are few things so perfect they cannot be improved." All his transcriptions support that philosophy, for he embroidered with spangles whatever caught his fancy. Even the simplest pieces have an intricacy of counterpoint, which is his trademark.

Alt Wien (Old Vienna), trans. for 2 pianos by the composer (GS 1935) 6 pp., 2½ min. Based on the motto "whose yesterdays look backwards with a smile through tears." Thematic material excellently distributed between the two performers; contrapuntal. M-D.

See also Albéniz; Bizet; Bohm; Chopin; Godard; Henselt; Kreisler; Rameau; Saint-Saëns; Schubert; Schumann, R.; Smith, J. S.; Strauss, Johann Jr.; Strauss, R.; Weber

Arthur Gold (1917–   ) USA, born Canada

See Barber; Copland; Thomson

Adolf Gotlieb (–   )

See Khachaturian

Louis Moreau Gottschalk (1829–1869) USA

Known as the American Liszt, Gottschalk ranked with the greatest European virtuosos of his time. His piano works require a solid technique. They display vitality, beauty, and charm. Many demand virtuosity of the highest degree, and all are laid out well for the piano. Gottschalk was the first important American composer to realize the beauty of native folk music.

The Banjo, trans. for 2 pianos by Jerome Moross (JF 1935; LC) 11 pp. Based on Stephen Foster's "Camptown Races" and the spiritual "Roll, Jordan, Roll." This version works very well. M-D.

Bamboula (West Indies Drum Dance), arr. for 2 pianos by Elizabeth Gest (EV 1943; LC) 8 pp. Based on a Louisiana Creole song known as "Quan patate la cuite." Spirited and effective. M-D.

————. Arr. for 2 pianos by Phyllis Gunther (Belwin-Mills 1975; LC) 22 pp. Thinner textures than in the Gest version. M-D.

Esquisses Créoles, originally for orchestra, trans. for duet by Lucien Lambert, on themes of Louis M. Gottschalk (Mackar & Noel 1898; LC) 15 pp. Uses themes from "The Banjo" and "Bamboula." Well written for the medium. Strongly rhythmic. M-D.

La Nuit des Tropiques 1858 or 1859, symphony for orchestra and additional band, arr. for 2 pianos by John Kirkpatrick with grateful borrowings from the unfinished arrangement for 2 or 3 pianos by N. R. Espadero (UCLA) 28 pp. *Andante; Allegro moderato.* Retains the Gottschalk stylistic glitter throughout. Composed under the inspiration of the friendly Antilles. John Kirkpatrick, in a short but penetrating study of Gottschalk's music, wrote that this symphony "demonstrates what a good piece he could write when he wanted to—it impresses one as perhaps the only time he really tried—the poetic atmosphere throughout is admirably realized—the line has surprising expansion." M-D.

Pasquinade (Caprice), arr. for 2 pianos by Phyllis Gunther (Belwin Mills 1975; LC) 16 pp. Contains a scintillating middle section. Usable. M-D.

Tournament Galop, arr. for 2 pianos by Phyllis Gunther (Belwin Mills 1975; LC) 16 pp. Covers the keyboard. M-D.

See also Rossini; da Silva; Songs, American; Verdi

Gould (–   )
See Rimsky-Korsakov

Morton Gould (1913–   ) USA
Gould's compositions contain popular music, jazz, and more-formal structures.

Boogie-Woogie Etude, trans. for 2 pianos from the solo-piano version by the composer (Belwin-Mills 1943) 13 pp. "Fast, driving tempo (steely hard)" (from the score). Catchy. Requires fine octave technique. M-D.

Dialogues, originally for piano and string orchestra, trans. by the composer for 2 pianos (Chappell) 22 min. Recitative and Chorale; Embellishments and Rondo; Dirge and Meditation; Variations and Coda. Dodecaphonic procedures used. M-D.

Interplay (American Concertette) 1943, originally for piano and orchestra, arr. for 2 pianos by the composer (Belwin-Mills) 13 min. With drive and vigor:

extremely rhythmic. Gavotte: a short, light dance. Blues: in a slow, nostalgic mood. Very fast: a brilliant, rapid finale. M-D.

Pavanne, from *American Symphonette* No. 2, originally for orchestra, trans. by the composer for duet (Mills 1944; LC) 11 pp., 3 min. This famous tune is treated nicely and works remarkably well. *Secco* (dry) style; highly recommended. Int. to M-D.

————. Trans. for 2 pianos by the composer (Mills 1944; LC) 10 pp. As effective as the duet version. M-D.

See also Foster; Kreisler; Songs, Mexican

Charles Gounod (1818–1893) France

Berceuse (Les Sabéennes), from *The Queen of Sheba,* Act II, trans. by Franz Liszt G.408. In collection *Twenty Transcriptions by Franz Liszt* (OD). Contains many harp-like (arpeggiated) sonorities. Each time the main theme returns it is treated differently. M-D.

Funeral March of a Puppet (Marionnetti), trans. for duet by William Scharfenberg (GS 1884; LC) 13 pp. Delightful and effective. M-D.

————. Trans. by Theodore Thomas (John Church 1877; LC) 11 pp. A little less "fussy" than the Scharfenberg version. M-D.

Waltz, from *Faust,* trans. by Franz Liszt, G.407 1861 (GS) 9 min. This is a gracious compliment from one devotee of the famous legend to another, for Liszt created his *Faust* Symphony even before Gounod's opera had its premiere in 1859. It was thus very much a "modern" work when Liszt published this transcription in 1861. Busoni wrote a fabulous cadenza for this work, entitled *Nach Gounod* (in his *Klavierübung,* Part 2, Bk. VII, of the 1st ed., or Bk. V of the 2d ed. [Br&H]), among others written for trill exercises. Since Liszt's transcription draws on one scene from the opera, it tends to be more like a paraphrase than a fantasy. According to Charles Suttoni: "A paraphrase differs from a fantasy in that it is usually not as multi-sectioned and generally draws on one particular scene or incident in the opera" ("Piano and Opera," p. 318). M-D to D.

See also Bach, J. S.

Percy A. Grainger (1882–1961) Australia

Grainger's genius is finally being appreciated. This multi-talented musician contributed many effective transcriptions to the repertoire. Some of them rank with those by Liszt, Busoni, and Rachmaninoff. See Percy A. Grainger, *Guide to Virtuosity* (GS 1933). Grainger used the *sostenuto* pedal in all his piano writing—even in song accompaniments. He studied Bach-Busoni transcriptions with Busoni in Berlin in the summer of 1903, and the use of the *sostenuto* pedal would certainly be an integral part of those lessons.

Children's March: Over the Hills and Far Away, arr. by the composer for 2 pianos (GS 1920; LC) 29 pp. This version can be used together with wind instruments and in chamber-music performances. Full sonorities; Grainger suggests using marimba mallets to strike the string at the end. M-D.

Country Gardens, arr. by the composer for 2 pianos (GS 1919–1932; LC) 7 pp. Grainger's most popular piece, and deservedly so. M-D.

English Waltz, arr. by the composer for 2 pianos (Schott 1947; LC) 18 pp. This is the fifth movement of the *Youthful Suite.* White-key glissandos hands together; some pedal. A delicious setting and a brilliant piece. M-D.

Faeroe Island Dance "set for one piano twosome" 1943 (Faber 1967) 9 pp. Based on two Faeroe Island dance-folksongs collected by Halmar Thuren: *Let's Dance Gay in Green Meadow; 'Neath the Mould Shall Never Dancer's Tread Go.* Much use of groups of 7 (3 + 4); many Graingerisms: "left side player"; "right side player"; "The high D with a star is not on the piano. For convenience play this note on the wood to right of keyboard." At the end, "don't slow off." Attractive. Int. to M-D.

Harvest Hymn, trans. by the composer 1938 (GS 1040; LC) 5 pp. "Heavily flowing"; uses many Graingerisms, such as, "in time feelingly, very clingingly," "slow off," "lingeringly," "louden." Builds to big climax. Int. to M-D.

Handel in the Strand: Clog Dance, arr. for 2 pianos by the composer (Schott 1947; LC) 12 pp. "The music seems to reflect both Handel and English musical comedy" (from the score). Includes a few snatches of Handel's *Harmonious Blacksmith.* Much fun for all; very effective. M-D.

Jutish Medley (GS 1928) 19 pp., transcription of five Danish folksongs. One of Grainger's largest piano works, this suite of five connected movements contains a set of variations in each movement. Represents Grainger's mature style; performance directions are meticulous—often indicating several different dynamic levels simultaneously. This transcription is written with the confident expectation of hands that can take tenths with ease. Uses all three pedals. This is No. 8 of Grainger's settings of Danish folk music. D.

Shepherd's Hey, based on English Morris Dance tunes using four variants collected by Cecil J. Sharp (GS 25381 1911) 7 pp. Meticulous performance indications: "The bigger printed notes should be heard well above the others"; "Chippy"; "The top notes as piercing as possible"; "It doesn't matter exactly what note the glissando ends on." Many pedal directions. Variation technique used throughout. A fetching tune and a good time for all. Large span required, although Grainger says, "All big stretches may be played broken (harped)." M-D.

See also Bach, J. S.; Brahms; Cook; Delius; Gershwin; Grieg; Powell; Rachmaninoff; Schumann, R.; Songs, English; Strauss, R.; Tchaikowsky

Enrique Granados (1867–1916) Spain

The Lover and the Nightingale, from the opera *Goyescas,* trans. for 2 pianos by Ethel Bartlett and Rae Robertson (JWC). A real audience pleaser! M-D.

El Pelele (Man of Straw), from *Goyescas,* arr. for 2 pianos by Frederico Longas (GS 1915; LC) 15 pp. Brilliant, effective, strong rhythms. M-D.

Rondella Arazovesa, arr. for 2 pianos by Phyllis Gunther (Belwin-Mills 1975; LC) 8 pp. Easier than the original. M-D.

Giovanni Battista Grazioli (1750–1820) Italy

Adagio in B-flat, trans. by Ignaz Friedman, in collection *Transcriptions of Ignaz Friedman,* vol. 1 (UE 17825) 4 pp. Requires a good *cantabile* style of playing. M-D.

Arthur de Greef (1862–1940) Belgium

Menuet Varié, originally for string orchestra, trans. for 2 pianos by the composer (Heugel 1913; LC) 5 pp. A charming piece in a most effective transcription. Cadenza in the mid-section. M-D.

Edvard Grieg (1843–1907) Norway

Arabian Dance, Op. 55/2, originally for orchestra, trans. for duet by the composer (CFP; LC) 15 pp. Works well. Int. to M-D.

Concerto in a, Op. 16, first movement, in Percy Grainger, *Concert Transcriptions of Favorite Concertos* (GS 1947; IU). This abridged solo piano version is mainly an arrangement of the principal themes and episodes. Includes footnotes not included in Grainger's edition of the complete work (for solo piano and orchestral reduction on a second piano). M-D.

Little Bird, Op. 43/4; *The Butterfly,* Op. 43/1; *Elegie,* Op. 38/6; *Melancholy,* Op. 47/5; trans. for the left hand by Paul Wittgenstein, in *School for the Left Hand,* vol. 3: *Transcriptions* (UE 12329). Charming; clever realizations. Pedaled and fingered. Int. to M-D.

Lyrische Stücke für die rechte oder linke Hand allein, arr. by Fritz Teichmann (CFP). Unusually effective. M-D.

Nocturne, Op. 54/4, arr. for 2 pianos by Ethel Bartlett and Rae Robertson (OUP 1958; LC) 7 pp. The tone coloring should be somewhat sombre for the most part, "except for the bird calls, which should have a brilliant bell-like quality" (from the score). A most colorful version. M-D.

Norwegian Melodies, Op. 63, originally for orchestra, trans. for duet by the composer (CFP; LC) 19 pp. Popular Song; Cow Keeper's Tune and Country-dance. Charming, good spacing of parts. M-D.

Peer Gynt Suite No. 1, Op. 46, trans. by the composer (CFP 9563) 20 pp. Morning-mood; The Death of Ase; Anitra's Dance; In the Hall of the Mountain-King. Includes pedaling and fingering. Very effective. Int. to M-D.

Sigurd Jorsalfar, Op. 56, originally for orchestra, trans. for duet by the composer (CFP; LC) 27 pp. Exploits the medium musically. M-D.

All these transcriptions by Grieg show that he was a real master at the piano.

Charles T. Griffes (1884–1920) USA

See Humperdinck

Ferde Grofé (1892–1972) USA
Grofé's works use jazz rhythms interwoven with simple ballad-like tunes.
On the Trail, from *Grand Canyon Suite,* arr. for 2 pianos by Domenico Savino
(Robbins 1936; LC) 18 pp. This picturesque piece is very effective in this
arrangement. Glissandos, tremolos, and fast repeated octaves add color.
M-D.

Rudolph Gruen (–   )
See Franck; Gliere; MacDowell; Moszkowski

Alfred Grünfeld (1852–1924) Austria
See Strauss, Johann Jr.

Karl Grunsky (1871–1943) Germany
See Bruckner

Felix Guenther (1886–1951) USA, born Austria
See Prokofiev; Respighi

David Guion (1892–1981) USA
Guion's best works use folkish material coupled with sophisticated imagination
and musical technique.
The Harmonica-Player, from *Alley Tunes: Three Scenes from the South,"* trans.
for 2 pianos by the composer (GS 1936; LC) 7 pp. Even more effective than
the original solo version. M-D.

Phyllis Gunther (–   ) USA
See Debussy; Gottschalk; Granados; Shostakovich; Songs, American

H

Jacques F. Halévy (1799–1862) France

Fantasy on "Reine de Chypre," Op. 157, trans. by Frederick Kalkbrenner (Schlesinger ca. 1842). Based on two themes from Act III that have no relation to each other. The mood of the first is negated by that of the second. Both themes were selected for their individual attractiveness. M-D to D.

Réminiscences de "La Juive." Fantaisie brillante, trans. by Franz Liszt G.409a (Hofmeister). Three major sections, logical form, concise dramatic content. Virtuosic, with bravura gestures. D.

Cristobal Halffter (1930–   ) Spain
See Albéniz

Ernesto Halffter (1905–   ) Spain
See Falla

Mark Hambourg (1879–1960) Russia
See Berlioz

Karl Hammer (–   ) Germany
See Hindemith

George Frideric Handel (1685–1759)

Concertino Barocco, based on themes of Handel, arr. by Denes Agay (GS 1975) 15 pp. Three contrasting movements, delightful. Int.

Fantasia on a Theme by Handel, by Michael Tippett 1942. Originally for piano and orchestra; trans. for 2 pianos by the composer (Schott 10122) 16 min. Theme from Handel's *Suites de pièces pour le clavecin,* 1733. Short, five clever variations, luxuriant tonal style, effective concluding fugue. M-D.

The Harmonious Blacksmith, air with variations, trans. for 2 pianos by Brian Easdale (OUP 1949; LC) 10 pp. Some interesting counterpoints have been added to the original. Uses very little pedal. M-D.

Passacaglia, arr. for 2 pianos by Pierre Luboschutz (JF 1951; LC) 15 pp. Many octaves and scales, full sonorities. M-D.

Passacaille, paraphrase for 2 pianos by Percival Garratt (Elkin 1956; LC) 8 pp. Thinner textures than in the Luboschutz version. M-D.

Sarabande and Chaconne, from *Almira,* concert arrangement by Franz Liszt, G.181 1879, in collection *Piano Transcriptions from French and Italian Operas* by Liszt (Dover) 17 pp. Only the melodies are by Handel—brief dances for Spanish nobility that occur in the opening act of his first opera,

Almira (1705). Liszt reversed the order of the dances and introduced his own varied treatment of them. The shift between the two movements is entrancing. M-D to D.

Suite, from *Water Music,* arr. by Alan Richardson (OUP 1954; LC) 7 pp. Bourrée; Air; Hornpipe. This delightful version has much appeal for younger and older pianists. Int.

Johana Harris (1913–   ) USA, born Canada
See Bach, J. S.

Roy Harris (1898–1979) USA
See Bach, J. S.

Hans Leo Hassler (1564–1612) Germany
Choral sur un thème de Leo Hassler (1601), "Wenn ich einmal scheiden soll," by George Templeton Strong 1929; originally for string orchestra, reduction for 2 pianos by the composer (Henn 1933; LC) 6 pp. The tune "O Sacred Head" is carefully presented in canon between the instruments. Beautifully worked out. M-D.

Herbert Haufrecht (1909–   ) USA
See Songs, American

Franz Joseph Haydn (1732–1809) Austria
Air with Variations, from *Symphony* No. 63 ("La Roxelane") Hob.I:63/2, transcription by Haydn not certain. In collection *Masters of the Theme and Variations* (Alfred 1987) 5 pp. Constant alternation of major and minor variations adds special interest. Technical problems include double notes, especially thirds and sixths, as well as repeated notes, large stretches, and arpeggios. A charming transcription. Int. to M-D.

Finale, from *String Quartet,* Op. 33/2, arr. by Harold Bauer (GS 1932; LC) 7 pp. *Presto,* 6/8. Delightful, would make a fun encore. M-D.

Two Pieces for a Musical Clock, arr. for 2 pianos by Joan Lovell (Elkin 1956; LC) 8 pp. Nos. 10 and 12 of a set of twelve pieces written for a musical clock that Haydn presented to Prince Nicolaus Esterházy. Delightful. M-D.

Quartet, Op. 64/5, *Adagio Cantabile,* trans. by Paul Wittgenstein for the left hand, in collection *School for the Left Hand,* vol. 3: *Transcriptions* (UE 12329). Includes footnotes for variants in performance. Effective. M-D.

Sonata in A-flat, *Adagio,* trans. by Paul Wittgenstein for the left hand, in collection *School for the Left Hand,* vol. 3: *Transcriptions* (UE 12329). Works very well. Special fingering, pedal indications. M-D.

Sonata in C, arr. for 2 pianos by Stanley R. Avery (OD 1951; LC) 31 pp. Tasteful additions. M-D.

Sonata, in D, arr. for 2 pianos by Claude Murphree (SB 1940; LC) 26 pp. Much imitation between players; measures numbered. M-D.

———. Arr. for 2 pianos by Eric Thiman (Augener 1935; LC) 20 pp. Additions

correspond to the style of the period. Cadenza added in final movement.
M-D.

Stephen Heller (1813–1888) born Hungary, lived mostly in France
See Mendelssohn; Schubert; Weber

Adolf Henselt (1814–1889) Germany
Love Song, Op. 5/11, trans. by Paul Wittgenstein for the left hand in *School for
    the Left Hand,* vol. 3: *Transcriptions* (UE 12329). Melodious, requires
    careful pedaling. M-D.
Si Oiseau j'etais (If I Were a Bird) Op. 2/6, trans. by Leopold Godowsky
    (Musica Obscura). Contains Godowsky's preparatory studies. M-D.
See also Donizetti

Ferdinand Hérold (1791–1833) France
Fantaisie on Themes from the Opera Le Pré aux Clercs, trans. by Sigismond
    Thalberg, Op. 57/3 (Br&H; SBTS) 15 pp. Focuses on the most melodious
    themes, but contains little thematic development. M-D.

Henri Herz (1803–1888) Germany
See Bellini; Rossini; Songs, Irish

Philip Heseltine (1894–1930) Great Britain
Pen name for Peter Warlock
See Delius

Myra Hess (1890–1965) Great Britain
See Bach, J. S.

Edouard Hesselberg (–   )
See Dett

James Hewitt (1770–1827) USA
See Songs, French

Mildred J. Hill (1859–1916) USA
Happy Birthday, Humorous Variations on a birthday song, trans. by Claus-
    Dieter Ludwig (Schott). In various styles, clever, fun for performer and
    listener. Int. to M-D.
See also Songs, American

Ferdinand Hiller (1811–1885) Germany
See Weber

Paul Hindemith (1895–1963) Germany
Der Damon (The Demon), Op. 28, dance-pantomime in two scenes by Max
    Krell 1922, arr. by Hermann Uhticke (Schott 1924) 27 pp., 34 min. Scene I:
    7 movements; Scene II: 5 movements. This piece reveals an immense
    kinetic rhythmic drive, some humor, and contrapuntal textures. The

arrangement is generally successful, but in No. 3 of Scene I, textures get very thick. M-D to D.

Nobilissima visione, Dance Legend in six scenes, 1938, trans. by the composer (Schott 1938) 56 pp., 35 min. Based on the life and philosophy of St. Francis of Assisi; set in a stark neo-medieval idiom in sinewy linear counterpoint. Requires complete technique plus a large span. D.

Quartet 1938, originally for clarinet, violin, cello, and piano; trans. by the composer for 2 pianos (Schott) 24 min. Mässig bewegt; Sehr langsam; Mässig bewegt—Lebhaft. This transcription has been made in a straightforward way and may be enjoyed by two skilled players. Much of it is very literal, and it is a little unimaginative in places. M-D to D.

Simfonische Metamorphosen Carl Maria von Weber'schen Themen (Symphonic Metamorphosis on Themes of Carl Maria von Weber) 1943, trans. for 2 pianos by Jon Thorarinsson (Schott 1952) 58 pp., 18 min. Allegro; Turandot Scherzo; Andantino; Marsch. The second movement contains a jazz fugato. The finale is "a magnificent fanfaronade of vigesimosecular Polyphony" (Nicolas Slonimsky, *Music Since 1900,* 4th ed. [New York: Charles Scribner's Sons, 1971] p. 779). Effective transcription; requires fine octave technique and large span. M-D to D.

Symphonie Mathis der Maler, arr. for duet by the composer (Schott 3286 1934) 47 pp. Engelkonzert; Grablegung; Versuchung des heiligen Antonius. Two performers at one instrument provide an effective way to underscore Hindemith's contrapuntal style. D.

Symphonische Tänze (Symphonic Dances), originally for orchestra 1937, trans. for duet by Horst-Günther Schnell (Schott 1939) 71 pp., 32 min. In four sections. Requires extraordinary contrapuntal playing plus lithe rhythmic energy. D.

Symphony in E-flat 1940, trans. for duet by Horst-Günther Schnell (Schott 1943) 77 pp., 36 min. In four classically contoured movements. Written in a propulsive rhythmic idiom with lyrical episodes. Transcription requires experienced ensemble players with great sensitivity to tonal balance. M-D to D.

Tanz der Holzpuppen (Dance of the Wooden Dolls), from *Tuttifäntchen,* Christmas fairytale in three scenes, with song and dance, 1922, trans. by the composer. In the *Hindemith Collection* (Schott 1989) 5 pp. A mixture of ragtime and foxtrot dance styles; clever and attractive. Presents a side of Hindemith not readily known. Int. to M-D.

Theme mit vier Variationen (The Four Temperaments) 1940, originally for piano and string orchestra, arr. for 2 pianos by Karl Hammer (Schott 1947) 54 pp., 28 min. Theme; Melancholy; Sanguine; Phlegmatic; Choleric. Shows an increase in virtuosity as regards techniques of orchestration and composition over earlier works. Also displays a greater profundity of polyphony. This work depicts in spacious neo-Baroque modalities the four "humors" of medieval biology—melancholy (in muted violins, followed by a manic-depressive march), sanguine (a hedonistic waltz), phlegmatic (in turgid motion), and choleric (in vigorously impassioned rhythms). Very effective arrangement. M-D.

Stefan von Hodula (–   ) Hungarian
See Songs, French

Richard Hoffman (1831–1909) USA, born Great Britain
See Verdi

Josef Hofmann (1876–1957) USA, born Poland
See Smith, J. S.

Lee Hoiby (1926–   ) USA
See Bach, J. S.

Gustav Holst (1874–1934) Great Britain
The Planets, originally for orchestra, arr. for 2 pianos by the composer (Curwen 1949; LC). Seven movements, each published separately. Inspired by the astrological significance of the planets. Holst's most famous work. The faster-moving parts are the most effective. Efficient transcriptions throughout. M-D to D.

Arthur Honegger (1892–1955) France
Although Honegger was born and died in France, he is considered Swiss.
Les aventures du Roi Pausole, trans. from the opera by the composer (Sal 1931; LC) 18 pp. Overture; Ritournelle de la Mule; Les adieux de Pausole; Air d'Aline; Le Chocolat Espagnol. Clever, attractive, a little awkward in spots. M-D.
Chant de Joie, originally for orchestra, trans. by the composer for duet (Senart 1924; LC) 11 pp. Honegger has rescored this version efficiently—the layout is clear, and the two parts are fairly equal. M-D.
Pacific 231, originally for orchestra, trans. for duet by the composer (Senart 1924; LC) 16 pp. Requires careful rhythmic control; does not have the "punch" of the original. M-D to D.
Pastorale d'Été, originally for orchestra, trans. for duet by the composer (Senart 1921; LC) 13 pp. This version lends itself well to the medium. A very pleasant piece with some lovely moments. M-D.

Wallace Hornibrook (–   ) USA
See Bach, J. S.

Mary Howe (1882–1964) USA
See Bach, J. S.; Songs, Spanish

Edwin Hughes (1884–1965) USA
See Bach, J. S.; Strauss, Johann Jr.

William H. Humiston (–   ) USA
See MacDowell

Johann Nepomuk Hummel (1778–1837) Hungary
See Gluck; Mozart

Engelbert Humperdinck (1854–1921) Germany
Overture to "Hansel und Gretel," trans. for 2 pianos by Charles T. Griffes (GS
1951; LC) 24 pp. Contains melodies of ingenious felicity. Charming,
colorful, and very effective. M-D.

Ernest Hutcheson (1871–1951) Australia
See Berlioz; Liszt; Wagner

I

Jacques Ibert (1890–1962) France

Divertissement, originally for chamber orchestra, reduced for piano by Lucien Garban (Durand 13553 1952) 27 pp. Introduction; Cortège; Nocturne; Valse; Parade; Finale. Some pedal directions. Colorful; wit and humor come through in this version. M-D.

Vincent D'Indy (1851–1931) France

D'Indy's style was greatly influenced by his teacher, César Franck.

Istar (Variations Symphoniques) Op. 42, trans. for duet by the composer (Durand 1897; LC) 27 pp. There are some interesting sections, e.g., *Tres animé; bien soutenu;* but by and large this version is lacking in good transcribing continuity. M-D to D.

Souvenirs, Op. 62 1906, originally for orchestra, trans. by Blanche Selva (Durand 7069 1908) 25 pp. Well carried out, pianistic; the original music lends itself to the piano. M-D.

Symphony on a French Mountain Air, Op. 25, arr. for 2 pianos, 6 hands, by the composer (Hamelle). One player at piano A, two at piano B. Complex, severe, and intellectual writing. M-D to D.

John Ireland (1879–1962) Great Britian

The Forgotten Rite originally for orchestra, trans. for duet by the composer (Augener 1918; LC) 9 pp. Mystical and expressive, syncopated melodic line. Requires expert ensemble. M-D.

Charles Ives (1874–1954) USA

Three Quarter-Tone Piano Pieces for 2 pianos 1923–24; possibly derived and arranged from piano pieces of 1903–1904 (G. Pappastavrou—CFP 66285) 26 pp., 11 min. Piano II is tuned ¼ tone higher than normal pitch. Largo: atmospheric, haunting, primarily diatonic. Allegro: jazzy dance tune sounds very twangy with these tunings; rhythms contrasted on "split" between the two pianos. Chorale: combines wit with serious exploration. "My Country 'Tis of Thee" appears in frantic fragmentation side-by-side with microtone remembrances of four-voice chorale style. Augmented and syncopated chords, ragtime elements, alternating melodic tones between the pianos. M-D.

See: George Pappastavrou, "Ives Quarter-Tone Pieces," *Clavier* 13 (October 1974):31–32.

Harry Perison, "The Quarter-Tone System of Charles Ives," CM 18 (1974):96–104.

J

Maxime Jacob (1906–1977) France

Sérénade 1923, originally for orchestra, trans. for duet by the composer (Jobert 1928; LC) 11 pp. In style of Poulenc with imitation; many trills; *ppp* ending. M-D.

Maurice Jacobson (1896–1976) Great Britain
See Warlock

Joseph Joachim (1831–1907) Germany

Ouvertüre zu Shakespeare's Heinrich IV, Op. 7, originally for orchestra, arr. for 2 pianos by Johannes Brahms (Simrock 1903; LC) 39 pp. Beautifully laid out between the instruments. The two performers have equal assignments. M-D.

Johann Ernst, Duke of Saxe-Weimar (1695[6?]–1715) Germany

Concerto No. 11 in B-flat, trans. by J. S. Bach BWV 982. Based on *Violin Concerto,* Op. 1/1.

Concerto No. 13 in c, trans. by J. S. Bach BWV 984.

Concerto No. 16 in d, trans. by J. S. Bach BWV 987. Based on *Violin Concerto,* Op. 1/4.

All contained in J. S. Bach, *Complete Keyboard Transcriptions of Concertos by Baroque Composers* (Dover 1987). See Bach, J. S.

Grant Johannesen (1921–   ) USA
See Poulenc

Alberto Jonás (1868–1943) USA, born Spain
See Schubert

Joseph Jongen (1873–1953) Belgium

Jongen was greatly influenced by César Franck and the Impressionists.

Fantaisie sur deux Noëls populaires Wallons, originally for orchestra, trans. by the composer (Durand 1911; LC) 41 pp. An expansive work that contains some successful moments. M-D to D.

Rafael Joseffy (1852–1915) USA, born Hungary

Joseffy was a great pianist, a pupil of Liszt and Tausig, and a famous teacher. He sometimes took liberties and prettified his Bach transcriptions with Chopinesque harmonies and other nineteenth-century pianistic devices.
See Bach, J. S.; Chopin; Delibes

Paul Juon (1872–1940) Russia
See Brahms

K

Dmitri Kabalevsky (1904–1987) USSR
See Bach, J. S.; Glinka

Frederick Kalkbrenner (1785–1849) Germany
See Halévy

Eugen Kapp (1908–   ) USSR, born Estonia
See Glinka

M. Karpov (–   ) USSR
See Khachaturian

Wilfried Kassebaum (–   ) Germany
See Schumann, R.

Robert Keller (–   ) Germany
Keller was the editor of Simrock's thematic catalog of Brahms's works.
See Brahms; Dvořák

Wilhelm Kempff (1895–   ) Germany
See Bach, J. S.

Jenö Kenessey (1906–   ) Hungary
See Kodály

Aram Khachaturian (1903–1978) USSR
Dance of the Rose Maidens from *Gayane Ballet*, trans. for 2 pianos by Adolf
  Gotlieb (Leeds 1947; LC) 7 pp., 2½ min. Colorful. M-D.
Lesginka, from *Gayane Ballet,* trans. for 2 pianos by Victor Babin (Leeds 1948;
  LC) 12 pp. Incisive rhythms and a broad secondary theme are characteristic
  of this Caucasian Dance. M-D.
Masquerade Suite 1946, arr. by A. Doloukhanian with the composer's approval,
  edited with special annotations by Harold Sheldon (Leeds 1948) 28 pp.
  Waltz; Nocturne; Mazurka; Romance; Galop (Polka). Extracted by
  Khachaturian from the incidental music to the play of the same name by the
  nineteenth-century Russian poet Lermontov. This music contains little evi-
  dence of Khachaturian's Armenian background, as it was written to convey
  the atmosphere of the Romantic period of the play. But here and there (as in
  the "Galop") the exuberance and rhythmic devices mark the vitality for
  which Khachaturian's music has become so well known. M-D.
Saber Dance, from *Gayane Ballet,* concert transcription by Vladimir Padwa

(Russian-American Music Publications 1948; LC) 9 pp. Full of exciting rhythms; requires first-rate pianism throughout. Effective. M-D to D.

————. Arr. for duet by M. Karpov (Leeds 1947; LC) 13 pp. Edited with special annotations by György Sandor.

————. Trans. for 2 pianos by Pierre Luboshutz (Leeds 1948; LC) 12 pp.

Waltz, from *Masquerade Suite,* arr. for 2 pianos by Mario Castelnuovo-Tedesco (Leeds 1951; LC) 16 pp. Like a big concert transcription. M-D.

Theodore Kirchner (1823–1903) Germany
Kirchner's writing was strongly influenced by Schumann.
See Brahms; Schumann, R.

John Kirkpatrick (1905–   ) USA
See Gottschalk

Johann Christian Kittel (1732–1809) Germany
(*Nachspiel* (Postlude). See Bauer

Karl Klindworth (1830–1916) Germany
See Tchaikowsky

Zoltán Kocsis (1952–   ) Hungary
See Berlioz; Wagner

Zoltán Kodály (1882–1967) Hungary
Dances of Galanta, trans. from the orchestral version by Jenö Kenessey (UE 10671 1935) 15 min. Originally written for the 80th anniversary of the Budapest Philharmonic Society. Folk influence, octotonic. Faithful transcription but loses much of its original color. M-D to D.
Dances of Marosszek 1930, originally for orchestra, trans. by the composer (UE 8213 1930) 12 min. Five dances with the first returning three times in varied moods. Based on peasant tunes; modal; catchy rhythms. M-D to D.
"Intermezzo," "Song," "Viennese Clock," three pieces from *Háry János,* concert transcriptions by Andor Foldes (UE; LC) 5 pp. Intermezzo: much short-long rhythmic usage. Song: contrasted sections, many scales and arpeggios, tremolos, *ppp* ending. Viennese Clock: portrays its title: very metronomic; clever. All M-D.

Stephen Kovacs (–   )
See Liszt; Strauss, Johann Jr.

Leo Kraft (1922–   ) USA
See Gliere

Fritz Kreisler (1875–1962) Austria
Caprice Viennois, arr. for 2 pianos by June Weybright (Foley 1943; LC) 10 pp. Arr. for students but still about M-D.

————. Trans. for 2 pianos by Jacques Miller (CF 1910; LC) 15 pp. Concert version. D.

Liebesfreud (Love's Joy), trans. by Sergei Rachmaninoff, in *Rachmaninoff—A Commemorative Collection* (Belwin-Mills) 5½ min. M-D to D.

————. Arr. for 2 pianos by Guy Maier (Foley 1942; LC) 9 pp. Arr. for students. Effective. Int. to M-D.

————. Arr. for 2 pianos by Marie von Ritter (CF 1910; LC) 9 pp. Clever. M-D.

Liebesleid (Love's Sorrow), trans. by Sergei Rachmaninoff, in *Rachmaninoff—A Commemorative Collection* (Belwin-Mills) 4½ min. The two violin and piano pieces, *Liebesfreud* and *Liebesleid,* are just as famous, and rightly so, in these Rachmaninoff versions. M-D.

————. Arr. for 2 pianos by Guy Maier (Foley 1942; LC) 9 pp. Arr. for students. Effective. Int. to M-D.

Midnight Bells, arr. for duet by Cecily Lambert (C. Foley 1945; LC) 9 pp. Pedaled and fingered; uses terms like "softly but full toned," "whimsically," "passionately," "serenely." Clever and attractive. Int.

————. Arr. for 2 pianos by Hermene Eichhorn (Foley 1944; LC) 7 pp. Colorful and attractive. Int.

The Old Refrain, arr. for 2 pianos by Cecily Lambert (Foley 1943; LC) 7 pp. Arr. for students. Attractive. Int. to M-D.

Rondino (on a theme of Beethoven), trans. by Leopold Godowsky (CF 1916). Clever. M-D.

Schöne Rosmarin, arr. for 2 pianos by Cecily Lambert (Foley 1943; LC) 9 pp. Arr. for students. Int. to M-D.

————. Arr. for 2 pianos by Morton Gould (CF 1934; LC) 13 pp. Concert transcription. M-D to D.

Johann Kuhnau (1660–1722) Germany

Kuhnau was not only one of the greatest musicians but also one of the most learned men of his time. He is credited with the invention of the Sonata as a piece in several movements, not a collection of dance tunes. Kuhnau was the most important German composer for the keyboard before J. S. Bach, whose predecessor he was as Cantor of Leipzig.

David and Goliath, concert version by Harold Bauer (GS 1927; Oberlin College Library). One of Kuhnau's *Biblical Sonatas.* 8 movements. Bauer introduced "octave couplings and changes of register . . . in the present edition with the design of reproducing as nearly as possible the effect of a performance on the harpsichord. A few cuts have been made" (from the score). M-D.

L

Max Laistner (1853–1917) Germany
See Chopin

Cecily Lambert (–   ) Great Britain
See Kreisler

Lucien Lambert (1858–1945) France
See Gottschalk; Kreisler

Wanda Landowska (1879–1959) Poland
See Lanner

Joseph Lanner (1801–1843) Austria
Lanner and Johann Strauss, Sr., are credited with the creation of the mid-nineteenth-century Viennese waltz.
Valses Viennoises, trans. by Wanda Landowska (GS 1926). Landowska used these pieces to display her own style of pianistic dexterity. She also recorded them on Ampico 6828-3. M-D.
Vindobona, Introduction and Waltzes, arr. for 2 pianos by Celius Dougherty and Vincenz Ruzicka (AMP 1944; LC) 24 pp. Sweeps over the keyboard with great aplomb! M-D to D.

Vally Lasker (–   )
See Songs, English

Eduard Lassen (1830–1904) Denmark
Lassen succeeded Liszt as music director at the Weimer Court in 1858.
Löse, Himmel, meine Seele, song, trans. by Franz Liszt, G.494 1861 (Sauer—CFP). Liszt infuses this mediocre music with forward-looking harmony and unusual registers. M-D.

Joan Last (–   ) Great Britain
See Corelli

Ernesto Lecuona (1896–1963) Cuba
Lecuona's compositions personify the Spanish musical idiom and are basically popular songs.
Cordoba, from the Spanish Suite *Andalucia* for piano, arr. for 2 pianos by E. C. Cabiati and Mario Carta (EBM 1949; LC) 12 pp. Exploits the medium well. Effective. M-D.

Danza Lucumi, from *Danzas Afro-Cubanas* suite for piano, arr. for 2 pianos by
   E. C. Cabiati and Mario Carta (EBM 1949; LC) 11 pp. Big sonorities but
   ends *pp.* M-D.

Christopher Le Fleming (1908–1985) Great Britain
See Bach, J. S.; Strauss, Johann Jr.

Lawrence Leonard (–   )
See Mussorgsky

Bennett Lerner (–   ) USA
See Copland

Theodor Leschetizky (1830–1915) Poland
See Donizetti

Amanda Vick Lethco (–   ) USA
See Clarke

Henry Levine (–   ) USA
See Brahms; Gershwin; Villa Lobos

Yuri Levitin (1912–   ) USSR
See Glinka

Mischa Levitzki (1898–1941) USA, born Russia
Levitzki was a pianist of uncommon elegance.
Valse, trans. for 2 pianos by Ralph Berkowitz (GS 1951; LC) 7 pp. Graceful and
   attractive; full of Slavic temperament. M-D.

Vladimir Leyetchkiss (–   ) USSR
See Stravinsky, I.

Anatol Liadoff (1855–1914) Russia
Four Russian Folk Songs, from Op. 58, trans. by Alexander Siloti (CF P1336
   1923) 10 pp. Legend of the Birds; I Danced with a Mosquito; Cradle Song;
   Dance. The original work, *Eight Russian Folksongs* (1906) for orchestra,
   included numerous arrangements of folk melodies. Highly developed sense
   of color and musical characterization; charming; an effective group. Int. to
   M.-D.

Dinu Lipatti (1917–1950) Switzerland, born Rumania
See Bach, J. S.

Franz Liszt (1811–1886) Hungary
Liszt was perhaps the greatest master of transcription. He wrote almost 400 piano
transcriptions, arrangements, fantasies, paraphrases, variations, reminiscences,
divertissements, etc. They are based on the music of other composers and on
national themes or melodies in the public domain (such as "God Save the
Queen"). They made available orchestral compositions that were infrequently
performed, as well as the music of composers whom Liszt was championing; and

they served as an outlet for a display of piano virtuosity. Liszt used the term "transcription" (or *übertragen für,* or *transcrit pour*) mainly for songs, such as his adaptations of Schubert's songs; the terms "paraphrase," "fantaisie," "réminiscences," or "illustrations" to describe free works based on operatic melodies, such as the *Réminiscences de Norma* or the *Rigoletto Concert Paraphrase;* and the designations *Klavierauszug, Klavierpartitur,* or *partition de piano* for piano reductions of orchestral scores, such as the *Klavierauszug* of the Beethoven Symphonies or the *Liebestod* from Wagner's *Tristan und Isolde.* Liszt's *partitions* were exact reproductions of the original work presented as accurately as possible within the limitation of the piano medium. Liszt transcribed some works (e.g., Berlioz' *Symphonie Fantastique*) as a challenge to his abilities as an arranger and performer, mainly because they were basically unsuited to the piano. Transcriptions were his way of communicating enthusiasm for things that appealed to him. It should be remembered that Liszt flourished at a time when mechanical means of reproducing sound were all but unknown, concert life was limited, and many communities had no symphony orchestra or opera company.

Liszt performed two-piano music (either two-piano compositions *per se* or piano concertos) with almost every important pianist of his day. He was an inveterate reviser and arranger of his own and other composers' works. Most of his original pieces exist in multiple versions and show in their various reworkings a progressive expansion and refinement of his musical conceptions. He had an uncanny instinct for the appropriate pianistic setting for each piece he transcribed. His piano transcriptions probably represent the greatest body of unperformed music in any instrumental repertoire, but no valid assessment of Liszt, the composer, can be made without reference to this music. We can only mention some of the most famous of these works, for a complete account would require its own book. Editio Musica Budapest is publishing a complete edition of Liszt's compositions—a gigantic task when one considers the sheer volume and diversity of his output. Series II (24 volumes), designated "Free Arrangements and Transcriptions for Piano Solo," was begun in 1987 and will include 359 compositions. G. numbers refer to the listing in *The New Grove,* 1981.

Album Leaf G.164, trans. by the composer, in collection *At the Piano with Liszt* (Alfred). This elegant piece dates from around 1841 and is a good example of Liszt's rewriting and rearranging his own works. Its first (longer) version was composed in 1839 with the title *Valse mélancolique.* In 1850 it became No. 2 of *Trois Caprices-Valses.* M-D.

Bénédiction de Dieu dans la Solitude, originally for solo piano, trans. for 2 pianos by Emil Sauer (Kistner 1906; LC) 31 pp. Lends itself well to the two-piano medium. A beautiful version. M-D to D.

Der blinde Sänger G.546, in vol. 17 of the NLA, *Piano Versions of His Own Works* III, 1983. Originally a melodrama composed in 1875 as a setting of Tolstoy's ballad "The Blind Man." In the melodrama the narrator is accompanied. Liszt transcribed the work in 1878 as it appears here. M-D.

Cadenza to the Hungarian Rhapsody No. II 1847, trans. by Sergei Rachmaninoff 1919? (Mercury 1955) 8 pp., edited and with an introductory note by Jan Holcman. Holcman reconstituted the work from Rachmaninoff's Edison recording. In Liszt's work, an opportunity for a "Cadenza ad libitum" is indicated before the final flourish. M-D.

La Campanella, arr. for 2 pianos by Colin Taylor (OUP 1939; LC) 22 pp. Gives even more opportunities than the solo version for producing intriguing bell effects from the piano. Exact fitting together of the chromatic scale passages is very important. M-D to D.

Christmas Song (Christ Is Born) G.502 1865, trans. by the composer, in collection *At the Piano with Liszt* (Alfred). Originally composed in 1863 as a chorus in three different versions. The piano transcription may well have been written at the same time. The lovely chorale-like melody is carefully punctuated with syncopated rests at measures 10, 13, and 19. Int.

Concerto Pathétique in e, G.258 1856, arr. for 2 pianos by the composer from his *Grosses Konzertsolo* (Br&H 2277; GS 1534) 51 pp. Allegro energico—Andante sostenuto—Allegro trionfante. Originally written for solo piano for a piano competition at the Paris Conservatory in 1849. A bold one-movement form similar to a symphonic poem in three contrasting sections. Exploits many pianistic problems. Brilliant sonorities, cadenza passages, orchestral effects, theme transformation, subdivided by tempo changes. Although the score is unusual in that it has no programmatic background, it displays the same unique pianistic approach that distinguishes Liszt's more-familiar piano works. Virtuosic throughout. M-D to D.

Fantasia on Hungarian Folk Melodies G.123 for 2 pianos, the second piano part arr. from the orchestral score by Hans von Bülow (GS 1056). This work uses the same material as *Hungarian Rhapsody* No. 14. It is appealing and has the same technical and character requirements as the solo version, which Liszt intended as a brilliant instrumental concert piece with dazzling colors, a purpose he achieved magnificently. M-D.

Forgotten Romance (Romance Oubliée) G.527, in collection *At the Piano with Liszt* (Alfred). A transcription of Liszt's *Romance Oubliée* (1880) for piano and viola (or violin or cello), which was an elaboration of *Romance* G.169 (1848) for piano, which in turn was an arrangement of the song "Oh pourquoi donc," G.301 1848. Liszt never tired of continually rearranging his own pieces. Int. to M-D.

From the Cradle to the Grave. This work was inspired by a neo-Gothic painting by Michael Zichy. It was published in 1883 in three versions for orchestra, for solo piano, and for duet. The solo version (GS 1984) preserves the markings from the 1883 edition and adds editorial suggestions in brackets. The Cradle; The Struggle for Existence; The Grave: The Cradle of Future Life. M-D to D.

Gaudeamus Igitur (Humoreske) G.509 1870, originally for orchestra, soloists, and chorus; arr. by the composer (Musica Obscura) 15 pp. This full-blown glittering transcription completely overshadows the original tune. Requires virtuosity. M-D to D.

Hungarian Rhapsody No. 2, arr. for 2 pianos by Stephen Kovacs (CF 1949; LC) 25 pp. A brilliant arrangement of a brilliant piece; black and white key glissandos at end. M-D to D.

Hungarian Rhapsody No. 16, G.622 1882; and *To the Spirit of Petőfi*, G.614 1877, trans. for duet by the composer (Ervin Major—EMB 1959) 23 pp. We have no reliable information on relations between the two Hungarian men of genius, Liszt and the poet Petőfi, whom he highly esteemed. In 1874 Liszt composed incidental music to Mór Jókai's poem on Petőfi, "The Love of the Dead Poet"; and three years later he used the same themes in the little piano piece *To the Spirit of Petőfi,* which he played often. He performed it at a concert in Budapest on March 26, 1879 for the benefit of the flood victims of Szeged, and a few days later in Vienna at the palace of Count Gyula Andrássy, the Foreign Minister. "From the Bösendorfer piano decorated with garlands of roses the Elegy to Petőfi sounded very captivating," so wrote a contemporary reporter. The piece was played by Ferenc Erkel at the second Liszt Memorial Concert at the Music Academy in Budapest on October 21, 1887. It then vanished from concert programs and was not heard for decades. Liszt augmented this piece with a few introductory and final bars and included it in his last Hungarian cycle, *Hungarian Historic Portraits*. M-D.

Hungarian Rhapsody No. 19, freely edited by Ferruccio Busoni (Br&H 4959 1920). Busoni added performance instructions and dynamics, changed some rhythmic figures, and cut over 120 measures to tighten the structure. M-D.

In domum Domini ibimus G.505, trans. by the composer during his last years from the original version for mixed choir accompanied by organ, brass, and timpani; in NLA vol. 17. This is the first publication of Liszt's transcription. Chordal; trills used as pedal points; octaves. M-D.

Liebesträume (Dreams of Love), G.541 1850, trans. by the composer from his songs G.307, 308, and 298 (NLA; CFP; Schott; Br&H; S&B; GS; WH; Ric; Sal). These three pieces have a similar sentiment, as the romantic title indicates. No. 1, in A-flat (K; UE): right-hand accompanied trills present a problem. No. 2, in E (UE; K; Willis): needs a broad singing quality, diversified accompaniment. No. 3, in A-flat (Alfred; Schott; UE; EMB; K): ingenious cadenzas are an extension of Chopin's ornamentation; requires some power. M-D.

Liebestraum III, arr. for 2 pianos by Ethel Bartlett and Rae Robertson (OUP 1944; LC) 12 pp. Requires a broad *cantabile* style. M-D.

Die Lorelei, trans. by the composer G.532 (GS). Introduction is very Tristanesque. This transcription is as effective as the original song; hauntingly beautiful ending. M-D.

Mephisto Waltz No. 1, G.514, trans. by Ferruccio Busoni 1904 (GS 1649) 10 min. Liszt composed four versions of the *Mephisto Waltz* for piano. No. 1 is the most famous and is one of his most graphic creations, from the first tuning of the fiddle to the final distant singing of nightingales. This transcription is very different from Liszt's original version. Busoni did not hope to improve or make this masterwork more effective; he merely wished to offer an alternative transcription with pianistic merits of its own, and in this he was most successful. The pianist should compare the two versions measure by measure. It provides a rare opportunity to compare the same work transcribed by two masters of the art. D.

————. Originally for orchestra G.110, trans. by the composer G.514 (CFP; Ric; Sal; GS; K; EMB; Schott; Durand). A virtuoso's delight and one of Liszt's most effective picturesque works. The middle episode contains soaring melodies and *rubato*. Calls for a wide range of technical resources, including strong fingers capable of handling broken octaves, granitic chord playing, and large skips. D.

See: Dmitry Feofanov, "How to transcribe the *Mephisto Waltz* for piano," JALS 11 (1982):18–27.

Mephisto-Walzer No. 2, G.515, in vol. 17 of NLA. Liszt composed this work in 1880–81 for orchestra, then revised it later in 1881 and transcribed it for piano solo and for piano duet. G.111, a solo version transcribed from the duet, is at times more savage than the better-known *Mephisto Waltz* No. 1, but it is an equally powerful and disturbing work. Makes much use of the tritone B–F. D.

Three Petrarca Sonnets, trans. by the composer from songs in *Années de Pèlerinage,* Vol II. *Sonetto 47 del Petrarca* (NLA; Ric): cadenza in double notes, melodic material greatly syncopated. *Sonetto 104 del Petrarca* (NLA; Schott; Ric; GS): declamatory, agitated, and emotional; contains some technical problems. *Sonetto 123 del Petrarca* (NLA; GS includes the three poems illustrated in the Sonnets and their translations): lyric, melodious, imaginative, easier than Nos. 47 and 104. All M-D.

Polonaise No. 2 E Dur Nouvelle Edition Augmentée d'une Cadence Finale par Ferruccio Busoni (Simrock 12604 1909). Busoni's hand does not appear until the end of the piece, where, deleting Liszt's last 26 bars, Busoni writes his own 39-bar cadenza-finale. His cadenza is full of difficulties but is effective and exciting; the fast *leggiero* runs and *brio* staccato octaves in the left hand blend well with Liszt's gestures. Busoni uses the polonaise rhythm with a chromatic staccato idea to build his cadenza. M-D.

Rakoczy March, arr. for 2 pianos by Ernest Hutcheson (JF 1928; LC) 22 pp. Contains occasional free use of the Berlioz and Liszt versions. Virtuosic, glissando, brilliant closing. M-D to D.

O Roma nobilis, originally for mixed choir with piano accompaniment 1879, trans. by the composer, in NLA vol. 17, *Piano Versions of His Own Works* III. A harmonized chant. Above the staves, Liszt gives the text from the choir and piano version. The first publication of the piano arrangement. Int.

Salve Polonia G.518, in NLA vol. 17, *Piano Versions of His Own Works* III. Composed in 1863 for orchestra and for piano duet. This transcription for solo piano was also presumably written in 1863. Liszt intended to use the work first as an interlude and later as the final movement of his unfinished oratorio, *St. Stanislas*. M-D to D.

Spanish Rhapsody G.254, arr. for 2 pianos by Ferruccio Busoni (Belwin-Mills 9511; GS; Siloti—K&S; CFP) 15 min. Enhances the effectiveness of the original solo piano work. Following a short cadenza for one of the pianists, a series of variations emerge based on the "Folies d'Espagne" theme. They build to a strong climax and then subside into a lively Jota aragonese. A piano cadenza leads to the second theme, which is developed before the first Jota tempo returns. These two contrasting themes are worked together with increasing excitement and lead to a dramatic statement of the "Folies d'Espagne." Lisztian fireworks close the piece. D.

Twelve Symphonic Poems, trans. by the composer for 2 pianos (Br&H). Vol. I: *Ce qu'on entend sur la montagne*, G.635; *Tasso*, G.636; *Les Préludes*, G.647; *Orpheus*, G.638; *Prometheus*, G.639; *Mazeppa*, G.640. Vol. II: *Festklange*, G.641; *Héroïde funèbre*, G.642; *Hungaria*, G.643; *Hamlet*, G.644; *Hunnenschlact*, G.645; *Die Ideale*, G.646. Liszt has transferred the orchestral sound to the two keyboards in a marvelous manner. M-D.

Totentanz (Dance of Death), trans. by the composer for 2 pianos G.652 (EMB; Sauer—CFP; K; Br&H; Paragon) 17 min. Also available for solo piano in vol. 16 of the NLA (EMB). This set of variations on *Dies Irae* (Day of Wrath) was planned in 1838, when Liszt saw Orcagna's *Triumph of Death* frescoes in Pisa; he finished it in 1849 but revised in 1853 and again in 1859. Liszt creates an unearthly atmosphere of mingled horror and fantasy. The virtuosity of the piano parts underscores the grotesque and savage character of the entire work. Glissandos, but no excessive technical demands in this highly effective work. M-D.

Ungarns Gott (Hungary's God), G.543, originally for baritone solo with ad lib. male choir and piano 1881, trans. by the composer. In NLA vol. 17, which also contains a version for left hand alone. Liszt quotes the first six lines of Petőfi's poem "God of the Magyars" at the beginning of the piece. Left-hand version also available in *Piano Music for One Hand* (GS). M-D.

Ungarisches Königslied G.544, trans. by the composer, in NLA vol. 17. All nine versions of this work, commissioned for the opening of the Royal Opera House in Budapest, probably date from 1883. M-D.

Valse Oubliée, arr. for 2 pianos by Colin Taylor (OUP 1948; LC) 12 pp. One of Liszt's most attractive short pieces. It should be played with a light touch, even in the *forte* passages. Slight *rubatos* are necessary here and there, but the waltz rhythm must never be lost. M-D.

Via Crucis G.504/a, trans. by the composer from his versions for choir and soloists with organ (or piano) accompaniment, and for organ. In NLA vol.

10, *Various Cyclical Works* II. Includes Vexilla Regis followed by fourteen stations of the cross. Original sung text is written above the staff. In Liszt's late style; not many notes but requires mature musicianship. M-D.

Piano Transcriptions from French and Italian Operas (Dover 1982) 247 pp. Handel: Sarabande and Chaconne from *Almira,* concert arrangement. Mozart: *Réminiscences de Don Juan (Don Giovanni).* Meyerbeer: "Valse Infernals," from *Réminiscences of Robert de Diable.* Rossini: Overture to *William Tell.* Donizetti: *Réminiscences de Lucia di Lammermoor,* and *Concert Waltz on Two Themes from Lucia and Parisini.* Bellini: *Grand Concert Fantasy from Sonnambula,* and *Réminiscences de Norma.* Verdi: *Concert Paraphrase of Rigoletto,* "Miserere" from *Il Trovatore,* and *Concert Paraphrase of Ernani.* Gounod: Waltz from *Faust,* concert paraphrase. Tchaikovsky: Polonaise from *Eugene Onegin.* M-D to D.

Twenty Piano Transcriptions by Franz Liszt (A. Spanuth—OD 1903) 156 pp. Alexander Alabieff: *The Nightingale (Le Rossignol).* Frédéric Chopin, *The Maiden's Wish (Mädchen's Wunsch),* Op. 74/1, Chant Polonais; *The Ringlet (Das Ringlein)* Op. 74/14, Chant Polonais. Robert Franz: *The Messenger (Der Bote)* Op. 8/1,3. Charles Gounod: Berceuse *(Les Sabéennes)* from *The Queen of Sheba (La Reine de Saba),* Act II. Felix Mendelssohn: *On Wings of Music (Auf Flügeln des Gesanges),* Op. 34/2. Niccolo Paganini: *La Campanella,* from *Grandes Etudes de Paganini.* Gioachino Rossini: *La Regatta Veneziana (Notturno)* No.2, from *Soirées Musicales de Rossini;* and Barcarole in G (*La Gita* in Gondola) No.4, from *Soirées Musicales de Rossini.* Franz Schubert: *Faith in Spring (Frühlingsglaube)* Op. 20/2; *Hark, hark! the Lark (Morgenständchen); My Peace Thou Art (Du bist die Ruh')* Op. 59/3, and *Valses-Caprices* in D-flat and in a, Nos. 4 and 6 from *Soirées de Vienne.* Robert Schumann: *Dedication (Widmung)* Op. 25/1; and *Spring Night (Frühlingsnacht)* Op. 39/12. Giuseppe Verdi; *Rigoletto,* Paraphrase on the Quartet, Act III. Richard Wagner: *Spinning Song (Spinnerlied)* from *The Flying Dutchman (Der fliegende Hollander),* Act II, Scene I; *O Thou Sublime, Sweet Evening Star (O du mein holder Abendstern)* from *Tannhaüser,* Act III, Scene 2; and *Elsa's Bridal Procession (Elsa's Brautgang zum Münster)* from *Lohengrin,* Act II, Scene 4.

See also Aliabiev; Bach, J. S.; Beethoven; Bellini; Berlioz; Bourgeois; von Bülow; Busoni; Chopin; Cui; Dargomizhsky; Diabelli; Donizetti; Franz; Glinka; Gounod; Halévy; Handel; Lassen; Mendelssohn; Meyerbeer; Mozart; Pacini; Paganini; Rossini; Rubinstein; Saint-Saëns; Schubert; Schumann, C.; Schumann, R.; Songs, English; Songs, French; Songs, German; Songs, Russian; Spohr; Tchaikowsky; Verdi; Wagner; Zichy

For Liszt's transcriptions for piano and orchestra, see Maurice Hinson, *Music for Piano and Orchestra* (Bloomington: Indiana University Press, 1981), pp. 169–71.

Harry Loevy (–   )
See Debussy

Frederico Longas (1893–1968) Spain
See Granados

Joan Lovell (–   ) Great Britain
See Bach, J. S.; Haydn

Jack Lowe (–   ) USA
See Morgenstern; Villa Lobos

Pierre Luboshutz (1891–1971) USA, born Russian
See Bach, J. S.; Cui; Glinka; Gluck; Handel; Khachaturian; Mussorgsky; Pro-
    kofiev; Rameau; Shostakovich; Strauss, Johann J.

Clarence Lucas (–   ) Great Britain
See Bach, J. S.

Claus-Dieter Ludwig (–   ) Germany
See Hill

Jean-Baptiste Lully (1632–1687) France, born Italy
Pièces de Clavecin 1689 (K. Gilbert—Heugel 1975). Contains all of D'An-
    glebert's keyboard works, including his transcriptions of Lully's composi-
    tions for orchestra: Ouuerture de Cadmus, from *Cadmus et Hermoine,*
    1673; Ritournelle des Feés de Rolland, from *Roland,* 1685; Menuet. dans
    nos bois, from *Trios pour le coucher du Roi;* Chaconne de Phaeton, from
    Phaéton, 1683; Courante Mr. de Lully; Double; Sarabande Dieu des Enfers,
    from *Ballet de la Naissance de Vénus,* 1665; Gigue; Menuet la Jeune Iris,
    from *Trios pour le coucher du Roi;* Ouverture de la Mascarade, from *Le
    Carnaval, Mascarade,* 1668; Les Sourdines d'Armide, from *Armide,* 1686;
    Les Songes agreables d'Atys, from *Atys,* 1676; Air d'Apollon du Triomphe
    de l'Amour, from *Le Triomphe de l'Amour,* 1681; Passacaille d'Armide,
    from *Armide,* 1686; Ouuerture de Proserpine, from *Proserpine,* 1680; and
    Chaconne de Galatée, from *Acis et Galatée,* 1686.

Witold Lutoslawski (1913–   ) Poland
See Paganini

M

Richard McClanahan (–   ) USA
See Bach, C. P. E.

Edward MacDowell (1861–1908) USA
MacDowell is considered by many to be America's first truly professional composer. His music adhered to the representative Romantic style prevalent in his day.

Hamlet-Ophelia, Op. 22, originally for orchestra, trans. for duet by the composer (GS 1885; LC) 27 pp. Excellently laid out for this medium. Fine sonorities, eminently successful. M-D.

Lancelot and Elaine, Op. 25, originally for orchestra, trans. for duet by the composer (GS 1888; LC) 27 pp. M-D.

Larnia, Op. 29, originally for orchestra, trans. for duet by the composer (A.P. Schmidt 1908; LC) 23 pp. M-D.

Polonaise, Op. 46/12, arr. for 2 pianos by Rudolph Gruen (AMP 1942; LC) 14 pp. Thickens some of the original sonorities. M-D.

Rolandslied, Op. 30, originally for orchestra, trans. for duet by the composer (A. P. Schmidt; LC). Two movements: Die Sarazenen; Die schöne Alda. M-D.

Suite, Op. 42, originally for orchestra, trans. for duet by the composer (A. P. Schmidt 1891; LC) 35 pp. In a Haunted Forest; Summer Idyll; The Shepherdess' Song; Forest Spirits. Excellently laid out for the medium. Fine sonorities, eminently successful; some delightfully "new" music that cries for investigation and performance. M-D.

Suite No. 2 "Indian," Op. 48 1897, arr. for 2 pianos by William H. Humiston and Ottilie Sutro (TP 1921). This version is effective and makes this suite available to a wider public. Some essential parts have been simplified and some non-essential parts eliminated. M-D.
See also Bach, J. S.

Lilias Mackinnon (–   ) USA
See Brahms

Colin McPhee (1901–1964) USA
Balinese Ceremonial Music, originally for flute and 2 pianos (1942), trans. for 2 pianos by the composer (GS 1940; LC). Three pieces, each published separately: *Pemoengkah*, 11 pp. *Gambangan*, 7 pp. *Taboeh Teloe*, 11 pp. These come off very well in this version. M-D.

Arthur Maddox (–   )
See Satie

Gustav Mahler (1860–1911) Austria, born Bohemia
Symphony No. 8, arr. for piano duet by Alban Berg (UE 3390 1912) 133 pp.
"The role of Alban Berg in the work of transcription was not publicized; his
name is not on the score at all, nor is it in the publisher's lists. According to
Berg's own correspondence, he was called in to take over the task from
another person, a pianist by the name of Albert Neufeld, who had begun the
task but had evidently not done a satisfactory job. The reason that neither
Berg's name nor Neufeld's was published in the score has never been
discussed in the literature; making an educated guess, I think that Neufeld's
name was suppressed because of the quality of his work, whereas Berg, I
think, chose voluntarily to have his name left out of it . . . the quality of the
score itself is debatable; Berg did the best he could, but I think it may have
been a no-win situation" (letter to the author from Susan M. Filler, May 8,
1988). The arrangement uses much tremolo and is not very pianistic. M-D
to D.

Guy Maier (1891–1956) USA
See Bach, J. S.; Brahms; Kreisler

Gian Francesco Malipiero (1882–1973) Italy
Impressioni dal Vero, originally for orchestra 1910–11, trans. for duet by the
composer (Senart 1918; LC) Part 1, 13 pp. Works well in this version.
Descriptive writing. M-D.
Pause del Silenzio, originally for orchestra 1917, trans. for duet by the composer
(Bongiovanni 1919; LC) 17 pp. A very beautiful work that expresses itself
well in this version. M-D.
Dialoghi I 1956, "Con Manuel de Falla (in memoria)," originally for small
orchestra, trans. for 2 pianos by the composer (Ric 129401 1957) 11 min.
Melodies consist of combinations of motives and ideas that are molded into
long phrases. Development of musical material through free association and
constant variation in what the composer calls a "free conversation" that
produces a cumulative formal structure. M-D.

Franco Mannino (1924–   ) Italy
See Bach, J. S.

Alessandro Marcello (1669–1747) Italy
Concerto No. 3 in d, originally for oboe, trans. by J. S. Bach BWV 974. In J. S.
Bach, *Complete Keyboard Transcriptions of Concertos by Baroque Com-
posers* (Dover 1987). M-D. See Bach, J. S.

Benedetto Marcello (1686–1739) Italy
Concerto No. 10 in c, trans. by J. S. Bach BWV 981. In J. S. Bach, *Complete*

Keyboard Transcriptions of Concertos by Baroque Composers, (Dover 1987). M-D. See Bach, J. S.

Sonata in B-flat, originally for harpsichord, trans. by Béla Bartók (CF 1930; CF) 14 pp. Lento: exploits dotted rhythms. Allegro non troppo: fugal. Allegro: martial. Maestoso: French overture rhythmic treatment. A very effective piece. M-D.

Igor Markevitch (1912–1983) France, born Russia

Markevitch wrote in a basically tonal style but it was laced with dissonant counterpoint.

Le Nouvel Âge 1937, originally a sinfonia concertante for orchestra, arr. for 2 pianos by the composer (Bo&H) 23 min. Ouverture; Adagio; Hymne. M-D.

Partita 1931, originally for piano and small orchestra, arr. for 2 pianos by the composer (Bo&H) 17 min. Ouverture; Choral; Rondo. Anti-tonal canonic and serial writing in the outer movements, strong writing in Choral somewhat similar in mood to the *Andante religioso* of the Bartók Piano Concerto No. 3. M-D.

See: Alex de Graeff, "Partita for Piano and Small Orchestra," *Tempo* 133/4 (September 1980):39–43.

Frank Martin (1890–1974) Switzerland

The reputation of Martin, one of Switzerland's foremost composers, is based on relatively few works, which constantly reappear in the concert repertoire. But this remarkably gifted composer produced a large oeuvre in a musical language that, while of his time, is uniquely his own. He totally assimilated various modern musical languages, from Debussy and Ravel to Falla and Schönberg, and used them as vehicles for wholly personal yet very disciplined poetic expression.

Etudes for Two Pianos 1955–56, trans. by the composer from his *Etudes for String Orchestra* (UE 1969). Overture; Etude I—pour l'enchainment des traits; Etude II—pour le jeu fugue ou "chacun et chaque chose à sa place." Distinctive harmonic treatment in that triads, conspicuously frequent, support and enrich melodies that use the whole chromatic scale. All twelve notes of the chromatic scale are arranged in such a way as to exploit their tonal implications. Fresh and grateful writing with influences of Hindemith, Ravel, and Shostakovitch. M-D.

Giovanni Martini (1706–1784) Italy

Gavotte (Les Moutons), arr. for 2 pianos by Sarah E. Pond (EV 1940; LC) 6 pp. This delightful arrangement captures the charm and spirit of the piece. Int. to M-D.

Daniel Gregory Mason (1873–1953) USA

Prelude and Fugue, Op. 20, originally for piano and orchestra, arr. for two pianos by the composer (JF 0292) 11 min. Rather sterile writing but there are a few spots of real ingenuity. The closing of the Fugue is very Lisztian in pianistic treatment. M-D.

Jules Massenet (1842–1912) France

Thaïs, from *comédie lyrique,* trans. by the composer (Heugel; LC) 3 pp. A graceful melody in a distinctive French style. A beautiful piece and one of the most frequently performed transcriptions in the repertoire. Int. to M-D.

Johann Mattheson (1681–1764) Germany

Air varié. See Bauer.

Minuet in C. See Bauer.

Nicolai Mednikoff (–   )

See Bach, J. S.

Felix Mendelssohn (1809–1847) Germany

Caprice on the Elfin March, from *Midsummer Night's Dream,* trans. by Stephen Heller, Op. 144/2 (Musica Obscura) 9 pp. Clever and effective; requires fleet fingers. D.

Capriccio Brillant in b, Op. 22, arr. for 2 pianos by the composer (GS; CFP; Br&H; Schott; Eulenburg; K; Augener; Hug). An introduction, similar to the one in the *Rondo Capriccioso,* Op. 16, leads to an Allegro with technical characteristics similar to those in the first movement of *Concerto* in g, Op. 25. The second subject is a jestful march, which is cleverly worked together with the main subject in a delightful development. Efficiently designed. M-D.

Lieder, trans. by Franz Liszt, G.547 1840 (Br&H). *Auf Flugeln des Gesanges* (On Wings of Song), Op. 34/4. *Sonntagslied,* Op. 34/5. *Reiselied,* Op. 19/6. *Neue Liebe,* Op. 19/4. *Fruhlungslied* (Durch den Wald), Op. 47/3: a brilliant solo. *Winterlied,* Op. 19/3. *Suleika,* Op. 34/4: a fine example of Liszt's wonderful power of enhancement; it glows with beauty. M-D.

Nocturne, from *A Midsummer Night's Dream,* trans. by Paul Wittgenstein in *School for the Left Hand,* vol. 3: *Transcriptions* (UE 12329). Carried out beautifully, highly effective. M-D.

On Wings of Song, Op. 34/4, trans. by Franz Liszt, G.547/1 1840 (Br&H; CFP; Musica Obscura; OD, in *Twenty Piano Transcriptions of Liszt*). The most popular of the nine Mendelssohn songs that Liszt transcribed. The overlapping in the second verse is not easy but quickly yields to slow practice. Int. to M-D.

————. Trans. by Stephen Heller, Op. 67 (Musica Obscura) 12 pp. Much use of arpeggio and scalar figuration; material tossed between hands. Very effective. M-D.

Rondo Brillant in E-flat, Op. 29 1834, arr. for 2 pianos by the composer (GS; CFP; K; Eulenburg; Augener; Hug) 12 min. A brilliant display piece for the pianist, full of dazzling staccato octaves, chords, and broken chords. Effective scoring throughout. Displays charm, delicacy, and a cool elegance. Deserves much more playing. M-D.

Scherzo from "A Midsummer Night's Dream," trans. by Sergei Rachmaninoff (Belwin-Mills). Seldom has the spirit of an orchestral showpiece been applied to the piano as effectively. The arrangement is very faithful to the original, though considerable ingenuity is exercised to suggest the constant repeated 16th notes of the winds without actually copying them. The effect of the opening, which is very pianistic yet marvellously orchestral, is a good example. A real finger twister, reserved only for spectacular virtuosos. D.

————. Trans. for 2 pianos by Isidor Philipp (GS 1943; LC) 23 pp. Efficient transcribing. M-D to D.

————. Arr. for 2 pianos by Ethel Bartlett (OUP 1950; LC) 12 pp. Requires utmost delicacy and strict rhythm. M-D.

Serenade and Allegro Giocoso in b, Op. 43 1838, arr. for 2 pianos by the composer (Simrock; CFP; Br&H; Augener). A short and effective work. The Serenade serves as a dialogue (piano and orchestra) introduction to the lively Allegro, which is delightfully efficient. Strong inspiration seems to be lacking. M-D.

String Octet, Op. 20, trans. for piano duet by the composer (CFP). The writing is always finely in tune with the resources and shortcomings of the piano. M-D.

String Quartet, Op. 44/3, Scherzo, trans. by Ignaz Friedman, Op. 97, in collection *Piano Arrangements of Popular Classics* (Allans 1225) 10 pp. Uses many thirds and sixths, staccato, trills, *pp* ending. Extremely effective in this version. M-D.

Symphony No. 1 in c, Op. 11, arr. by Ferruccio Busoni for 2 pianos, 8 hands (Br&H 1253). Efficiently managed, but routine arranging for Busoni. M-D.

Wedding March and Dance of the Elves, from *A Midsummer Night's Dream,* trans. by Franz Liszt, G.410 1849–50 (Br&H 12369; Friedman—Br&H 380; Friedman—UE 11505) 9 min. Here Liszt, a pianist who played many roles, is a one-man orchestra, simulating the qualities of woodwind, brass, and strings. D.

See also Songs, Irish

Herbert Merrill (–   ) Great Britain
See Walton

Claudio Merulo (1533–1604) Italy
See Bauer

Giacomo Meyerbeer (1791–1864) Germany
Caprice on Themes from the Opera Le Prophète by Meyerbeer, trans. by Sigismond Thalberg, Op. 57/9 (Br&H; SBTS) 15 pp. A potpourri of highlights from this opera; full of typical Thalberg keyboard gestures that exploit the piano. M-D to D.

Chorus of the Bathers, from *Les Huguenots,* trans. for left hand by Paul Wittgenstein. In *School for the Left Hand,* vol. 3: *Transcriptions* (UE 12329). Much filigree accompaniment supports the flowing melody. M-D.

Fantasy and Fugue on the Chorale "Ad nos, ad salutarem undam," from *Le Prophète,* trans. by Franz Liszt for duet G.624 (Br&H) 22½ min. A work of gigantic proportions based on the chorale from Act I, in which three Anabaptists exhort the people to be rebaptized. In the opening section the chorale is stated and developed in an extended fantasy. The second section, an *adagio* of sublime and rhapsodic beauty, is among the finest works Liszt composed. A statement of the chorale melody is followed by a virtuoso cadenza, which leads to the final fugue. Measure by measure, the fugue builds relentlessly to a tremendous climax in which the chorale theme is restated in triumphant majesty. D.

————. Transcription of the Liszt transcription by Ferruccio Busoni (Br&H 3863). Pure Liszt in style and organ effect. D.

Fantaisie on Les Huguenots of Meyerbeer, trans. by Sigismond Thalberg, Op.20 (Musica Obscura; SBTS) 21 pp. First performed on April 16, 1836, six weeks after the opera had opened in Paris. Built on three of the most successful parts of the opera and divided into five major sections. Melody is ornamented with florid counterpoint and chords above and below; orchestral sonorities. Requires a dazzling technique. D.

Fantasy on Meyerbeer's "Robert le Diable," Op. 6, trans. by Sigismond Thalberg (Artia) 11 min. Thalberg included themes from several arias and ensemble pieces in this "tour de force." D.

Grande Fantaisie Dramatique, Réminescences des Huguenots, trans. by Franz Liszt, G.412, 2d rev. ed. (Hofmeister 1828). Shorter than the original (Schlesinger) version, with a number of alterations. Long and elaborate; every note of the transcription comes from the opera, though it is sometimes difficult to locate the source. D.

Grand Fantaisie on the opera Les Huguenots of Meyerbeer, trans. for duet by Sigismond Thalberg, Op. 43 (Musica Obscura; Schlesinger; LC) 27 pp. Contrasting sections, virtuoso scales, arpeggios. Both players range all over the keyboard. D.

Illustrations du "Prophète," trans. by Franz Liszt, G.414 (Br&H) 35 pp. Four separate pieces; No. 2, *Les patineurs,* comes from a set of dances in Act III. A large fantasy; gigantic ending with runs, chords, enormous volume, and bravura display. D.

Réminiscences de Robert le diable, "Valse infernale," trans. by Franz Liszt, G.413 1841, in collection *Piano Transcriptions from French and Italian Operas* (Dover 1982). Liszt adds to the original, revises and freely reorders Meyerbeer's material, and ingeniously combines various themes. This transcription was the most dazzling of all of the potpourris based on themes from this opera, for which Parisians developed an insatiable appetite. In June 1892, reviewing a piano recital in London, George Bernard Shaw wrote: "He gave us a chance of hearing one of those prodigious opera fantasias by Liszt which few pianists can play and fewer understand. The one selected, that on Robert, is a pungent criticism of Meyerbeer as well as a *tour de force* of adaptation to the pianoforte. To anyone who knows the opera and knows the composer thoroughly, no written analysis of Robert could be half so interesting as this fantasia in which Liszt, whilst vividly reproducing Meyerbeer's cleverly economized and elaborate scraps of fantasy, grace and power, picks up the separate themes apparently at random, and fits them to one another with a satirical ingenuity which brings out in the most striking way how very limited and mechanical the Meyerbeerian forms were." D.

Shadow Dance, from *Dinorah,* concert paraphrase by Edward Schütt (TP 1924; LC) 7 pp. *Allegretto* introduction to Tempo I. A pleasant waltz. Fingered and pedaled. M-D.

Aleksander Michalowski (1851–1938) Poland
See Chopin

Francisco Mignone (1897–1986) Brazil

Congada, from the opera *O Contratador de Diamantes* 1921, arr. for 2 pianos by the composer (OMB) 4 min. The congada is a dance type which deals with the coronation and royalty theme among African tribes, particularly those of Angola. ABA; main theme is strongly Lydian and appears over an open-fifth ostinato, which retains its rhythmic character throughout. A show piece, exotic and effective. M-D.

Dansa Campestre, arr. for duet by the composer (Arthur Napoleão 1971) 6 pp. Sectional construction, MC, strong rhythms, some bitonal usage, rich sonorities. Int. to M-D.

No Fundo do Meu Quintal (In the Depth of My Garden) 1945, originally for solo piano, trans. by the composer for 2 pianos (Ric BA 1976) 1 min. Introduction; interlude; coda. Delicate; plaintive square tune appears twice. Int. to M-D.

Darius Milhaud (1892–1974) France

Milhaud used a variety of techniques, both old and new. Polytonality, contrapuntal textures, folk song, and jazz are all utilized in generous measure. In addition, contrasting moods of tenderness and gaiety were popular with this prolific composer. The deep impression made on him by Latin America inspired a number of his works.

Le Bal Martiniquais, Op. 249 1944, trans. by the composer for 2 pianos (MCA) 24 pp. Chanson Créole: chordal, short and lyrical, in calypso style, pandiatonic. Beguine: rhythmic, brilliant. The orchestral version of this visit to Martinique is more effective. Based on several folk tunes from the French West Indies. Would serve well as a dessert piece to end a program. M-D.

La Boeuf sur le Toit 1919 (The Nothing Doing Bar), reduced for duet by the composer (ESC 855 1976). This ballet of Jean Cocteau was originally cast in 2-piano form and then orchestrated. This score, for piano, 4 hands, is effective on 2 pianos. Based on South American (mainly Brazilian) folk tunes. Titled sections immediately follow each other. Much variety in the distribution of melody and accompaniment. Rondo-like tango theme recurs between each two sections. Players are able to imagine what is taking place on stage since all of the Cocteau scenario is indicated in the score. M-D.

Carnaval à Nouvelle Orléans, Op.275 1945 trans. by the composer for 2 pianos (MCA) 28 pp., 9 min. *Mardi gras! chic a la paille* (Creole expression of joy): vigorous. *Domino noir de Cajan* (The domino is a carnival costume): lyrical and fast, unusual meter. *On danse chez Monsieur Degas* (They are dancing at Monsieur Degas's): dancelike rhythms. *Les mille cents coups* (a Creole exaggeration of the French "400 blows," an expression of excitement): catchy syncopations. Cross-rhythms; coloration and dynamic contrasts are cleverly divided between the two instruments. The whole work displays strong South American influence but is based on French tunes from Louisiana. More effective in the orchestral version. M-D.

Le Carnaval d'Aix 1926, originally for piano and orchestra, orchestral reduction for second piano by the composer (Heugel; Millikin University Library) 40 pp., 15½ min. Suite of twelve short pieces, the first six and one or two others are excellent on two pianos. Le Corso; Tartaglia; Isabelle; Rosetta; Le bon et le mauvais tuteur; Coviello; Le capitaine; Polichinelle; Polka; Cinzio; Souvenir de Rio (tango); Final. Contains some of the flavor of *Scaramouche.* Fairly dissonant and somewhat humorous. M-D.

Divertissements, trans. for 2 pianos by Victor Babin (ESC 1954; LC) 24 pp. La Française; L'Espagnole; L'Italienne; La Provençale. Fluent writing. M-D to D.

Fantaisie Pastorale, Op.188 1938, originally for piano and orchestra, reduction for 2 pianos by the composer (Sal) 22 pp., 10 min. Lacks key signature but is freely tonal around F, mainly homophonic. Flowing double glissando in thirds, octotonic. M-D.

Kentuckiana, Op.287 1948, trans. for 2 pianos by the composer (EV) 22 pp., 6½ min. Built on twenty Kentucky mountain tunes. Quodlibet effect, shifting meters, predominantly contrapuntal. The resulting complex texture creates rhythmic problems, seems unable to control the thematic profusion. Milhaud's ways with American folk tunes are so similar to his ways with French airs that this suite might be called a "Suite Française." Began as a work for the Louisville Orchestra. M-D.

La Libertadora, Op.236 1943, trans. for 2 pianos by the composer (Ahn & Simrock 1960) 20 pp., 7 min. Five original dances each reflecting a Latin American style. Vif: folk-like tunes give this an exuberant character; 2/4 is used occasionally with the mainly 3/4 meter. Animé: opening reminiscent of Debussy's *Gardens in the Rain;* glissando opens the door for a new tune in the upper register; first theme returns with parts reversed. Modéré a tango with one idea developed in different keys with a constantly recurring accompaniment figure of 16th note, 8th note, 16th note. Vif: a lively dance in varied rhythms; frequent interaction between instruments; Spanish rhythm; hemiola treatment; concludes *pp*. Animé: uses samba rhythm; tunes are Latin American inspired; excitement builds at the conclusion, where a syncopated fragment of the samba rhythm is repeated in octaves three times (the last in canon). Both pianos have accented octaves to conclude this truly exciting work. Written at the same time Milhaud was writing his opera *Bolivar,* about the great South American liberator, and that seems to be the relationship with this work. Arranged rather conservatively and resembles duet style. Piano I often has strict melody while Piano II has accompaniment exclusively in the bass clef. Sometimes this procedure is reversed. Can be played at one piano if players are careful to switch parts when necessary. Good high school pianists could play and would enjoy this piece. M-D. Solo arrangement by the composer also available (Ahn & Simrock).

Les Songes (Daydreams), Op. 237 1943, trans. by the composer for 2 pianos (Sal) 19 pp. Scherzo: facile writing, mainly pentatonic, many tempo changes. Valse: short, nostalgic, moderate tempo, recalls Satie's *Gymnopedie*. Polka: animated and brilliant, more contrapuntally complicated. This suite, derived from a ballet of the same name composed in 1933, can serve as a refreshing substitute for the overworked *Scaramouche*. M-D.

Suite, Op. 300 1951, originally for 2 pianos and orchestra, arr. for 3 pianos by the composer (Heugel) 74 pp., 18 min. Entrée; Nocturne; Java fuguée; Mouvement perpetuel; Final. Uses polytonality for dramatic tension; strong contrapuntal and rhythmic usage with some rhythmic patterns piled up in a manner comparable to the stacking of polytonalities. The Java is a popular French dance in an alternating 3/4 and 2/4 time. Extended, appealing, but not Milhaud's strongest writing. M-D.

Première Suite Symphonique 1914, trans. for duet by the composer (ESC 1923; LC) 27 pp. Vif; Lent; Très animé. Transcription works well but thematic material is very slim. M-D to D.

Jacques Miller (1900–   ) USA, born Russia
See Kreisler

Robin Miller (–   )
See Scarlatti

Stanislaw Moniuszko (1819–1872) Poland
Moniuszko's masterpiece was *Halka,* the first genuinely national Polish opera.
Réminiscences de Halka, trans. by Carl Tausig (Musica Obscura) 11 pp. A glittering work; for virtuosos only! D.
Trois Transcriptions de Concert d'Après St. Moniuszko, Op. 28, trans. by Ignaz Friedman (Piwarski; LC). *Printemps; Chant du Soir; Dumka.* Effective in a kind of turn of the century (nineteenth to twentieth!) salon style. M-D.

Thomas Moore (1779–1852) Ireland

Moore was a famous Irish poet, ballad singer, and song composer.

Variations in D major on a National Air by Moore duet by Frédéric Chopin (Ekier—PWM). At the age of 16, while he was still attending the Warsaw Conservatory, Chopin found the melody in a collection entitled *National Airs and Other Songs* compiled by Moore. This particular air was published with the English lyrics "Oh come to me when daylight sets," but Moore stated that the tune was actually Venetian—in fact, it is known today as the "Carnival of Venice." Most pianistic interest is given to the Primo part. Chopin's autograph manuscript has changed hands many times and fragments were lost. Some convincing restoration has been made by the editor. M-D.

Sam Morgenstern (–   ) USA

Toccata Guatemala, arr. for 2 pianos by Arthur Whittemore and Jack Lowe (CF 1957; LC) 13 pp. Incisive Latin American rhythms, full chords, glissandos. M-D.

Jerome Moross (1913–1983) USA

See Gottschalk; Songs, American

Ignaz Moscheles (1794–1870) Bohemia

See Songs, Irish

Moritz Moszkowski (1854–1925) Poland

Maleguena from the opera *Boabdil,* arr. by Jacob M. Velt (EBM 1940; LC) 8 pp. The maleguena rhythm is handled tastefully; contrasting section, brilliant coda. M-D.

Valse Brillante in E, trans. for 2 pianos by Rudolph Gruen (AMP 1934; LC) 20 pp. Concert version. M-D.

See also Bizet; Chopin; Mendelssohn; Offenbach

Wolfgang A. Mozart (1756–1791) Austria

Adagio, from *Wind Serenade* in E-flat K.375, trans. for left hand by Paul Wittgenstein in *School for the Left Hand,* vol. 3; *Transcriptions* (UE 12329). Clever and effective; numerous tenths; footnotes for variants in performance. M-D.

Adagio and Fugue in c, K.546 and K.426, for 2 pianos (Badura-Skoda—GS; Krause—Br&H). Mozart composed the *Fugue* K.426 for 2 pianos in 1783; when he arranged it for string orchestra he added the *Adagio* K.546 as a prelude. Paul Badura-Skoda has arranged the *Adagio* for 2 pianos. Some surprising harmony in the *Fugue,* perhaps the greatest fugue that has been written since Bach. In an elaborate foreword Badura-Skoda explains the musical thoughts that governed this presentation. M-D.

Caprice on Favorite Airs from the Operas "Figaro" and "Don Juan," Op. 64, trans. by Johann B. Cramer (André 1823). Cramer identifies the Mozart themes in the score. This Caprice is a potpourri of three themes but Cramer does not relate them to each other in the various sections. He opens the piece with his own introduction and combines original thematic ideas with the popular opera themes. Scale fragments, arpeggios, and sequences are used extensively, as well as embellishments of the vocal line. M-D.

Chorale Prelude, from *The Magic Flute,* arr. for duet by Geoffrey Carroll (Willis 1987) 7 pp. *Adagio;* most of the chorale "Ach Gott, vom Himmel sieh' darein" is given to the Secondo part, which has some moving left-hand octaves. Effective. Int.

Concerto in F, K.242 1776, originally for 3 pianos and orchestra, arr. by the composer for 3 pianos (Badura-Skoda—Eulenburg; K; Br&H), and for 2 pianos (Br&H). Allegro; Andante; Rondeau. Although originally composed to be performed with orchestra, this work can be effective unaccompanied, with all the pianos playing tutti passages. Related in chamber music style to concertos of J. C. Bach. Three levels of difficulty, with Piano I the most involved. Piano II features some interesting solo lines, while the performer at Piano III must be alert to counting rests. Cadenzas in all movements. Amiable and pleasing but reaches no great heights of inspiration. M-D.

Deutsche Tänze, K.600, 602, and 605 1791, trans. by Carl Czerny (K. Hermann—CFP 11417 1939), 16 pp. A combination of thirteen contrasting numbers from these collections, concluding with a full-page coda. Int.

Sechs Deutsche Tänze, K.509 1787, trans. by E. H. Mueller von Asow (Dob DM 27 1955) 11 pp. A few octaves and thickened chords have been added. Int. to M-D.

Duettino Concertante, trans. by Ferruccio Busoni in 1919 for 2 pianos, after the finale of the *Piano Concerto* in F, K.459 (Br&H). Busoni changes some triplet passages to 16ths. Contains constant and witty interplay between the two instruments, plus an infectious chatter and some brilliant concertante passages. M-D.

Fantasia for Musical Clock Work, K.608, trans. for 2 pianos by Ferruccio Busoni (IMC 585; Br&H 5220; LC) 16 pp. The two-piano idiom lends itself admirably to a mechanical subject, for the effort of synchronizing the two instruments tends in itself to produce a mechanical style. The contrapuntal texture here manifests such clarity and independence of parts that it anticipates the neo-Classic style of Stravinsky. One of Busoni's most faithful Mozart transcriptions. M-D.

Fantasina on Mozart's Figaro, Op. 124, trans. by Johann Nepomuk Hummel (Haslinger ca. 1833; LC). "Fantasina" is the diminutive of "fantasy." This piece is based only on one aria from the opera, "Non più andrai." Hummel had studied with Mozart as a child, and it appears he wanted to reflect a spirit of Mozart in this little fantasy. The theme is set simply and without any interference. Makes few technical demands on the pianist. M-D.

Fantasia on the Serenade and Minuet from Don Juan (Don Giovanni), trans. by Sigismond Thalberg, Op. 42 (Schott; LC) 25 pp. Sparkling passage-work with careful regard for phrasing and expression; skillfully and effectively written. Schumann heard Thalberg play this work in February 1841 and commented on the "highly artistic" manner in which Mozart's themes were used. The piece uses a few themes, an extensive introduction, and progresses to a grand climactic conclusion. D.

Fantaisie on Two Motives from Mozart's "Marriage of Figaro," trans. by Franz Liszt, arr. by Ferruccio Busoni 1912 (Br&H 3830) 12 min. Liszt began this work in 1842, performed it at least one in Berlin in 1843, but left it incomplete. It is a fanciful elaboration of Figaro's "Non più andrai" followed by Cherubino's "Voi che sopete." The piano writing is symphonic. The coda blends both pianistic and symphonic styles.

Grand Fantaisie et Variations sur deux motifs de Opera "Don Juan" de Mozart, trans. by Sigismond Thalberg, Op.14 (Haslinger 184?; LC) 29 pp. The first theme is treated to a remarkable variety of figurations and techniques. The second theme ("La ci darem la mano") gets even more virtuoso treatment. M-D to D.

The Magic Flute—Chorale Prelude, arr. for duet by Geoffrey Carroll (Willis 1987) 7 pp. Parts are well divided between the players, with the Secondo having the chorale "Ach Gott, von Himmel sieh' darein." Clever counterpart adds interest. Int. to M-D.

Magic Flute Overture, trans. for 2 pianos by Ferruccio Busoni (Br&H 5241; IMC 449) 19 pp. Stylistically sound, no extra padding. Absolutely faithful, bar by bar, to the original; adaptations of orchestral effects. Fun to play, interaction between the two pianos is diverting for audience. M-D.

Maurerische Trauermusik, K.477, arr. for 2 pianos by Otto Vrieslander (Heinrichshofen 1949; LC) 64 pp. Much syncopation. Chromatic, poignant, beautiful. M-D.

Menuet, from *Symphony* in g, K.550, trans. by Charles Alkan (Musica Obscura). Menuet uses left-hand full chords; Trio is thinner but the texture thickens near the end. M-D.

Overture: Die "Entfuhrung aus dem Serail," K.384, trans. by Ferruccio Busoni 1904 (Br&H). Busoni wrote a concert ending for this transcription. M-D to D.

Overture: Don Giovanni, K.527, trans. by Ferruccio Busoni 1908 (Br&H). Busoni composed a concert ending for this transcription. M-D to D.

Réminiscences de Don Juan, trans. for 2 pianos by Franz Liszt, G.656 1841, published 1877 (Br&H; E. Szegedi—EMB Z7810 1978) 50 pp., 16 min. The EMB edition includes a preface in Hungarian, German, and English. A breathtaking transcription by Liszt in most brilliant fashion for paired pianos. Structurally more cohesive and technically more brilliant than Liszt's original solo version, G.418. The antiphonal potential of the two instruments is magnificently exploited in this version, especially in the "La ci darem la mano" section. D.

Réminiscences de Don Juan, from Mozart's "Don Giovanni," trans. by Franz

Liszt, G.148 1841 (Busoni—Br&H) 16 min. Also in collection *Piano Transcriptions from French and Italian Operas* (Dover 1972). The most ambitious and most successful of all the Liszt operatic pieces. It is no mere potpourri, but a synthesis of the character of Don Giovanni, displayed by means of sophisticated variation technique. The work begins at the end of the opera, with the Don being dragged down to the Underworld by his Stone Guest, then we have the vocal duet "La ci darem la mano" (with two stunning variations), a reprise of the opening material, and finally a spectacular elaboration on Don Giavonni's first-act champagne aria, "Finch han dal vino." Busoni noted that this monumental work has "the almost symbolic significance of a pianistic summit." D.

Réminiscences de "Don Juan," Konzert-Fantaisie über Motive aus Mozarts "Don Giovanni" für das Pianoforte, Grosse Kritisch-Instrucktive Ausgabe von Ferruccio Busoni (Br&H 4960 1918). Contains both the Liszt transcription of *Réminiscences de Don Juan* and Busoni's version of that transcription. In an essay entitled "Mozarts 'Don Giovanni' und Liszts 'Don Juan-Fantaisie,' " Busoni appeals to pianists to duplicate the transparency of the Mozart score in this Liszt *Fantaisie*. Busoni placed his version under Liszt's for comparison. For Busoni, the operatic paraphrase was a psychological compression of the opera and its drama into the medium of the piano. Many of Busoni's deviations from the Liszt text are based on Liszt's own version of the same work for two pianos, which Busoni considered superior. D.

Serenade from Mozart's "Don Giovanni," trans. by Ferruccio Busoni 1920 (Br&H). In the early 1920s Busoni produced his enormous piano pedagogy work *Klavierübung*. In vol. 3, dedicated to the study of staccato playing (*Lo Staccato)*, he included this fine transcription of Don Giovanni's serenade "dehveni alla finestra." The original features a solo mandolin. Here Busoni conspires to stretch the hands so as to give the effect of two outer staccato parts with the lyrical melody taken in the middle, as if by the third hand. M-D.

Study No. 6 (on themes from *The Magic Flute),* from *Kurze Stücke zur Pflege des Polyphonen Spiels,* trans. by Ferruccio Busoni (Br&H).

Variations on "La ci darem" from Mozart's Don Giovanni, by Carl Czerny, Op. 825/7 (Musica Obscura) 4 pp. Four-bar introduction leads to theme. Variation of the melody plus an Allegro in 6/8 follow. M-D.

————. Trans. by Frédéric Chopin, Op. 2, 1827, trans. for 2 pianos. In Chopin, *Complete Works for Piano,* vol. 15: *Works for Piano and Orchestra* (PWM). This piece does not differ very much in form from many pieces of the period called "fantasy" or "fantasy and variations." It inspired Schumann to make his famous statement, "Hats off, Gentlemen, a genius." The piece was designed to show off Chopin's virtuosity and his genius for handling a favorite popular tune. Chopin uses only the opening 2/4 part of Mozart's theme and restructures it slightly. A 63-bar introduction presents a fantasy-like treatment of thematic fragments with elaborate pianistic figuration. Five contrasting variations follow, concluding with a lively polacca. M-D to D.

See also Reger; Songs, French

Gottlieb Muffat (1690–1770) Germany
See Bauer

Claude Murphree (ca. 1900–1958) USA
See Haydn

Modest Mussorgsky (1839–1881) Russia

Coronation Scene, from *Boris Godounov,* arr. by Frederick Block (EBM 1953; LC) 7 pp. The peal of Moscow's bells is effective. Much use of tremolo; triplet figures build to climax. M-D.

———. Arr. for 2 pianos by Pierre Luboshutz (JF 1951; LC) 8 pp. Effective. M-D.

The Fair at Sorochinsk: Hopak, trans. by Sergei Rachmaninoff, In *Rachmaninoff—A Commemorative Collection* (Belwin-Mills) 2 min. A brilliant dance made more fluent in this transcription. M-D.

Pictures at an Exhibition, trans. by Harold Bauer (GS 2131 1950) 45 pp. Additions are tasteful, and a few bare spots are "filled out," although some of the "bare spots" color Mussorgsky's style considerably. M-D to D.

———. Arr. for piano and orchestra by Lawrence Leonard, reduction for 2 pianos (Br&H 1980; SBTS) 64 pp. A free transcription, but no notes have been added other than octave transpositions. The big central Promenade omitted from Ravel's orchestral version is here intact. D.

Siege of Kazan, from *Boris Godunov,* arr. by Frederick Block (EBM 1953; LC) 5 pp. Colorful setting, dancelike, attractive. M-D.

N

John Jacob Niles (1892–1980) USA
See Songs, American

Gustav Nottebohm (1817–1882) Germany
See Beethoven

O

Siegfried Ochs (1858–1929) Germany

Ochs was a famous choral conductor as well as a composer. One of his best-known works is the comic opera *Im Namen des Gesetzes* (1888). *5 Variationen über "Kommt ein Vogel Geflogen,"* trans. by Ferruccio Busoni (Schott 7511 1987) 13 pp. plus 5 pp. of facsimile. Busoni treats the little tune by Ochs "in the style of" Chopin, Wagner (Nibelungen), Scarlatti, Schumann, and Mendelssohn. Delightful and humorous! Int. to M-D.

John Odum (–) Great Britain

See Bach, J. S.

Jacques Offenbach (1819–1880) France

Barcarolle from "Tales of Hoffman," Op. 27, trans. by Moritz Moszkowski (CFP 9460) 7 pp., 5½ min. Effective, inventive, and appealing. M-D.

———. Trans. by Ferruccio Busoni "à trois mains," in *Klavierübung,* 2d ed., Bk. IV (Br&H). This delightful little two-page piece is frequently used as an encore, sort of a parting joke. M-D.

Silvio Omizzolo (–)

See Beethoven; Rossini

P

Paul Pabst (1854–1897) Germany
Pabst studied with Liszt before moving to Moscow to accept a piano position at Nikolai Rubinstein's Conservatory. Pabst produced a great deal of music in various forms, but his most successful works were in the operatic paraphrases modeled after those of his mentor.
See Tchaikovsky

Giovanni Pacini (1796–1867) Italy
Divertissement on "I tuoi frequenti Palpiti," from *Niobe,* trans. by Franz Liszt G.419 (USSR, in vol. 4 of complete edition: *Operatic Transcriptions* I). Dazzling and pianistic throughout. Requires complete technique for mastery. D.

Ignace Jan Paderewsky (1860–1941) Poland
Fantaisie Polonaise, Op. 19, originally for piano and orchestra, arr. for 2 pianos by the composer (Bo&Bo 1895) 21 min. One movement divided into three large sections. Based on Polish folk songs. Includes double glissandos, complex textures, and brilliant figuration. D.

Vladimir Padwa (1900–   ) USA, born Russia
See Khachaturian

Niccolò Paganini (1782–1840) Italy
Paganini's violin virtuosity and his music inspired many musicians (including Brahms, Chopin, Liszt, Rachmaninoff, and Schumann). In his early years Liszt worshipped Paganini.
Introduzione, Capriccio (Paganinesco), trans. by Ferruccio Busoni. In *An die Jugend* (Zimmermann 1909); and in *Klavierübung,* 2d. ed. only, Bk. 10: *Etuden nach Paganini-Liszt* (Br&H), where it is titled *Introduzione e Capriccio.* The *Introduzione* is a transcription for left hand alone of the opening of *Caprice* No. 11 in C, from Paganini's *Capricci per violino solo,* Op. 1; it returns in grand style in E at the end. The middle section, *Capriccio,* is a transcription of *Caprice* No. 15. Strong Liszt influence. D.
Six Paganini Etudes, trans. by Franz Liszt G.141 (NLA; Sal; Br&H; CFP; Ric; K; GS; Durand). The first version of these pieces (1832–33) was one of Liszt's earliest attempts to transcribe music for another medium for the piano. Five of these etudes are transcriptions from Paganini's *Twenty-four Caprices* for unaccompanied violin, Op. 1. No. 3, *La Campanella,* the most famous of the set, contains chiming chords, dazzling technical effects in the

101

upper register of the keyboard, and difficult repeated notes. No. 3 is also in collection *Twenty Transcriptions of Liszt* (OD).

————. Edited and trans. by Ferruccio Busoni (Br&H, available separately). Many pianists are familiar with Busoni's transcription of *La Campanella*, but it is not well known that Busoni also edited and transcribed the other Paganini etudes. M-D to D.

La Campanella, trans. by Franz Liszt, arr. for 2 pianos by Colin Taylor, in the two-piano series of Bartlett and Robertson (OUP 1939) 22 pp. This fascinating piece comes through wonderfully in this brilliant arrangement. M-D to D.

Willard Palmer (1916–   ) USA
See Bach, J. S.; Clarke

Albert Ross Parsons (1847–1933) USA
See Bach, C. P. E.

Ernst Pauer (1826–1905) Austria
See Wagner

Flor Peeters (1903–1981) Belgium
12 Choral Preludes, Op. 114, originally for organ, trans. by the composer (CFP 6895a, b 1966). Vol. I: Nos. 1–6; Vol. II: Nos. 7–12. Fairly well-known chorales treated in three and four parts. No fingering, and very little pedal indicated. Int. to M-D.

Leonard Pennario (1924–   ) USA
See Chopin; Field

Martin Penny (–   )
See Byrd

Giovanni Battista Pergolesi (1710–1736) Italy
Three Days My Nina, trans. by Sigismond Thalberg (Musical Scope). Once a repertoire piece of Joseffy and Busoni. M-D.

Vincent Persichetti (1915–1987) USA
Concertino, Op. 16 1941, originally for piano and orchestra, arr. for 2 pianos by the composer (EV) 9 min. This one-movement, neoclassic work is spiced with dissonant counterpoint. Superb craft, brilliant conclusion, effective in this medium. M-D.
See also Brahms

Ad. Pescio (–   )
See Raff

Egon Petri (1881–1962) Germany
See Bach, J. S.; Buxtehude

Isidor Philipp (1863–1958) France, born Hungary
See Bach, J. S.; Bach, W. F.; Berlioz; Chopin; Frescobaldi; Mendelssohn; Strauss, Johann Jr.

Riccardo Pick-Mangiagalli (1882–1949) Italy
See Bach, J. S.

Gabriel Pierné (1983–1937) France
Fantaisie-Ballet, Op. 6, originally for piano and orchestra, arr. for 2 pianos by the composer (Leduc; BrM) 17 pp. Sectionalized, strong dance influence. M-D.

Karl Hermann Pillney (1896–   ) Austria
Escapaden eines Gassenhauers (Escapades of a Street Song), Paradoxical variations for listeners with a sense of musical humor (Br&H 6510). Pillney has arranged this little tune in the style of J. S. Bach, Handel, Mozart, Schubert, Mendelssohn, Rossini, Verdi, Reger, Schönberg, and Liszt. Fun for all. Int. to M-D.
See also Bach, J. S.

Johann Peter Pixis (1788–1874) Germany
See Bellini

Sarah E. Pond (–   )
See Martini

Francis Poulenc (1899–1963) France
With Poulenc, color was as important an element of composition as linear drawing is to the painter. He possessed a unique inventive gift and a rich imagination.
Aubade 1929, originally for piano and 18 instruments, reduced by the composer for 2 pianos (Sal). This multi-section work is a hybrid between a concerto and a ballet. Numerous short motives; sharp contrast between the wit and brilliance of some sections and the Gallic melancholy of others; some sections reminiscent of the music hall. Improvisatory style. M-D.
Capriccio (d'après Le Bal Masque), trans. for 2 pianos by the composer (Sal) 5 min. Varies from the earlier *Caprice,* based on same work, by an eight-bar introduction and a brief quasi-cadenza inserted at rehearsal number 14. This ready-made and accessible work deserves more playing. Thick polytonal chords mixed with scalar figuration and lyric melodies. A witty and delightful lampooning of French music hall ditties and the cancan. Requires an infectious rhythmic bounce and a proper saucy flair. M-D.
Les Animaux Modèles (The Model Animals) 1940–41 ballet, trans. by Grant Johannesen (ESC 8515 1984) 35 pp. Dawn; The Bear and His Two Friends; Grasshopper and Ant; The Amorous Lion; An Elderly Man with Two Girlfriends; Death and the Woodcutter; Two Roosters; Noonday Repast.

Neo-archaic setting of old Gallic dance music. Poulenc's tendency toward witty pastiche, sometimes harmonious, sometimes not, is evident in this score. I doubt if Poulenc could have done it any better. Exceedingly pianistic and extremely effective. M-D.

L'Embarquement pour Cythère 1951, trans. for 2 pianos by the composer (ESC) 11 pp., 2½ min. Originally written as the score for the film *Le Voyage en Amérique*. This amusing little rondo must not be taken seriously—it only tips its hat and winks over its shoulder at the Watteau painting that inspired it. The simple main tune is wistful and catching; a little dissonance is cleverly sprinkled in this Valse Musette. Themes alternate from one piano to the other. Int.

Pastourelle 1927, trans. by the composer from the ballet *L'Eventail de Jeanne* (Heugel). Enticing melody. Int.

John Powell (1882–1963) USA

Powell was greatly influenced by American folk music. Some of his titles disclose a whimsical propensity.

In the Hammock (Scene Sentimentale), Op. 19, arr. for 2 pianos by the composer (GS 1920; LC) 9 pp. Int. to M-D.

Natchez-on-the-Hill, Op. 30 bis, for piano, arr. for 2 pianos by Percy Grainger (GS 1933; LC) 23 pp. Charming and effective. M-D.

Charles Proctor (–   ) Great Britain
See Bach, J. S.

Sergei Prokofiev (1891–1953) USSR

Divertimento, Op. 43 bis 1925–29, originally for orchestra, trans. by the composer, in *Collected Works* (K) 24 pp. Four movements; melodic line moves between hands in the second movement, *Larghetto*. Large span required. M-D to D.

March, Op. 99, originally for band, trans. for 2 pianos by Pierre Luboshutz (Leeds 1948; LC) 12 pp., 2½ min. Feisty and fresh sounding. M-D.

March, from the opera *Love for Three Oranges,* arr. for 2 pianos by Felix Guenther (EBM 1957; LC) 8 pp. A delightful piece, witty and sarcastic. M-D.

Peter and the Wolf, Op. 67, originally for orchestra, trans. by the composer (MCA). Delightful and very accessible. The texture is rarely complex; and with the possible exception of some metronome markings that must be taken figuratively, the entire score is quite performable. Many demanding passages, such as those in which the right hand plays the flute part (representing the little bird), especially when this theme is combined with others, such as the march of the hunters, near the end of the work. M-D.

Romeo and Juliet, Op. 75, trans. by the composer from the ballet 1937 (MCA; IMC). Folk Dance; Scene; Minuet; Juliett—the little girl; Masks; The Montagues and the Capulets; Friar Laurence; Mercutio; Dance of the Maids from the Antilles; Romeo and Juliet before Parting. Short sketches that are effective as a group or separately. Most of the melodies are direct and uncomplicated, utilizing harmonies and chromaticism not associated with Prokofiev's piano sonatas. Int. to M-D.

Scherzo and March, from *Love for Three Oranges,* Op. 33, trans. by the composer. In vol. 8 of *Complete Piano Works* (K) 3½ min. These favorite transcriptions show not only Prokofiev's superb imagery but also his technical in conveying their provocative dazzle and humor. M-D.

See also Buxtehude; Schubert

Joseph Prostakoff (1911–   ) USA, born Russia
See Bach, J. S.

Arthor Pryor (1870–1942) USA
See Cook

Giacomo Puccini (1858–1924) Italy

Sailor's Chorus, from *Madame Butterfly,* trans. for left hand by Paul Wittgenstein, in *School for the Left Hand,* vol. 3: *Transcriptions* (UE 12329). Melody and chords are well spread out; pedaled and fingered. M-D.

Henry Purcell (1659–1695) Great Britain

The Old Bachelor, arr. by Thomas F. Dunhill from the original music to Congreve's play (1693) (OUP 1933; LC) 15 pp. Rondeau; Slow Air; Boree; First Hornpipe Minuet; Jig; Second Hornpipe; March. This charming suite should be investigated and performed. In fine style and good taste. Int.

Three Fantastic Variations on Lilliburlero, for 2 pianos, by Madeleine Dring 1948 (Lengnick) 27 pp., 9 min. Henry Purcell is supposed to be the composer of the seventeenth-century tune "Lilliburlero." Three conventional variations in 4/4 with much triplet use. Octotonic, MC. M-D.

Q

Roger Quilter (1877–1953) Great Britain

Three English Dances, Op. 11, originally for small orchestra, trans. for duet by
the composer (Boosey 1910; LC) 21 pp. Allegretto semplice; Allegro
scherzoso; Allegro non troppo, ma con spinto. Modal, flowing, attractive.
M-D.

R

Sylvia Rabinof (ca. 1918–   ) USA
See Bach, C. P. E.; Bach, J. S.

Sergei Rachmaninoff (1873–1943) USA, born Russia
In the art of transcription Rachmaninoff was in his happiest vein. Not only did his profound and practical command of the piano enable him to translate musical sound from any medium to the keyboard in terms of his own unique pianism, but in treating ready-made themes and structures he was freed from the problems of form, which tormented him throughout the composition of every major work. His transcriptions especially radiate rare joyousness and flights of fancy. Rachmaninoff followed the example of Liszt and Godowsky in writing his transcriptions. What could be more welcome to music lovers than new and imaginative treatment of melodies they already loved? Rachmaninoff's transcriptions are not only unique in sound and brilliance but also supremely expressive.

Capricco bohémien, Op. 12, originally for orchestra 1894, trans. by the composer for duet 1892 (Gutheil 1895; LC) 39 pp. Rachmaninoff had a special feel for these gypsy tunes. The layout of this version is splendiferous! M-D to D.

Concerto No. 2 in c, Op. 18, concert transcription of third movement by Percy Grainger. In *Concert Transcriptions of Favorite Concertos* (GS 1947; IU). Strange as it may seem, this abridged transcription displays a finer style of piano writing than does the original version. It presents a fabulous lesson in writing for the piano. Rachmaninoff admitted, in an interview published in *The Etude* in 1923, that his Second Piano Concerto was "uncomfortable to play." Grainger has made this movement more comfortable! M-D.

————. Arr. for 2 pianos by the composer (Foley 1938). Moderato; Adagio sostenuto; Alegro scherzando (rondo: ABABAB). Frequent important interludes. Highly effective fugato in the finale. Simple rhythmic structure of the whole work helps one to grasp its contents quickly. A melancholic mood pervades most of this work until the ending, which is a strong affirmation of faith. Impeccable craftsmanship in every bar. M-D to D.

Floods of Spring, Op. 14/11, trans. by Duncan Stearns (Willis). This work blossoms and spreads the joy of this beautiful song in a glorious manner. M-D.

Italian Polka, arr. for 2 pianos by the composer (Belwin-Mills 1938). Rachmaninoff supposedly heard this tune played outside the hotel in Florence by strolling musicians. M-D.

————. Trans. for piano solo by Alexander Siloti (Bo&H). Transposed to the key of d.

Lilacs, Op. 21/5, arr. by the composer 1914 (Br&H 1919); revised and trans. by the composer (Foley 1941) 5 pp. Rachmaninoff has made this song even more beautiful in this version. Delightful, poetic. Rhythmic pattern of accompaniment triplets pulsate against the double melody. The original song was one of Rachmaninoff's finest compositions. This transcription won the composer enormous popularity in Russia. Exquisite writing. M-D.

Margeritki (Daisies) Op. 38/3, song, arr. by the composer (Foley 1940). Extensive coda provides a kind of poetic commentary on what has gone before. M-D.

Prelude in C-sharp minor, Op. 3/2, arr. for 2 pianos by the composer (CF 1938; LC) 9 pp. Also in Charles Foley, *Album for Two Pianos* (Belwin-Mills). Beautifully effective. Int. to M-D.

Symphonic Dances, Op. 45 1940, arr. by the composer for 2 pianos (Foley; Schott) 102 pp., 26 min. Non Allegro; Andante con moto (Tempo di valse); Lento assai—Allegro vivace. A strong work in its own right and not an outline or study for the orchestral version. Approached in the same manner as the Ravel piano works that were transformed into orchestral masterpieces. Displays adventurous pungent harmonies (notably the shifting, ambiguous harmonization and sinister, unsettling chromatic figures in the lilting central waltz), contrasts of texture, and rhythmic subtleties, often suggesting jazz influence. D.

See also Bach, J. S.; Behr; Bizet; Kreisler; Liszt; Mendelssohn; Mussorgsky; Rimsky-Korsakov; Tchaikovsky

Joachim Raff (1822–1882) Germany, born Switzerland

Gavotte and Musette, from *Suite* Op. 200, for piano and orchestra, arr. for 2 pianos by Ad. Pescio, rev. by Harold Bauer (GS 1931; Wright State University Library) 21 pp. Neoclassic style, moderately thick textures, brilliant closing. M-D.

The Mill, trans. for 2 pianos by George Anson (EV 1948; LC) 11 pp. The "pitter patter" mill runs constantly. Fine transcription. Int.

See also Bach, J. S.

Jean-Philippe Rameau (1683–1764) France

Gavotte with Variations, trans. for 2 pianos by J. Doebber (IMC 1957; LC) 8 pp. Gavotte and five variations are very effective in this version. Much staccato usage. M-D.

A Gay Melody (Air Trés Gai), arr. for 2 pianos by Pierre Luboshutz (JF 1937; LC) 19 pp. Would make a charming program opener. Int. to M-D.

Le Rappel des Oiseaux, trans. by Ignaz Friedman. In collection *Transcriptions of Ignaz Friedman,* vol. 1 (UE 17825). Very fast and light.

Musette in G, trans. by Ignaz Friedman. In collection *Transcriptions of Ignaz*

Friedman, vol. 1 (UE 17825) 2 pp. Has many large-spread chords, a few ornaments. M-D.

Trois Pièces, trans. by Leopold Godowsky (Schlesinger 1906; NYPL). *Rigaudon; Elegie; Tambourin.* These transcriptions maintain the charm of the originals. M-D.

Sam Raphling (1910–1988) USA
See Stravinsky, I.

Maurice Ravel (1875–1937) France
Ravel translated some of his most important orchestral works into piano music, usually for duet or for two pianos. He lavished a great deal of care on these transcriptions and tried to make them as playable as possible. His synthesizing genius produced a uniquely personal style that exploits the use of modal melodies and the intervals of the seventh and the ninth. Ravel extended the pianistic traditions of Franz Liszt but expressed himself in a quintessentially French way.

Bolero, arr. by Roger Branga (Durand 11671 1929) 8 pp. Requires exceptional dynamic control to be effective. M-D.

————. Arr for 2 pianos by the composer 1930 (Durand) 30 pp. The second pianist may "stop" (press on the strings) the opening ostinato with the left hand and simulate the timbre of the snare drum if the constant repetition becomes monotonous. Colors and hypnotic spell must be uncannily evoked. M-D to D.

Daphnis et Chloé, Danse Gracieuse et Légère de Daphnis, trans. by the composer (Durand) 4 pp. Full of lyrical beauty and picturesque sonority. Highly effective. M-D.

L'Heure Espagnole, Comédie Musicale, Fantaisie for piano, arr. by Léon Roques (Durand 8489 1912) 11 pp. All scenes are indicated; very little added by Roques. Effective. M-D.

Introduction and Allegro 1906, originally for harp, string quartet, flute, and clarinet; arr. for 2 pianos by the composer (Durand 2906; LC) 25 pp., 13 min. This work sounds especially congenial on two pianos—the solo harp, after all, is not that dissimilar. Ravel has forged this piece into a beautiful transcription. M-D.

Ma mère l'Oye, originally for duet, trans. by Jacques Charlot (Durand 7430 1910) 18 pp. These five charming pieces are colorful and effective in this transcription. No fingering or pedal indications. Large span would be helpful. Int. to M-D.

————. No. 4, *Les Entretiens de la Belle et de la Bête,* trans. by the composer (Durand). This delightful waltz tells the story of Beauty and the Beast. Very effective but more difficult than the original. M-D.

Pavane pour une infante défunte, arr. for duet by Ralph Berkowitz (EV 1941; LC) 90 pp. Effective version; includes all material from original but is much easier. No measure numbers. Int. to M-D.

————. Trans. for 2 pianos by Mario Castelnuovo-Tedesco (Leeds 1950; LC) 8 pp. Usable. Int. to M-D.

Pièce en Forme de Habanera, originally for violin and piano, concert transcription by Maurice Dumesnil (Leduc 1955) 3 pp. Gorgeous melody, pianistic. Overlapping hands; no pedaling or fingering indicated. M-D.

Rapsodie Espagnole 1907, originally for orchestra, arr. for 2 pianos by the composer (Durand) 16½ min. Prelude à la nuit; Malaguena; Habanera; Feria. All the specifics of the orchestral version are as graphic as they are with the symphonic counterpoint. This arrangement achieves the same stunning brilliance as the original does. Requires a brilliant, symphonic approach. M-D.

————. No. 3, *Habanera,* trans. by the composer (Durand) 3 pp. Contains a rare charm in its warm sonorous mist and floating harmonies; perpetual suspense; everything evaporates. Large rolled chords, hands interlocked for some passages. M-D.

La Valse 1919–20, originally for orchestra, trans. for duet by Lucien Garban (Durand 9895 1920) 42 pp. Pianistic and well divided between the players. Requires a taut measured quality and strong rhythmic projection. M-D to D.

————. *Mouvement de Valse Viennoise,* arr. for 2 pianos by the composer (Durand) 42 pp., 17 min. A sinister re-creation of Johann Strauss's nineteenth-century Vienna. Requires tight control and a fiendish, measured quality. D.

————. Arr. by the composer (Durand). Ravel's solo version is highly effective and requires virtuoso technique. D.

See also Debussy

Gardner Read (1913–   ) USA

Sonata da Chiesa, Op. 61a, trans. for 2 pianos by the composer (Seesaw 1971) 20 pp. Intrada; Canzona; Ricercare. Eclectic style, chordal, contrapuntal, modal. Driving rhythms in the Ricercare. M-D.

Max Reger (1873–1916) Germany

Variations and Fugue on a Theme by Mozart, Op. 132a, originally for orchestra, trans. by the composer (Simrock; CFP 1915) 57 pp., 27 min. Theme is from Mozart's *Sonata* in A, K.331. D.

See also Bach, J. S.; Chopin

A. Reitlinger (–   )

See Strauss, Johann Jr.

Ottorino Respighi (1879–1936) Italy

Fountains of Rome, originally for orchestra, trans. by the composer for duet (Ric; LC) 27 pp. Very effective but no comparison with the original. M-D.

Notturno, arr. for 2 pianos by Felix Guenther (EBM 1947; LC) 12 pp. Colorful; much added to the original but still a beautiful setting. M-D.

The Pines of Rome, originally for orchestra, trans. by the composer for duet (Ric; LC) 37 pp. More effective than the *Fountains*. M-D.

Josef Rheinberger (1839–1901) Liechtenstein

Duo, Op. 149a, after the *Suite* for organ, violin, cello, and string orchestra; trans. for 2 pianos by the composer (K&S). Similar in style to Brahms. M-D.

Rhené-Baton (1879–1940) France

Menuet pour Monsieur, frère du Roy, Op. 5 1901, originally for orchestra, arr. for 2 pianos by the composer (Durand 1909; LC) 12 pp. Colorful, flowing, tuneful. M-D.

Alan Richardson (1904–1978) Great Britain
See Handel

Wallingford Riegger (1885–1961) USA

Canon and Fugue, Op. 33 1954, originally for strings, trans. for 2 pianos by the composer (SP; AMC; UCLA) 7 pp. Canon: in d; *Allegro non troppo.* Fugue: makes a fine climax. M-D.

Nikolai Rimsky-Korsakov (1944–1908) Russia

Ballet Dance, from *The Czar's Bride,* arr. by Frederick Block (EBM 1952; LC) 6 pp. These delightful tunes are not blown out of proportion with too many trappings. Straightforward presentation. Int.

Cortège de Noces (Wedding Procession), from *Coq d'Or,* arr. by Frederick Block (EBM 1952; LC) 5 pp. Colorful march. Some tremolo used, octotonic staccato writing, active coda. M-D.

Cradle Song, arr. for 2 pianos by Victor Babin (Bo&H 1942; LC) 7 pp. Sweetly effective, flowing. M-D.

Dance of the Tumblers, arr. for 2 pianos by Victor Babin (Bo&H 1942; LC) 21 pp. Scherzo quality throughout; the two piano parts are carefully balanced. Staccatissimo usage, colorful ending. M-D.

———. A concert transcription for 2 pianos by Abram Chasins (JF 1938; LC) 19 pp. D.

A Song of India, from the opera *Sadko,* trans. by Alexander Siloti (CF 1927) 4 pp. Siloti suggests a slower tempo for this piano solo than for the operatic performance. Entire piece built on a pedal tone on *A.* Int.

Tsar Saltan: The Flight of the Bumblebee, trans. by Sergei Rachmaninoff. In *Rachmaninoff—A Commemorative Collection* (Belwin-Mills) 1 min. The device Rinsky-Korsakov uses to represent a bee's buzz is simplicity itself: a continuously droning chromatic scale. The piece is light and brief, a masterpiece of pianistic magic. D.

The Flight of the Bumblebee, arr. by Gould and Shefter for 2 pianos (EMB).

Robert Riotte (–   ) Germany
See Gärtner

Marie von Ritter (–   )
See Kreisler

Julie Rivé-King (1854–1937) USA
See Strauss, Johann Jr.

Rae Robertson (1893–1956) Great Britain
Robertson and his wife, Ethel Bartlett, were a well-known two-piano team from
the 1930s to the 1950s. Together they edited an Oxford University Press series of
works for two pianos.
See Franck; Granados; Grieg; Liszt; Strauss, Johann Jr.

Jean Jules Roger-Ducasse (1873–1954) France
Au jardin de Marguerite, originally a symphonic poem for double chorus and
orchestra, trans. for 2 pianos by the composer (Durand 1912). Choeur de la
dispute des fleurs; Interlude; Prelude et choeurs.
Le joli Jeu de furet, orginally for children's choir and orchestra, trans. for 2
pianos by the composer (Durand) 19 pp.
Suite Française, originally for orchestra, reduced for 2 pianos by the composer
(Durand 1909–10; LC) 41 pp. Overture; Bourrée; Recitatif et Air; Menuet
vif. An expansive work, requires much ensemble experience. M-D to D.
Variations plaisantes sur un thème grave 1907, originally for harp and orchestra,
trans. for 2 pianos by the composer (Durand 7875) 29 pp. Well laid out
between the instruments. M-D to D.
See also Debussy

Leon Roques (–   ) France
See Debussy; Ravel

Lawrence Rosen (–   ) USA
See Barber

Moriz Rosenthal (1862–1946) Poland
See Chopin (*13 Transcriptions for Piano Solo of Chopin's Minute Waltz,* Op.
64/1); Strauss, Johann Jr.

Michelangelo Rossi (17th cent.) Italy
Tre Correnti, originally for organ or harpsichord, trans. by Béla Bartók (CF
1930; LC) 7 pp. No. 5 in F, No. 1 in e, and No. 2 in D, from *Dieci Correnti
per Cembalo od Organo.* Many octaves; large span required. M-D.
Toccata No. 1 in C, originally for organ or harpsichord, trans. by Béla Bartók
(CF 1930; LC) 7 pp. No. I from *Dieci Toccate per Cembalo od Organo*
Many octaves, full chords, numerous ritards and accelerendos. Last section
is fugal; big ending. M-D.
Toccata No. 2 in a, originally for organ or harpsichord, trans. by Béla Bartók
(CF 1930; LC) 9 pp. No. IX from *Dieci Toccate per Cembalo od Organo.*
Some octave doubling; insignificant changes suggested in smaller sized
notes; sectional, big conclusion. M-D.

Gioachino Rossini (1792–1868) Italy

Rossini's opera tunes have fascinated other composers for decades.

Cuyus Animam, from *Stabat Mater,* trans. by Franz Liszt G.553 (OD; LC) 9 pp.
Fast left-hand octaves; contains a few *ossias.* Extensive coda dies away to
ppp ending. M-D to D.

La Danza (Tarantella), trans. for 2 pianos by Franz Liszt G.424/9 (Schott; LC)
7 pp. *Presto e brillante;* Liszt cadenza near opening; a wild, brilliant, and
effective dance. M-D.

————. Trans. for 2 pianos by Silvio Omizzolo (Ric 1955; LC) 8 pp. Much
easier version than the Liszt version. Int. to M-D.

Fantasie on motifs on "La Donna del Lago" de Rossini, by Sigismond Thalberg,
Op. 40 (Br&H 184?; LC) 23 pp. Sectionalized. The Romance and the
Choeur des Bardes are the most effective sections. Extravagant treatment
with many virtuosic tricks of the trade. Trans. by Thalberg, for duet, Op. 40
(Schlesinger; LC) 29 pp.

Fantasie on Rossini's Barber of Seville, by Sigismond Thalberg, Op. 63 (MTP).
Themes carefully selected to present a dramatic and cogent viewpoint. M-D
to D.

Fantasy on "Semiramide," by Sigismond Thalberg, Op. 51 (Br&H; SBTS)
27 pp. Full of arpeggios, chromatic figuration, and melody tossed between
the hands. D.

Fantasie on themes from "Moise," by Sigismond Thalberg, Op. 33 (MTP;
Troupenas; LC; SBTS) 21 pp. Octaves everywhere, *Sentimento* tunes,
sectionalized, *Veloce* chromatic figuration, full tenth chords arpeggiated. In
the finale the melody is played by both hands in the midst of sweeping
arpeggios. Intricate and brilliant. Virtuosic, generates enormous sound. D.

Fantasie on Themes from the Opera La Gazza Ladra by Rossini, by Sigismond
Thalberg, Op. 57/6 (Br&H; SBTS) 14 pp. Many fast octaves, repeated
chords, filigree figuration, *Più presto* coda. M-D to D.

March of the Greeks in Rossini's Opera "The Seige of Corinth" with Variations,
by Jean Baptiste Duvernoy (Musica Obscura) 4 pp. March theme followed
by three variations. Int.

Soirées Musicales de Rossini, trans. by Franz Liszt, G.424 1837 (Schott). The
twelve pieces in this set are songs Rossini composed for evening parties
with his friends. No. 2, "La Regatta Veneziana" (Notturno), and No. 4,
Barcarolle in G, are available in the collection *Twenty Transcriptions of
Franz Liszt* (OD). All twelve are transcribed in a straightforward manner,
well suited to their graceful and charming character. Unpretentious; worthy
of revival. M-D to D.

Mi Manca la Voce, from the opera *Moise,* trans. by Sigismond Thalberg, Op. 36
(Schlesinger; SBTS) 5 pp. A *cantabile* melody is played mostly by the
thumbs while the accompaniment is spread out among the other fingers.
Andante tempo allows much freedom in the vocal line.

Overture to William Tell, trans. by Franz Liszt, G.552 1838, in collection *Franz*

Liszt—Piano Transcriptions from French and Italian Operas (Dover)
28 pp. Liszt played this work at his first solo recital in Paris, a city where he
astonished and dazzled his audience. D.

———. Arr. for duet by Louis M. Gottschalk (Weekley & Arganbright—Kjos
West 1983) 16 pp. Rossini's attractive tune plus Gottschalk's brilliant
arrangement make this a "hit." The editors have deleted the long and
generally less-familiar opening section and begin with the familiar "Lone
Ranger" section. M-D.

Variations on "Non più mesta" from La Cenerentola, trans. by Henri Herz 1831
(MTP). Extended introduction in which broken thirds and repeated notes are
interspersed with fast arpeggios and difficult cadenza figuration. Six variations, with Var. 6 serving as a summation of all that has gone before; the
audience is treated to broken octaves, skips, repeated chords, difficult
dotted note work, and numerous other hurdles. D.

Albert Roussel (1869–1937) France

Evocations, Op. 15 1910–11, originally for orchestra, trans. for 2 pianos by the
composer (Durand 8143; LC) 21 pp., 42 min. *Les Dieux dans l'ombres des
Cavernes:* a musical depiction of the impact that viewing images of Hindu
deities has on Europeans. *La Ville rose:* a scherzo inspired by the ancient
town of Jaipur. *Aux bords du fleuve sacre:* deals with the attractions of
nature in the holy city. Shows a fondness for acidulous harmonies and rather
dense textures. Influence of Indian music seen in the flat second, raised
fourth, and flat sixth degrees of the scale. Throughout his life, Roussel, a
well-practiced traveler, was fascinated with the Near and Far East, and
Evocations is but one of many compositions reflecting this fascination. D.

Pour une fête de printemps, Op. 22 1920, trans. for 2 pianos by the composer
(Durand 9939; LC) 23 pp., 12 min. Atmospheric symphonic poem with
pleasing fresh sonorities that arise naturally from the melodic and contrapuntal thought. Displays more sense than sensibility, more integrity than
imagination. Bitonal usage creates an impression of tension and heightens
the poignancy of the emotional situation. M-D to D.

Anton Rubinstein (1829–1894) Russia

Romance in E-flat, freely trans. for 2 pianos by Silvio Scionti (TP 1943; LC)
9 pp. Pedaled and fingered. Much added to the original but the sonorities
are in the correct style. M-D.

Two Songs, trans. by Franz Liszt, G.554 1881 (Kistner; Musica Obscura) "O!
wenn es doch immer so bliebe" (O! would it last forever!): dedicated to
Mrs. Rubinstein in memory of "The good old times" she and the composer
had together, hence the meaning of the title and its dedication. "Der Asra"
(from Op. 32) was originally 46 measures; Liszt's version is 144 measures.
Impressionistic. M-D.

See also Beethoven

Walter Rummel (1887–1953) Belgium
Rummel was well known as a pianist who devoted himself to promoting Claude
Debussy's works. He gave the first performance of Debussy's *Etudes* on December
14, 1916. His Bach transcriptions are well-respected.
See Bach, J. S.

Leslie Russell (–   )
See Bach, J. S.

Vincenz Ruzicka (–   )
See Bach, J. S.; Lanner

S

Camille Saint-Saëns (1835–1921) France

Le Carnaval des Animaux 1886, trans. by Lucien Garban (Durand 13538 1951) 37 pp., 14 min. Excellent transcription; exquisite music blended with humor of a high order. No. 13, *The Swan*, requires fine control of *legato* melody and 16th-note accompaniment in the right hand. M-D. Also trans. for duet by Lucien Garban (Durand) and for 2 pianos by Ralph Berkowitz (Durand). *The Swan* is available for piano, duet, and 2 pianos (all Durand).

Cypres et Lauiers, Op. 156 1919, originally for organ and orchestra, trans. for 2 pianos by the composer (Durand; LC) 31 pp. Requires fine octave and tremolo technique. M-D.

Danse Macabre, Op. 40, originally for orchestra, trans. by Franz Liszt, G.555 1876 (K; Musica Obscura) 21 pp. Takes considerable liberties with the original, much to its advantage. M-D to D.

———. Trans. for 2 pianos by the composer 1874 (Durand 2099) 13 pp. This descriptive transcription is almost as effective as the original version. M-D.

Duo, Op. 8 1859 (d'après les Duos pour piano et orgue), arr. for 2 pianos by the composer (Durand).

Etienne Marcel, waltz, arr. for 2 pianos by Claude Debussy (Durand). Originally in the opera.

Introduction and Rondo Capriccio, Op. 28, originally for violin and orchestra, trans. for 2 pianos by Claude Debussy (Durand; IMC). M-D.

La Jeunesse d'Hercule, Poème Symphonique, Op. 50 1877, originally for orchestra, trans. for 2 pianos by the composer (Durand 2330; LC) 17 pp. M-D.

Marche du Couronnement, Op. 117, originally for orchestra, trans. by the composer for duet (Durand 1902; LC) 19 pp. This rip-roaring piece sounds extremely well when played by two fine pianists. M-D.

Marche Héroïque, Op. 34, arr. for duet by the composer (Durand; LC) 19 pp. This arrangement works as well as the original. The martial quality is even more noticeable in this version. M-D.

———. Arr. for 2 pianos, 8 hands by the composer (Durand 2907).

Minuet and Gavotte, Op. 65, from the *Septet,* trans. for 2 pianos by the composer (IMC 1954; LC) 12 pp. Charming and graceful writing. Would make a delightful encore. Int. to M-D.

Phaëton, Op. 39 1873, originally for orchestra, reduced for 2 pianos by the composer (Durand 1958; LC) 15 pp. M-D.

Le Rouet d'Omphale, Poème Symphonique, Op. 31 1871, originally for orchestra, reduced for 2 pianos by the composer (Durand 2033; LC) 33 pp.

Suite Algérienne, Op. 60, originally for orchestra, arr. for duet by Gabriel Fauré (Durand 1880; LC) 49 pp. Prélude, Rhapsody Mauresque, Rêverie du Soir; Marche Militaire Française. This picturesque suite comes to life in this arrangement, but much color is lost as compared with the original. Rêverie du Soir is by far the most successful movement in this version. M-D.

Sur les bords du Nil (Marche Militaire), Op. 125, originally for military band, trans. for duet by the composer (Durand 1908; LC) 17 pp. This version works well and sounds properly martial. M-D.

The Swan (Le Cygne), from *Carnival of the Animals,* trans. by Alexander Siloti (CF; LC 1924) 4 pp. Melody moves between the hands with continuous 16th-note accompaniment in right hand and continuous 8ths in the left. Requires careful delineation of dynamics in right hand. M-D.

————. Trans. by Leopold Godowsky (Musica Obscura) 7 pp. Freely transcribed. M-D to D.

Symphonie No. 2 in a, Op. 55 1878, trans. by Claude Debussy (Durand 1908; UCLA) 31 pp. The transcriptions by Debussy are outstanding and show the high regard he had for his countryman. M-D.

Tarentelle, Op. 6 1851, for flute and clarinet with orchestra or piano, arr. for 2 pianos by the composer (Richault; LC) 29 pp. Romps continually but contains attractive moments. M-D.

See also Bach, J. S.; Beethoven; Chopin

Karel Salmon (1897–1974) Israel, born Germany

Suite on Greek Themes 1943, trans. for 2 pianos by the composer (IMI 1966) 68 pp., 18 min. Based on a collection of Greek folk songs and dances. Syrtos thrakikos: a slow dragging dance. Theme and Variations. Intermezzo—the Lemon Tree: constant repetition of theme in various textures. Finale—Horra Hellenica: two sections, Greek and Jewish elements intermingle; at the end the themes appear simultaneously. Salmon's most popular piece. D.

Lionel Salter (1914–   ) Great Britain
See Songs, Scottish

Olga Samaroff (1882–1948) USA
See Bach, J. S.

Gustave Samazeuilh (1877–1967) France
See Chabrier; Debussy; Fauré

György Sándor (1912–   ) USA, born Hungary
See Shostakovich

Pablo Sarasate (1844–1908) Spain
Gypsy Dance, originally for violin and piano, arr. for duet by A. Louis Scarmo-

lin (Pro-Art 1945; LC) 7 pp. This version is exciting and effective. Too fast a tempo can result in twisted fingers. Int. to M-D.

Erik Satie (1866–1925) France

Parade—Ballet réaliste, trans. by the composer (Rouart Lerolle 1917; LC) 21 pp. This transcription is extremely effective—colorful and full of wit. M-D to D.

Socrate, originally a symphonic drama, arr. for 2 pianos by John Cage (ESC 8554 1984; IU) 61 pp. Portrait de Socrate (Le Banquet), 1947; Bords de l'Ilissus (Phèdre); Mort de Socrate (Phédon). Movements II and III were completed with the assistance of Arthur Maddox in 1968. The text of *Socrate* is omitted so that the music itself can be enjoyed. Well laid out; contains highly interesting sonorities. M-D.

Emil Sauer (1862–1942) Austria, born Germany

Boîte à Musique (Spieluhr), originally for solo piano, arr. for 2 pianos by the composer (Schott 1932; LC) 10 pp. One of Sauer's most charming pieces; colorful musical representation of a music box. Subtler and more flexible mid-section with fast scale passages adds color. Requires careful rhythm control. M-D.

See also Liszt

Domenico Savino (1882–1973) USA, born Italy
See Grofé

Domenico Scarlatti (1685–1757) Spain, born Italy

Pastorale, K.9; *Gigue* in G; and *Capriccio,* K.20; trans, by Carl Tausig (Schott). For their day, not terribly overblown. *Gigue* has large skips, hand crossings, 3 against 2, *ff* ending. M-D. *Capriccio* available separately (Musica Obscura) 5 pp.

Pastorale K.446 (L.433), trans. by Ignaz Friedman, in collection *Transcriptions of Ignaz Friedman,* vol. 1 (UE 17825) 4 pp. Free transcription with flowing arpeggiated chords and elaborate decoration. Requires a good hand span and judicious use of pedal. M-D.

Five Pieces, K.332 (L.141); K.109 (L.138); K.212 (L.135); K.193 (L.142); K.70 (L.50); trans. by Béla Bartók (Belwin Mills 3858) 23 pp. Bartók had much interest in Baroque music; these are just a few of the Scarlatti sonatas he transcribed. Includes pedal marks, fingering, and many dynamics. Effective on the piano. M-D.

A. Louis Scarmolin (1890–1969) USA, born Italy
See Sarasate

Dirk Schaefer (–   )
See Strauss, Johann Jr.

William Scharfenberg (–   )
See Gounod

Xaver Scharwenka (1850–1924) Poland
Suite de Danses, Op. 41, trans. by the composer for duet (CFP; LC) 35 pp. Alla
    Marcia; Menuetto; Gavotte; Bolero. Effective and much fun in this version.
    M-D.

William Scher (–   )
See Chopin

Otto Schlaaf (–   ) Germany
See Gärtner

Rudolf Schmidt-Wurnstorf (1916–   ) Germany
See Delius

Florent Schmitt (1870–1958) France
Schmitt wrote over 120 compositions. Most are difficult to perform, full of
massive sonorities and bold dissonances, and epic in style. Only a few have been
played in the United States.
Antoine et Cléopatre, originally for orchestra, trans. for duet by the composer
    (Durand 1921; LC) 50 pp. This extensive work sounds somewhat like Fauré
    (Schmitt's teacher). The expressive writing has much to offer. The com-
    plete work in this version would be tedious; individual movements would be
    more successful, especially the one called "Orgie et danses." D.
Étude pour le Palais Hanté (Haunted Palace), d'Edgar Allan Poe, Op. 49,
    originally for orchestra; reduction for 2 pianos by the composer (Durand
    1904) 15 min.
La Tragédie de Salomé, Op. 50, originally a ballet, trans. by the composer for
    duet (Durand 1911; LC) 58 pp., 26 min. "Danse de l'Effroi" is the most
    effective movement in this version. M-D to D.
————. Trans. for 2 pianos by the composer (Durand).
Musiques de plein air, Op. 44, originally for orchestra, trans. for duet by the
    composer (Durand 1914; LC) 37 pp. *La Procession dans la Montagne.*
    Danse désuète. Accalmie (published separately). Contains some very beau-
    tiful music. This version works well. M-D to D.
J'entends dans le lointain, Op. 64 1917, originally for solo piano, arr. for 2
    pianos by the composer (Durand) 6 min.
Symphonie concertante, Op. 82 1932, originally for piano and orchestra, arr. for
    2 pianos by the composer (Durand) 30 min. This three-movement work
    shows strong Fauré influence, considerable structural power, rich color, and
    impressive eloquence. M-D.

Artur Schnabel (1882–1951) Austria
See Brahms

Horst-Günther Schnell (–   ) Germany
See Hindemith

Johann Jean Schobert (1720–1766) Germany
Minuet in E-flat. See Bauer
Capriccio. See Bauer

Arnold Schoenberg (1874–1951) Austria
Klavierstück, Op. 11/2, trans. by Ferruccio Busoni 1909 (UE 2992). One of the most extraordinary concert interpretations that Busoni published. In his Preface he says: "This composition demands of the player the most refined touch and pedal; an intimate, improvised, 'floating,' deeply felt presentation; the performer's loving abandonment in its content, whose interpreter—merely a piano arranger—deems it an artistic honor to be present." Schoenberg tends to improvise in this piece, and this quality of free extemporization allowed Busoni to treat the text flexibly and imaginatively. M-D to D.
Five Orchestra Pieces, Op. 16 1909, arr. for 2 pianos by Anton Webern (CFP 3378) 34 pp., 17½ min. *Vorgefuhle; Vergangenes; Farben; Peripetie; Das obligate Rezitativ.* Not twelve-tone but atonal. Effective distribution of material between pianists. In the last piece Schönberg arrived at a musical style that eliminated thematic repetition almost completely. Development of intervallic material is fragmented in all five of these works. Subtly expressive and rhythmically complex. D.

Hermann Schroeder (1904–1984) Germany
Schroeder's style leans toward neo-Baroque writing.
Sechs Weihnachtslieder (Six Christmas Carols) arr. for duet (Otto Heinrich Noetzel 1956; LC) 15 pp. Includes "Uns kommt ein Schiff, geladen"; "Es flog ein Täublein weisse"; "Lieb Nochtigall, wach auf"; "Susani"; "Still, still"; "Stille Nacht, heilig Nacht." A delightful set in every way. Familiar as well as unfamiliar carols; expertly arranged. Int.

Godfrey Schroth (1927–   ) USA
See Debussy

Franz Schubert (1797–1828) Austria
Schubert's superb melodies have always had a great attraction for arrangers and transcribers. They had special appeal to Liszt, who transcribed over 50 of Schubert's songs.
Alt-Wien, transcriptions of Schubert Dances, by Ignaz Friedman, vol. I (UE 1928) 6 pp.; vol. II (UE 1928) 6 pp. These two volumes are actually two charming waltz suites based on Schubert dances. The Schubert tunes are clearly heard. Requires large span. M-D.
Andantino und Variationen D.823, arr. for duet by Carl Tausig, ed. with a Preface by Gary Wolf (Musica Obscura) 13 pp. This is the second movement of the *Divertissement* (à la française). Ernest Hutcheson, in *The Literature of the Piano,* 3d ed. (New York, 1964), considers this "an example of a perfect transcription." Theme *(Andantino)* and four variations. M-D.

Andantino varié, Op. 84/1, on a French motive, originally for duet, adapted for 2 pianos by Harold Bauer (GS 1928; Oberlin Conservatory of Music) 23 pp. Textures are kept lighter than in Bauer's arrangement of Op. 103. M-D.

Ballet Music from Rosamunde, concert arrangement by Leopold Godowsky (CF 1923). Attractive melodies and rhythms woven together. M-D.

Du bist die Ruh, trans. for left hand by Paul Wittgenstein. In collection *School for the Left Hand,* vol. 3: *Transcriptions* (UE 12329). This is a transcription of the Liszt transcription, and it works well in this medium. M-D.

Frühlingsglaube (Faith in Spring); *Hark, Hark! The Lark; Du bist die Ruh* (My Peace Thou Art). Three songs trans. by Franz Liszt, in collection *Twenty Transcriptions by F. Liszt* (OD). *Frühlingsglaube:* the two musically identical stanzas are framed and linked by a prelude, interlude, and postlude; the first stanza is virtually the equivalent of Schubert's vocal and piano score; the second is more richly varied, with the melody appearing mostly in the middle, in the upper part of the left hand; Liszt inserts a short cadenza before the closing ritornello. *Hark, Hark! The Lark:* fanciful treatment; highly effective; one of Liszt's best song transcriptions; *dolcissimo ppp* ending. *Du bist die Ruh:* sets three Stanzas, two of them identical; plus instrumental prelude, interludes, and postlude; inserts an independent variation without words between stanzas 2 and 3. All M-D.

Three Concert Transcriptions on Themes of Schubert, J. Strauss and Delibes, trans. by Ernst von Dohnányi (Rosavölgyi 1930). The Schubert themes are from *Valses Nobles.* Concert versions that were typical though outstanding products of the period—when love of the piano and its sound were an esthetic tradition. M-D to D.

Éloge des Larmes (Praise of Tears), trans. by Stephen Heller (Musica Obscura) 4 pp. This lovely song transcription always keeps the melody intact. Includes pedal marks that "are indispensable to the execution" (from note in score). M-D.

The Erlking, trans. by Stephen Heller (Musica Obscura) 11 pp. Very close to the original until the final section, where Heller uses broken octaves most effectively. M-D.

Fantasia in f, Op. 103, arr. for 2 pianos by Harold Bauer (GS 1928; Oberlin Conservatory of Music) 44 pp. Textures are generally thickened, but the arrangement is pianistic and effective. M-D.

Die Forelle (The Trout), trans. by Stephen Heller (Musica Obscura) 11 pp. Much of the melody is given to the left hand, while the right hand pursues varied figurations. M-D to D.

Franz Schuberts Märsche, trans for duet by Franz Liszt G.426, in Series II, Vol. 7, of the NLA (c.1988) 35 pp. *Trauermarsch:* based on *Six grandes Marches,* Op.40/5 (D.819). *Grande Marche de François Schubert:* based on Op.40/3 and on the trio of *Grande Marche Funèbre,* Op.55 (D.859), composed on the occasion of the death of Czar Alexander I in 1825; Liszt inserted the latter before the return (measures 225–69). The construction of the third piece, *Grande Marche caractéristique de François Schubert,* is the most varied: measures 1–177 contain arrangements of *Deux Marches carac-téristiques*, Op. posth. 121/1 (D.886); measures 178–227 are based on the trio of the Op. posth. 121/2. In measures 228–63 the first part of Op.40/2 is stated in F-sharp minor instead of the original G minor, whereas measures 264–309 include the arrangement of the trio of Op. 40/1 in F-sharp major instead of the original A-flat major. The return begins in measure 317, and, from measure 370 on, the trio of Op.40/1 is heard again as a kind of closing theme, in a completely different arrangement from the previous one (measures 264–309). M-D to D. (In 1859–60 Liszt transcribed the three marches for orchestra [G.363]; and he subsequently made a version for piano duet of the orchestral version, which he named *Vier Märsche von Franz Schubert* [G.632].)

Funeral March (Trauermarsch), originally for duet, trans. by Franz Liszt G.426 (Musica Obscura) 11 pp. Introduction; March; Trio; March returns. Includes una corda pedal indication. M-D. Also in Series II, Vol. 7, of the NLA.

Heiden-Roslein, trans. by Alfred Cortot (Foetisch Frères 1947) 2 pp. Simple but elegant treatment. M-D.

Hungarian March, Op. 54, originally for duet, trans. by Franz Liszt (Musica Obscura) 10 pp. Strong rhythms, hand-crossings, fast chromatic sixths and octaves in both hands, inside parts use tremolo, fast thick repeated chords at conclusion. Large span required. M-D to D.

Impromptu in E-flat, Op. 90/2, arr. for left hand alone by Johannes Brahms (Br&H 1927). Flows naturally; unusually effective. M-D.

Elf Ländler, arr. by Johannes Brahms for duet (Schott 1934). The eleven slow waltzes are absolutely charming in this version. Int. to M-D.

Marche Militaire No. 3, concert transcription by Alberto Jonás, Op. 21/6 (CF 1932; LC) 15 pp. "Freely arranged for concert performance." Glissandos in opposite directions, tremolos, moves over keyboard quickly, virtuosic. D.

Meeresstille, trans. for left hand by Paul Wittgenstein, in collection *School for the Left Hand*, vol. 3: *Transcriptions* (UE 12329). A transcription of the Liszt transcription. Effective; many arpeggios. M-D.

Military March, Op. 51/1, arr. for duet by Max Vogrich (GS 1901; LC) 23 pp. Based on the arrangement for concert use by Carl Tausig, this greatly expanded version works to an impressive conclusion. M-D.

The Miller and the Torrent, trans. by Sigismond Thalberg (Musica Obscura) 4 pp. Based on a simplified version of the song by Carl Czerny. Straightforward and charming. Int.

6 Melodien von Franz Schubert, trans. by Franz Liszt G.563, Series II, Vol. 7 of the NLA (c.1988) 22 pp. "Lebe wohl!"; "Mädchens Klage"; "Das (Züargen-) Sterbeglöcklein"; "Trockne Blumen"; "Ungeduld" (first version); "Die Forelle" (first version). When Liszt was arranging these songs (in 1844 at the latest), he must have been unaware that the first song was not by Schubert but by August Heinrich von Weyrauch, a composer and poet born in Riga in 1788. Liszt retained the metric and harmonic construction of the songs in his arrangements but varied the verse-settings considerably. Vol. 7 also contains a second version of "Die Forelle," G.564, with different, more simply constructed figurations in the accompaniment. M-D to D.

Rondo Brillante, Op. 84/2, arr. for 2 pianos by Harold Bauer (GS 1928; Wheaton College Library) 23 pp. More spread out over keyboard than original; pianistic. M-D.

Twelve Schubert Songs, freely trans., each with a foreword apropos transcriptions, arrangements, and paraphrases, by Leopold Godowsky (CF 1927). "Wohin?"; "Das Wandern"; "Heidenröslein"; "Gute Nacht"; "Morgengruss"; "Wiegenlied"; "Die Forelle"; "Die Junge Nonne"; "Litanei"; "Liebesbotschaft"; "An Mignon"; "Ungeduld." M-D.

Songs, trans. by Franz Liszt, edited and fingered by W. Scharfenberg. Vol. I (GS 128 1897) 77 pp.: "Am Meer"; "Auf dem Wasser zu singen"; "Ave Maria"; "Das Wirthshaus"; "Die Post"; "Erlkonig"; "Gretchen am Spinnrade"; "Horch, Horch! die Lerch' "; "Lob der Thranen"; "Meeresstille"; "Sei mir gegrusst"; "Ständchen." Vol. II (GS 129 1897) 74 pp.: "Aufenthalt"; "Das Wandern"; "Der Leyermann"; "Der Müller und der Bach"; "Der Wanderer"; "Die junge Nonne"; "Du bist die Ruh' "; "Frühlingsglaube"; "Lebe wohl!"; "Rostlose Liebe"; "Tauschung"; "Trockne Blumen"; "Ungeduld." In both volumes the song texts are overlaid on the piano score. Masterpieces of the art of transcription. M-D to D.

Müller-Lieder von Franz Schubert, trans. by Franz Liszt (second version), G.565 1846, Series II, Vol. 7 of the NLA (c.1988) 20 pp. "Das Wandern"; "Der Muller und der Bach"; "Der Jäger"; "Die böse Farbe"; "Wohin?"; "Ungeduld" (third version). Based on Nos. 1, 19, 14, 17, 2, and 7 of the song cycle *Die schöne Müllerin* D.795, written to poems by Wilhelm Müller. Liszt created five works out of the original six songs by combining the music of the third and fourth songs in a ternary form. He adhered strictly to the harmonies and the melodies of the songs except in "Der Jäger," for which he wrote an eight-measure variation on the piano accompaniment starting with measure 10, and a variation on the voice part starting with measure 18. M-D.

Soirées de Vienne (Valses Caprices d'après Franz Schubert), trans. by Franz Liszt, G.427 1852. Nos. 1–9 (Sauer—CFP 2126); Nos. 2, 4, 6 (third version), 7, 8 (Friedman—UE 11504); No. 6 (second version) (Spanauth—GS). Liszt rescued from oblivion many of Schubert's dances for piano, which he arranged with ornamental elaborations as nine *Soirées de Vienne.* Several dances are alternated, developed, and varied; and, while it is true that some of Schubert's originals are occasionally played, Liszt's versions are accomplished with such good taste that it is sheer snobbery that they are rarely heard today. M-D to D.

Variations on a Beloved Vienna Trauer-Walzer of Franz Schubert, by Carl

Czerny, Op. 12 (Musica Obscura) 8 pp. Introduzione a Capriccio: brilliant; leads directly to the simple theme. Four variations: the last is the most extensive and serves as a coda. M-D.

Waltzes, arr. for 2 pianos by Sergei Prokofiev. In vol. 11 of *Collected Works of Sergei Prokofiev* (K) 71/2 min. This suite was arranged by Prokofiev during his travels abroad in 1920 and published in 1923. He selected his examples from various sets of Schubert's waltzes. The suite is constructed on the principle of contrasts, with the opening theme recurring often as a unifying factor. The result is a rondo-like form, which reminds one of the opening piece of Schumann's *Faschingsschwank aus Wien,* Op. 26. Prokofiev and the noted Soviet pianist Samuel Feinberg played this suite as an encore in Moscow on February 4, 1927. Int. to M-D.

Wanderer-Fantasia, trans. by Franz Liszt for 2 pianos, G.653 1850 or 1851 (Joseffy—GS; UE; Cranz) 22 min. Liszt took a great deal of interest in this piece; both the piano writing and the form of the work show a strong affinity with his own aims. He did not change the formal construction of Schubert's work, but only enriched the transition to the second subject with a cadenza. The form is that of a sonata in four movements played without pause: Allegro con fuoco—Adagio—Presto—Allegro. The slow movement is a series of variations on Schubert's own song "Der Wanderer," Op. 4/1 (D.493) 1816. M-D to D.

Adolf Schultz-Evler (1852–1905) Poland
See Strauss, Johann Jr.

Clara Schumann (1819–1896) Germany
Why Will You Others Ask?, trans. by Franz Liszt (Musica Obscura) 2 pp. Song text appears over the piano part. Following; simple harmonies. Int. to M-D.
See also Schumann, R.

George Alfred Schumann (1865–1952) Germany
See Beethoven

Robert Schumann (1810–1856) Germany
Andante and Variations, Op. 46 1843, trans. by the composer for 2 pianos (CFP; GS; Durand; Heugel; Augener) 33 pp., 12½ min. One of the great works for two pianos, although it is even more effective in its original version for two pianos, two cellos, and horn. The variations are not numbered and are to be played without interruption, yet they are well defined and easily distinguished. They frequently go far afield from the theme. Especially lovely is the quiet coda, which conveys the impression of an evaporating cloud of sound. This work established a prototype for Romantic feeling and could well serve, beyond the purely musical realm, as a striking example of the artistic ideals of its period. Ernest Hutcheson calls it "beautiful, pianistically grateful, and universally popular." The premiere was given by Clara Schumann and Felix Mendelssohn in the Leipzig Gewandhaus on August 19, 1843. M-D.

Concerto in a, Op. 54, first movement. In *Concert Transcriptions of Favorite Concertos,* by Percy Grainger (GS 1947; IU) 25 pp. One of a series of four transcriptions of single concerto movements. They are mainly arrangements of principal themes and episodes. Includes many directions such as "linger," "top notes to the fore," "melody to the fore," and "cut to (sign) if you wish." Some parts of the original simplified. Grainger knew these transcriptions of well-known concertos were a way of bringing fine music to lay music lovers. The footnotes are a mine of pianistic information. M-D.

Du bist wie ein Blume, Op. 25/24, trans. by Leopold Godowsky (CF 1921). Fluent, lovely. M-D.

Six Etudes in the form of a Canon, Op. 85, trans. for 2 pianos by Claude Debussy (IMC 1952; Jobert) 23 pp. Excellent examples of Debussy's art of transcription. M-D.

Introduction and Allegro appassionato, Op. 92. *Concert allegro* with introduction, arr. for 2 pianos by Harold Bauer (GS 41249 1946) 96 pp. Most of the arranging is in the second piano part. M-D.

Melody and *Little Study,* from *Album for the Young; Melancholy,* Op. 99/7, trans. for left hand by Paul Wittgenstein. In *School for the Left Hand,* vol. 3: *Transcriptions* (UE 12329). Carried out well; effective. Int. to M-D.

Quartet in E-flat, Op. 47 1842, arr. for duet by Johannes Brahms (Fürstner 1887; LC). This Piano Quartet is one of the most important works in the literature for its original combination. Brahms was obviously interested in the equal division of interest between the four instruments; in this arrangement he manages mainly to assign one instrumental part to each hand. Effective but a little awkward at places. Unsurpassed in Romantic fervor and beauty. D.

Sketches for the Pedal Piano, Op. 58 1845, arr. by Wilfried Kassebaum (Heinrichshofen N4106) 19 pp. The pedal piano, a piano fitted with a pedalboard, attracted a limited amount of interest during the nineteenth century (Charles Henri Alkan and Charles Gounod also wrote for the instrument) before disappearing entirely from the musical scene. This explains why these four pieces have gradually fallen into oblivion. Clara Schumann arranged some of these pieces for two hands in 1896. This edition dispenses with unessential octave doublings. Kassebaum has reproduced, as closely as possible, the tonal concept of the original version while keeping the musical texture within the normal stretch of the hands. M-D.

Variations on a Theme by Schumann, by Johannes Brahms, Op. 23 1861, arr. by Theodore Kirchner (Goebels—Schott 09735 1982) 23 pp., 15 min. Originally written for duet. This arrangement for solo piano is exquisite. The theme was composed by Schumann during the night of February 17, 1854 and was his last musical thought. He claimed to have heard it from the spirits of Schubert and Mendelssohn. The piece is like a requiem. The theme is worked out differently in each variation; and the final variation, bathed in sadness and resignation, is like a death march. Ends with the return of the theme accompanied by poignant harmonies. M-D.

Widmung (Dedication) and *Frühlingsnacht* (Spring Night), trans. by Franz Liszt,

G.566 and G.545. In collection *Twenty Transcriptions by Franz Liszt* (OD). Liszt leaves the melodic content unchanged in *Widmung*. M-D. A much simpler setting of *Widmung* :s in *At the Piano with Liszt* (Alfred). Int.

Eduard Schütt (1856–1933) Austria, born Russia
See Meyerbeer; Strauss, Johann Jr.

Silvio Scionti (1882–1973) Italy
See Bach, J. S.; Rubinstein; Smith

Cyril Scott (1879–1970) Great Britain
Danse Nègre Op. 58/5, trans. for 2 pianos by the composer (Elkin 1935; LC) 13 pp. *Molto vivace,* rhythmic, and flowing. More effective than the original. M-D.
Lotus Land, arr. for two pianos by the composer (Elkin 1948; LC) 8 pp. Dreamy and limpid. M-D.
Two Pieces from Impressions from the Jungle Book (Rudyard Kipling), trans. for 2 pianos by the composer (Schott 2647 1928; LC) 16 pp., 6 min. *The Jungle:* Adagio. *Dance of the Elephants:* Allegro. Clever and effective. M-D.
See also Bach, J. S.

Blanche Selva (1884–1942) France
See Franck; d'Indy

Giovanni Sgambati (1841–1914) Italy
Sgambati was a pupil of Liszt's and a friend of Wagner's. He was head of the Accademia di Santa Cecilia in Rome.
See Gluck

Rodion Shchedrin (1932–   ) USSR
See Glinka

Vassarion Shebalin (1902–1963) USSR
See Glinka

Shefter (–   )
See Rimsky-Korsakov

Dmitri Shostakovich (1906–1975) USSR
Dance, from *The Golden Age* ballet, concert transcription by György Sándor (Am-Rus Music Corp. 1942; LC) 6 pp. Dry, brittle; exploits upper register at opening, glissandos, large skips in left hand; colossal ending. M-D to D.
Festive Overture, arr. by the composer for 2 pianos, Op. 96 (K) 32 pp. Full of sarcasm, pastiche, and grotesque naturalism. Octotonic, tremolos, wide dynamic range. Int. to M-D.
Polka, from *The Golden Age* ballet, arr. for 2 pianos by Pierre Luboshutz (JF 1941; LC) 9 pp. Most appealing. M-D.

————. Arr. for 2 pianos by Phyllis Gunther (Belwin-Mills 1975; LC) 8 pp. Much easier than the Luboshutz version. Int. to M-D.

Prelude and Fugue in D-flat, Op. 87/15, arr. for 2 pianos by the composer (USSR) 10 pp. *Allegretto.* Highly effective. M-D.

Presto Scene, from the opera *Lady Macbeth of Mtsensk,* arr. by Frederick Block (EBM 1943; LC) 6 pp. Many broken octaves; exploits extremes of the keyboard. M-D.

Tarantella, arr. for 2 pianos by the composer (Sikorski 1964; USSR) 11 pp. From the film *The Gadfly* of 1955. *Presto,* a few changing keys but tonal; brilliant and effective. M-D.

Waltz, Op. 30, from the film *Golden Mountains,* trans. for 2 pianos by Pierre Luboshutz (Leeds 1948; LC) 16 pp. Dashing, brilliant ending. M-D.

See also Glinka

Jean Sibelius (1865–1957) Finland

Belsazar, Op. 51, from suite for small orchestra, trans. by the composer (Schlesinger 1907; LC) 14 pp. Oriental Procession; Solitude; Night Music; Khadra's Dance. Exploits lower register of the keyboard; lovely tunes; colorful. Int. to M-D.

Karelia Suite, Op. 11, originally for orchestra, arr. by Otto Taubmann (Br&H 2236) 19 pp. Intermezzo: tremolo, exploits one main rhythm; large span required. Ballade: lyric, long pedals, tremolo. Alla marcia: repeated syncopated notes and chords. M-D.

Theme from "Finlandia," originally for orchestra, arr. for duet by Chester Wallis (BMC; LC) 7 pp. Secundo requires good dynamic control so as not to swamp Primo. Otherwise very usable. Int.

Valse Triste, Op. 44, arr. by the composer (Alfred; Br&H 2224 1904) 6 pp. This piece comes from *Kuolema* (Death), the incidental music to a drama written by the composer's gifted brother-in-law, Arvid Jarnefelt. Includes many pedal marks and interpretive directions. One of Sibelius's most popular compositions. Int. to M-D.

————. Arr. for duet by Chester Wallis (BMC; LC) 7 pp. A workable arrangement of a charming piece. Int.

Alexander Siloti (1863–1945) USA, born Russia

Siloti entered the Moscow Conservatory at the age of 12 and studied with, among others, Tchaikowsky. When he was 20 he studied with Liszt, and he carried the "grand manner" into the twentieth century. In 1922 he settled in the USA and taught at The Juilliard School until his retirement in 1942. He transcribed numerous works, especially those of Bach.

See Bach, J. S.; Glazounoff; Gluck; Liadoff; Rachmaninoff, Rimsky-Korsakov; Saint-Saëns; Songs, Russian; Strauss, Johann Jr.

See: Benning Dexter, "Remembering Siloti, a Russian Star," AMT 38/5 (April–May 1989):18–21.

Francisco Manuel da Silva (1791–1865) Brazil

Grande Fantaisie Triomphale sur l'Hymne National Brésilien, arr. by Louis
Moreau Gottschalk (Arno Press) 21 pp. (Da Silva composed the Brazilian
national anthem in 1831.) This grandiose piece opens with a *maestoso*
introduction. The main tune goes through many transformations, utilizing
numerous Lisztian pianistic techniques. One section simulates the roll of
drums. The *ossias* Gottschalk used to play are more difficult than the
normal score. Glitters all over! Gottschalk mentioned this piece in one of his
letters: "My fantaisie on the national anthem of Brazil, of course, pleased
the emperor, and tickled the national pride of my public. Every time I
appear I must play it" (quoted in Gilbert Chase, *America's Music* [New
York: McGraw-Hill, 1955], p. 320).

Homer Simmons (1900–   ) USA

Phantasmania 1923–24, originally for orchestra, trans. by the composer for 2
pianos (GS) 17 min. Jazz influence; fluctuating tempos. A fun piece but not
easy. M-D.

See also Songs, American

Christian Sinding (1856–1941) Norway

Suite, Op. 35, trans. for duet by the composer (CFP 1896; LC) 43 pp. Tempo di
marcia; Andante funebre; Allegretto; Finale. An effective set; layout for the
medium is clever and works well. M-D.

Leo Smit (1921–   ) USA
See Bernstein

John Stafford Smith (1750–1836) Great Britain
The ascription of the music to J. S. Smith is doubtful.

The Star-Spangled Banner, piano version by Josef Hofmann (CF 1918; LC)
2 pp. *Maestoso;* in C, with full chords. Includes pedaling. *Molto rit e cresc.*
at end. M-D.

————. Arr. for 2 pianos by Silvio Scionti (OD 1942; LC) 3 pp. It works! M-D.

————. Concert version by Leopold Godowsky (GS 1921). Except for the
opening phrase, this is the same as the "Epilogue" to No. 30 of Godowsky's
Triakontameron suite. M-D.

Raymond Songayllo (1930–   ) USA
See Berlioz

SONGS

This section includes folk songs, national songs, patriotic songs, work songs,
and chorales.

American

An American Hiking Tune (Arkansas Traveler), trans. by Duncan Stearns (Willis
1987) 9 pp. Moves over keyboard, glissandi, syncopation. Pedaled and
fingered. Colorful and effective. M-D.

Deep River, trans. for 2 pianos by Homer Simmons (Axelrod 1942; LC) 5 pp. A colorful and elegant setting of this moving American spiritual. M-D.

Frère Jacques' Concert, arr. for 2 pianos by Elizabeth Gest (JF 1956; AMC) 4 pp. One piano has the tune while the other decorates; fun for all. Int.

Improvisation on Children's Songs, by David Ward-Steinman (Lee Roberts 1967) 7 pp. Includes "Happy Birthday" (two settings); "Twinkle, Twinkle Little Star," and "Frère Jacques." MC. Int.

"My Little Mohee"; "Green Beds"; "The Story of the Bee." American folk tunes arr. for 2 pianos by John Jacob Niles (GS 1947; LC). Published separately. Attractive and well worked out. Int.

Paraphrase on "Three Blind Mice," arr. for 2 pianos by Elizabeth Gest (EV 1939) 7 pp. Attractive, clever, continuous variation treatment, *pp* closing. Int. to M-D.

Square Set, by Herbert Heufrecht, originally for string orchestra, arr. for 2 pianos by the composer (AMP 1972). Reel; Clog Dance; Jig Time. Composed as a result of Haufrecht's travel to the Catskill Mountains. Folk tunes include "Ta-ra-ra-Boom De Ay" and "Wilson's Clog." The I and V chords in "Jig Time" simulate the push and pull of an accordion. Light-hearted writing. M-D.

They All Sang Yankee Doodle, trans. by Dave Brubeck (AMP 1976) 39 pp. In this a set of variations on "Yankee Doodle," the tune is interwoven with other folk and national melodies for a musical collage. Brubeck explains his approach to this piece in "Composer's Notes." Exploits many pianistic devices, MC. M-D.

See also Dahl

Argentinian

Aires Criollos, arr. by Julian Aguirre (Ric 1953) 7 pp. Three short contrasting pieces using traditional Latin American tunes, rhythms, and harmonies. Int.

2 Books of Argentine National Airs, arr. by Julian Aguirre (Ric). Book I: Op. 17, 5 Tristes. Book II: Op. 36, 5 Canciones. Unusual rhythms and haunting melodies. M-D.

Chilean

12 Tonadas, based on popular Chilean tunes and arr. by P. Humberto Allende (Sal 1918–22). Short pieces that go through a circle of major and minor keys. Each piece begins in a minor key, then goes to the parallel major in a faster tempo. Some of the finest piano music inspired by folk music of the region. Int. to M-D.

See also Grainger

English

The Bailiff's Daughter, trans. for 2 pianos by Anis Fuleihan (CF 1957; LC) 8 pp. A charming work based on an English ballad. M-D.

Elegy No. 4, "Turandots Frauengemach" (The Apartments of Turandot), based on "Greensleeves," trans. by Ferruccio Busoni (Br&H; in collection *En-*

cores of Great Pianists, Lowenthal—GS). Busoni used this melody, think-
ing it was an oriental tune, in his opera *Turandot.* G major is established,
then "Greensleeves" is heard in E minor, and the piece closes on an abrupt E
major chord. The dynamics are restrained, and the melody is surrounded
with light staccato decorations, which also help blur the tonality with notes
distant from the expected harmony. So the work is kind of a fantasy on
"Greensleeves." Olga Samaroff played this piece. M-D.

God Save the Queen, paraphrase by Franz Liszt, G.235 1841 (Hin c.1953). Liszt
hints at the theme in the introduction and then presents it twice, first
pianissimo and then with a great deal of bravura. There is a fanfare-like
cadenza, and the closing bombastic pages bring out the theme in various
ways. M-D to D.

Green Bushes (Passacaglia), by Percy Grainger, trans. by the composer for 2
pianos, 6 hands (Scott 3923 1923). From an orchestral work based on an old
English folk song. Piano I is played by one pianist, Piano II by two. Clever
and fun. Int. to M-D.

In a Nutshell, suite, trans. for 2 pianos by Percy Grainger (GS 1916). Arrival
platform humlet; Gay but wistful; Pastoral; The Gum-Suckers March. Int.
to M-D.

Lincolnshire Posy, originally for military band, arr. for 2 pianos by Percy
Grainger (Schott 1940; LC) 28 pp. Includes the folk songs "Dublin Bay,"
"Harkstow Grange," "Rufford Park Poachers," "The Brisk Young Sailor,"
"Lord Melbourne," "The Lost Lady Found." Delightful and exceedingly
pianistic for both players throughout. M-D.

Oh Dear! What Can the Matter Be?, arr. by Felix Swinstead (JWC 1931; LC)
7 pp. This delightful arrangement was often played by Myra Hess. Cleverly
juxtaposes keys of E-flat and E. M-D.

The Running Set, originally for orchestra, arr. for 2 pianos by Vally Lasker and
Helen Bidder (OUP 1936; LC) 20 pp. Founded on traditional dance tunes
"The 'Running Set' is a dance of British origin still performed in the
remoter parts of the USA" (from the score). Delectably delightful dances.
M-D.

Two Musical Relics of My Mother, trans. for 2 pianos by Percy Grainger (GS
1924; LC) 9 pp. Hermund the Evil: Faeroe Island dance. *As Sally Sat
a-Weeping.* English folk songs. M-D.

Finnish

Finnish Folk Tunes, arr. for duet by Ferruccio Busoni Op. 27 (CFP). Two
settings, artfully arranged, somewhat long. The first is mainly fast and
treats a number of tunes. The second serves as a slow movement but ends
with a *Vivace* finale. Light and witty treatment, some contrapuntal melodic
usage. M-D.

French

Fantasia con Variazioni sull'aria "Au clair de la lune," by Muzio Clementi, Op.
48 (Zanibon 1982) 16 pp. Facsimile of the 1821 edition published by

Clementi in London. The only fantasy Clementi composed; stresses the elements of a true fantasy. It consists of the well-known air followed by nine contrasting variations. Thematic material is treated freely by changing the harmonic and rhythmic elements. The short Presto at the end may be considered a coda. M-D.

La Cloche Sonne, arr. by Franz Liszt, G.238 1850, in collection *At the Piano with Liszt* (Alfred). Arrangement of an old French song (The Tolling Bell). Very atmospheric; open-fifth sonorities. Int.

Flourish, based on an old French soldier song, "Le Port Mahon est pris," arr. for 2 pianos by Harold Bauer (GS 1923; LC) 11 pp. Tremolo chords between hands, arpeggios, trills, glissando ending. Festive. M-D.

Mark My Alfred, by James Hewitt, in *A Collection of Early American Keyboard Music* (Willis). Printed in New York in 1808, based on the folk tune "Ah, vois dirai-je, Maman." Ten variations full of charm and humor. M-D.

Variations on a Nursery Rhyme, by Ernst von Dohnányi, Op. 25 1913, for piano and orchestra, arr. for 2 pianos by Stefan von Hodula (Simrock; SBTS) 65 pp., 22 min. Based on the old French song "Ah, Vous Dirai-Je, Maman." (In the United States it is known as the Alphabet Song.) After a mock-serious introduction the theme is stated by the piano in unison. Eleven clever variations follow, and the set is completed by a robust fugue and an altered restatement of the theme. The work is a clever assimilation of virtually every nineteenth-century musical trend. Dohnányi was one of the most famous pianists of his time, so it is not surprising to see this extremely effective and brilliant writing for the solo instrument. The whole work reflects the composer's dedication of this work "to the enjoyment of lovers of humor, and to the annoyance of others." M-D.

Variations on "Ah, vous dirai-je Maman," by J. C. F. Bach (in *At the Piano with the Sons of Bach*—Alfred 1990; Barbe—Hug 1966). Bach varied the melody slightly and developed eighteen contrasting variations. Int. to M-D.

————. Anonymous 1795 (F. Goebels—Schott 6916). Charming and clever. M-D.

————. *Variations for Agnes,* by Fred Coulter, in collection *12x11* (Hinson—Hinshaw 1979). Fresh approaches to this durable and delightful folk song. The style is intentionally simple (!), orally and technically. Careful attention should be paid to cross-phrasing between the voices. M-D.

12 Variations on Ah, vous dirai-je, Maman, K. 265 (300e), by W. A. Mozart 1774 (Alfred; CFP; Henle; IMC; Schott; VU). Uses scales, arpeggios, varying touches; one of Mozart's most charming sets. Int. to M-D.

Four Transcriptions on French National Themes, trans. by Franz Liszt. In collection *Franz Liszt—Rare and Familiar* (E. Mach—AMP 1982). "Vive Henri IV," G.239 1870–80: stately and marchlike; written in theme and variation form. M-D. "La Cloche Sonne" (The Bell has Struck), G.238 1843: short lyrical piece with bell-like open fifths in the accompaniment. Int. "La Marseillaise," G.237 1872: this demanding piece treats the French national hymn in virtuosic fashion. M-D. "Pastorale du Béarn," G.236 1844: variation treatment of simple flowing theme. M-D.

German

11 Chorales, arr. by Franz Liszt G.50, in Vol. 10 of the NLA, *Various Cyclical Works* II. At the end of the 1870s Liszt planned to make a collection of piano arrangements of sacred songs for Cardinal Gustav Hohenlohe-Schillingsfürst. These chorales are the only part of the project he completed. *Crux ave benedicta; Jesu Christe; Meine Seel' erhebt den Herrn; Nun danket alle Gott!; Nun ruhen all Wälder; O Haupt von Blut und Wunden; O Lamm Gottes!; O Traurigkeit; Vexilla Regis; Was Gott tut, das ist wohlgetan; Wer nur den lieben Gott lasst walten.* These arrangements are generally kept rather simple, with a few octaves in the left hand and full chords in the right hand. Int. to M-D.

Hungarian

Christmas Songs from Hungary, trans. by Halsey Stevens (ACA 1956) 5½ min. Nine songs; all short, two- or three-voice textures; modal; arrestingly attractive. Int. to M-D.

Two Improvisations on Hungarian Folk Songs, by Denes Agay (TP 1973) 7 pp., 4 min. The Peacock. Gipsy Tune: modal, the more fetching of the two, attractive. Int.

See also Brahms

Irish

Variations brilliantes sur "The Last Rose of Summer," by Henri Herz, Op. 159 (Musica Obscura) 8 pp. Introduction presents fragments of the theme of the Irish folk song before it is heard *Andantino expressivo.* Three variations and a finale of repeated notes, tremolos, and a glissando in thirds round out this set. M-D.

Fantasy on the "Last Rose of Summer," by Felix Mendelssohn, Op. 15 (Br&H; in *Mendelssohn Complete Works for Pianoforte Solo,* vol. I, Dover; in *Masters of the Piano Fantasy,* Alfred). The Irish folk song is not elaborated, but its simplicity is emphasized by other materials that contrast with it in tempo, mode, and figuration. To close the piece, rather than repeat the melody, Mendelssohn constructed an original *Andante* that reflects it in general melodic shape. M-D.

Recollections of Ireland, originally for piano and orchestra, trans. by Ignaz Moscheles, Op. 69 (Cramer 1827). This charming work uses much improvisation and is influenced by the form of many opera fantasies of the day. The three tunes used as the basis of the piece are "Groves of Blarney," "Garry Owen," and "St. Patrick's Day." A free introduction gives an idea of things to come; each tune is then heard and treated individually. A spirited finale pulls together all thematic fragments. M-D to D.

Israeli

Mosaics 1968, six piano pieces on Hebrew folk themes by Denes Agay (MCA) 21 pp., 12½ min. Five short pieces followed by a set of eleven variations over an eight-bar melody that progresses to a brilliant but not too demanding climax. Beautifully laid out for the piano. M-D.

Mexican

Bolero Modern, arr. for 2 pianos by Morton Gould (EBM 1938; LC) 12 pp. Based on Mexican Folk Song "Ay! Ay! Ay!" The bolero accompaniment is contained in Piano II, melody in full chords in Piano I. Gradual *crescendo* from beginning to end (Ravel influence?), works to large climax. Requires fine octave technique. M-D.

Russian

Abschied (Farewell) (Russian folk song), trans. by Franz Liszt, G.251 1885, in collection *Liszt Miniatures* (GS 1899). Based on an old Russian folk song, "The Steppe of Mozboksk," and dedicated to one of Liszt's pupils, Alexander Siloti, who probably gave Liszt the original song. Sparse, economical late style. Int.

Four Russian Folk Songs, from Op. 58, by Anatol Liadoff, trans. by Alexander Siloti (CFP 1336 1923) 10 pp. Legend of the Birds; "I Danced with a Mosquito"; Cradle Song; Dance. The original work was *Eight Russian Folk Songs* (1906) for orchestra, which included numerous arrangements of folk melodies. Highly developed sense of color and musical characterization, charming, an effective group. Int. to M-D.

50 Russian Folk Songs, harmonized and arr. for duet by Peter I. Tchaikowsky (Leeds 1949, LC) 59 pp. Tchaikowsky was always interested in folk material and incorporated many folk themes in his compositions. Some of the folk songs in this collection are well known, but many are less familiar. Students will find it excellent for ensemble practice. Easy to Int.

Scottish

Scottish Reel, trans. by Lionel Salter (Lengnick 1947; LC) 16 pp. Uses the tunes "Green Grow the Rashes," "Loch Rynach," "Sweet Molly," "Perth Assembly," "Colonel McBain," "Wind that Shakes the Barley," "Countess of Sutherland," "Pease Strae." "The nature of this piece demands that the tempo remain absolutely constant throughout" (from the score). Int.

Spanish

Castellana (Romansca on Spanish Themes), by Mary Howe, originally for 2 pianos and orchestra, arr. for 2 pianos by the composer (AMC) 42 pp. Sectionalized; Spanish rhythms and lush harmonies. M-D.

Three Spanish Folk Tunes, trans. by Mary Howe 1926 (BMC; AMC; LC) each 7 pp. Available separately. Habanera de cinna; Spanish Folk-Dance; Petenera (Folk Songs). Somewhat dated but contains a certain amount of charm. Int. to M-D.

Kaikhosru Shapurji Sorabji (1892–1988) Great Britain
See Chopin; Strauss, Johann Jr.

John Philip Sousa (1854–1932) USA
Sousa's Great Marches in Piano Transcription, trans. by the composer; selected,
   with an introduction by Lester Levy (Dover 1975) 111 pp. 24 marches,
   including some of the most famous: *The Stars and Stripes Forever; Semper
   Fidelis; The Washington Post; Manhattan Beach; The High School Cadets;*
   and *El Capitan.* Reproductions of the original sheet music. Int. to M-D.

Ludwig Spohr (1784–1859) Germany
Rose, Softly Blooming, trans. by Franz Liszt G.570 (Musica Obscura) 5 pp. A
   lovely romance with a few lyrical embellishments. Includes Liszt's pedaling. M-D.

Duncan Stearns (–   ), USA
See Songs, American; Rachmaninoff

Eric Steiner (–   ) USA
See Bach, J. S.

Halsey Stevens (1908–1988) USA
See Songs, Hungarian

Ronald Stevenson (1928–   ) Scotland
See Britten

Gregory Stone (–   ) USA
See Foster; Gershwin

Sherman Storr (–   ) USA
See Telemann

August Stradal (1860–1930) Czechoslavakia
See Bach, W. F.

Johann Strauss, Jr. (1825–1899) Austria
The Strauss dances offer ample themes that can easily be developed, extended,
transformed, or restructured. Because of their nature, these dances (mainly
waltzes) are bright and cheerful and allow the composer-pianist to indulge in
pianistic display without being criticized for destroying their original thematic
character. Johann, Jr., elevated the waltz to new heights of polish and witty
phrasing.
Artist's Life, Op. 316, trans. for 2 pianos by Abram Chasins (JF 1933; LC)
   28 pp. Virtuoso concert transcription. Every nook and cranny of the keyboard is investigated! Glittering. M-D to D.
The Bat, a fantasy on themes from *Die Fledermaus,* trans. for 2 pianos by Pierre
   Luboshutz (JF 1951; LC) 34 pp. A fun piece, but it requires superb
   technique and ensemble experience. M-D to D.

Blue Danube Waltz, trans. for 2 pianos by Christopher Le Fleming (JWC). M-D.

By the Beautiful Blue Danube, Concert Arabesque by Adolf Schulz-Evler (GS; CF). This effective transcription with its virtuoso encore writing shows off the technique of the performer and captures the mood of the original (for orchestra) in a completely different setting. D.

————. Freely adapted and arr. by Abram Chasins for 2 pianos (JF 1926; LC) 23 pp. Chasins works over the Schulz-Evler version and adds more to these four waltzes. Naive melodies set with dizzying chromatic harmony. This ingenious arrangement preserves the joyous moods of the original, but instead of imitating the richness of the orchestration, Chasins chooses the clearer, more sparkling sound of the pianos. Virtuoso treatment. M-D to D.

————. Paraphrase by Eduard Schütt (Musica Obscura) 17 pp. Quasi-improvisational virtuosic treatment. D.

Carnival de Vienne (Humoresque) on themes of Johann Strauss, trans. by Moriz Rosenthal (CF 1925) 21 pp. A pianistic jigsaw puzzle of themes. D.

Fantasia on Johann Strauss Waltzes Beautiful Blue Danube, Die Fledermaus (The Bat) and Joys of Life, arr. by Moriz Rosenthal (Schott 1930) 15 pp. Virtuosic, in the grand nineteenth-century transcription tradition! D.

Fantaisie sur les valses de Johann Strauss, trans. for 2 pianos by Alexandre Tansman (ESC 1964). This concert waltz is Impressionistic with Strauss melodies heard in rapid succession. M-D.

Fledermaus Fantasy, trans. for 2 pianos by Abram Chasins (OD 1927; SBTS) 28 pp. A brilliant treatment of the main themes. Fast harmonic rhythm, contrasting sections, glissandos, *Furioso* closing, delightful. Eminently pianistic. D.

"Fledermaus" Paraphrase, Concert Paraphrase on Airs from *Die Fledermaus,* by Stephen Kovacs (GS 1942; LC) 17 pp. Improvisatory introduction increases in dynamics and activity, leads to main theme *Allegro con brio.* Black key glissandos, tremolo chords between hands. *Furioso* coda. D.

Soirée de Vienne, Op. 56, paraphrase on waltz motives by J. Strauss, Jr., from *Die Fledermaus,* by Alfred Grünfeld (Bo&Bo 1927). These brilliant arrangements were very popular at one time. M-D to D.

Symphonische Metamorphosen on *Fledermaus,* by Leopold Godowsky (Cranz 1912; LC) 16 pp. Uses every "trick of the trade" in a phantasmogoric setting as only Godowsky could do! The original melodies and moods are expanded by polyphonic amplification, harmonic complexities, and virtuoso stunts. D.

Frühlingstimmen (Voices of Spring), trans. by Alfred Grünfeld (Bo&Bo 1927).

————. Trans. by Ignaz Friedman, Op. 410 (UE 1925) 20 pp. Brilliant transcription dedicated to Wilhelm Bachaus, who must have delighted audiences with the impressive technical command required for this piece. D.

————. Trans. by Eduard Schütt (Musica Obscura) 13 pp. Moves over entire keyboard, glissandos, *pp* ending. D.

Duo zu zwei Klavieren uber den Frühlingsstimmen—Walzer von Johann Strauss, by Hans Tornieporth (Schott 3711 1940; LC) 24 pp. A virtuoso concert transcription. M-D to D.

Geschichten aus dem Wiener-Wald (Tales of the Vienna Woods), Op. 325, paraphrase de concert, by Julie Rivé-King (Kunkel 1881; rev. ed., Shattinger 1902; LC) 19 pp. A very graceful and tasteful work. Cadenza, soaring arpeggios over the melody. D.

Tales from the Vienna Woods, trans. for 2 pianos by Christopher Le Fleming (JWC). Effective and not too display-oriented. M-D.

Morgenblätter (Morning Leaves), paraphrase by Eduard Schütt (Musica Obscura) 14 pp. Strong melodic themes; bright; keeps to the original character of the waltz. D.

Moto Perpetuo, arr. for 2 pianos by Rae Robertson (OUP 1950; LC) 15 pp. Should be "played with a light lilting rhythm, at the speed of a rather fast Polka" (from the score).

O schöner Mai (Oh, Beautiful May), paraphrase on waltz motives of Johann Strauss by Eduard Schütt (Musica Obscura) 10 pp. Dance music is used for virtuoso display. D.

Concert Paraphrase on the Wiener Blut Waltz, by Edwin Hughes (GS 1921; LC) 19 pp. Long introduction, arpeggio figuration, change of keys (C, F, D-flat, etc.). Fast alternation of octaves between hands in a scintilating, surging close. D.

Paraphrase on "Weiner Blut," by Dirk Schaefer (Alsbach 1929; LC) 15 pp. Chromatic, many brilliant passages, virtuosic. D.

Persischer Marsch, Op. 289, trans. by Alfred Grünfeld (Cranz).

Rosen aus dem Suden (Roses from the South), concert paraphrase by Eduard Schütt (Musica Obscura) 14 pp. The waltz theme is given just about every treatment possible; climactic conclusion. D.

Schatz Waltz (Treasure Waltz), trans. by Ernst von Dohnányi, in *Three Concert Transcriptions on Themes of Schubert, J. Strauss and Delibes* (Rozsavölgyi 1930). Contains much decoration and some "delicious" moments. D.

Symphonic Metamorphosis on Kunstlerleben (Artist's Life), Op. 316, arr. by Leopold Godowsky 1912 (PIC; Musica Obscura). The last word in terpsichorean counterpoint. The simple Strauss waltz is completely transformed, imprisoned in a labyrinth of horrendous complexities. Every aspect of piano playing is utilized with exquisite decadence. D.

Trois Valses-Caprices sur des Motifs de Johann Strauss, by Isidor Philipp (Heugel 1930; LC, No. 3 only) 7 pp. *Les Feuilles du Matin et La Chauvresouris; Aimer, Boire et Chanter; Le Beau Danube Bleu.* Uses four staves for some of the piece, repeated-note accompaniment, glissandos, *stringendo* coda. D.

————. Arr. for 2 pianos by A. Reitlinger (Heugel 1901; LC). Glitters. M-D.

Twelve Themes from Famous Waltzes, trans. by Alexander Siloti (CF).

3 Valses-Caprices d'après J. Strauss, trans. by Carl Tausig (Musica Obscura). *Nachtfalter; Man Lebt nur Einmal; Waldstimmen.* Sparkling concert arrangements. Also published separately. M-D to D. A second set includes two more *Valses Caprices* (Musica Obscura) 34 pp. D. These works are some of the earliest examples in the long line of concert paraphrases of Strauss waltzes that became so popular in the late nineteenth and early twentieth centuries.

Valses Caprices No. 2, *On ne vit qu'une fois,* arr. by Carl Tausig, rev. by Isidor Philipp (Heugel) 14 pp. Virtuosic figures, glissandos, lilting. M-D to D.

Valse Fantaisie—Homage to Johann Strauss, trans. by Kaikhosru Shapurji Sorabji 1925 (OUP) 15 min. A light-hearted, simultaneously loving and deprecating pastiche that explores and pays tribute to the waltz rhythms of Strauss. Dance melodies are encircled with exuberant decoration. Opening gossamer cadenza leads to a wild series of waltzes strung together in a cycle. Elegant thematic opening, decadence sets in, and by the end thematic elegance has become gauche and satirically clumsy. Ends *ffff* in seven registers (octaves). D.

Variations sur la Valse Charmante de Johann Strauss "Le Duc de Reichstadt," Op. 249, arr. by Carl Czerny (Musica Obscura) 17 pp. Straightforward theme, five variations, and Finale—Allegro molto. Concludes in a burst of brilliant figurations. M-D.

Wine, Woman, and Song, Caprice de Concert for piano after the Waltz of Johann Strauss, trans. by Isidor Phillip (GS 1938) 15 pp. Uses all the "tricks of the trade" in a virtuosic, but at times graceful, romp through this delicious tune. D.

Richard Strauss (1864–1949) Germany

Ramble on the Last Duet in Strauss's Rosenkavalier, trans. by Percy Grainger (Fürstner/GS 1928). Grainger never compromises the sumptuousness of the original; with clever use of the *sostenuto* pedal he brings to our ears the world of Strauss totally in terms of the Grainger sound. A fabulous *tour de force!* Perhaps the most fastidiously notated piano writing in all virtuoso literature. Contains extremely detailed pedaling (especially the *sostenuto* pedal) and meticulous instructions. D.

Serenade, Op. 17/2, originally a song, freely trans. for 2 pianos by Abram Chasins (JF 1938; LC) 11 pp. Light, *vivace,* very effective, *ppp* ending. M-D.

————. Trans. by Walter Gieseking (Fürstner). Beautifully effective. M-D.

————. Trans. by Leopold Godowsky (CF 1922). Also effective but more difficult than the Gieseking version. M-D.

Suite in B-flat, Op. 4 1883, for 13 brass instruments, arr. for duet by the composer (Fürstner, 1911; LC) 51 pp. Allegretto; Romanze; Introduction und Fuge. This version is most successful, especially the Romanze and the Fuge. M-D.

Igor Stravinsky (1882–1971) USA, born Russia

Agon 1957, originally a ballet, trans. for 2 pianos by the composer (Bo&H) 20 min. A difficult score in which seventeenth-century dance forms are passed through the Stravinsky filter and emerge purposely distorted and dissonant. *Agon* is also a pivotal work, being one of the first Stravinsky scores to contain elements of serial technique. The pianists are required to be more like traffic cops than emotionally responsive interpreters. D.

Circus Polka (composed for a young elephant), arr. for 2 pianos by Victor Babin (AMP 1943; LC) 12 pp. This version is more colorful and effective than the original. M-D.

Concerto in E-flat ("Dumbarton Oaks") 1937–38, reduced from original chamber orchestra instrumentation for 2 pianos by the composer (Schott 2791) 12 min. Tempo giusto; Allegretto; Con moto. Highly effective but this reduction never quite approximates the colorfulness of the original orchestration. Requires a dazzling account of the score with each melodic fragment carefully delineated. M-D to D.
See: Herbert Eimert, "Stravinsky's Dumbarton Oaks," *Melos*, 14/9 (July 1947):247.

The Firebird, trans. by Guido Agosti (Schott). Three movements only: Dance Infernal; Berceuse; Finale. Exciting, effective, very popular in the 1940s. M-D to D.

————. Trans. by Sam Raphling (Lyra Music). Sonorous and effective. D.

Madrid, from *Four Studies for Orchestra,* trans. for 2 pianos by Soulima Stravinsky (Br&H 1951; LC) 10 pp. Glissandos; works well. Requires large span. M-D.

Three Movements from Petrouchka, arr. for 2 pianos by Victor Babin (Bo&H 1953) 31 pp. Russian Dance; Petrouchka; The Shrove-tide Fair. Requires first-rate pianistic equipment plus ensemble experience. M-D to D.

Trois Mouvements de Petrouchka, trans. by the composer 1921 (Bo&H; IMC). Danse Russe; Chez Petrouchka; La Semaine grasse. Virtuoso paraphrases of three scenes from the ballet. Brilliant orchestral writing for the piano that requires prodigious stretches and glittering display. Highly effective and demanding. D.

Le Sacre du Printemps (The Rite of Spring) 1911–12, trans. for duet by the composer (Bo&H) 83 pp. This boiled-down reduction was made by Stravinsky before the orchestration was completed. He recommended that it be played on "two separate pianos," which made it much more exciting. On June 9, 1912 he played it with Debussy, who took the Secondo part. On the following November 5, Debussy wrote to Stravinsky: "Our reading at the piano of *Le Sacre du Printemps* is always in my mind. It haunts me like a beautiful dream, and I try in vain to reinvoke the terrific impression. That is why I wait for the stage performance like a greedy child impatient for promised sweets." The simpler the musical substance, the less well it comes off in this reduction. The more complex, rhythmically varied, richly colored passages come off brilliantly. Stravinsky knew exactly what he was doing in this piano(s) version, and most of it is thrillingly and surprisingly idiomatic. D.

———. Trans. by Sam Raphling (Lyra Music 1984). Efficient and effective. D.

———. Trans. by Vladimir Leyetchkiss (GS 48633) 58 pp. Remarkably faithful to original score; very little tremolo used. Large span required. D.

Scherzo à la russe 1944, trans. for 2 pianos by the composer (Schott 10646) 17 pp., 4 min. The orchestral version was created for Paul Whiteman's orchestra. Vigorous rhythms and nationalistic melodies, reminiscent of the dances in the ballet *Petrouchka*. Jazz ensemble, a *tour de force* in this two-piano version. M-D to D.

Septet 1953, reduction for 2 pianos by the composer (Bo&H) 24 pp., 11 min. (Untitled: Quarter note = 88); Passacaglia; Gigue. Makes use of the technique of preconceived tone rows but is not strictly dodecaphonic. Contains an amazing degree of thematic integration. This reduction is remarkably pianistic. M-D.

See: Erwin Stein, "Stravinsky's Septet," *Tempo* 31 (Spring 1954).

Tango, trans. for 2 pianos by Victor Babin (Mercury 1941; LC) 8 pp. This version is spread out nicely, and the parts fit together artistically. M-D.

Soulima Stravinsky (1910–   ) Switzerland
See Stravinsky, I.; Tchaikowsky

Joseph Strimer (1881–1962) USA, born Russia
See Tchaikowsky

George Templeton Strong (1856–1948) USA
Le Roi Arthur, Poème symphonique 1916, originally for orchestra, 2-piano reduction by the composer (Henn 1921) 57 pp. M-D.
See also Hassler

Benjamin Suchoff (1918–   ) USA
See Bartók

Carlos Surinach (1915–   ) Spain
Acrobats of God: Five Dances, trans. by the composer from his ballet of the same title (AMP) 12 min. Fanfare; Antique Dance; Bolero; Minuet; Spanish Galop. Rhythmic emphasis in the faster movements while the slower ones emphasize much embellishment in the melodic treatment. Int. to M-D.

Ottilie Sutro (1872–1970) USA
Ottilie and her sister Rose were an outstanding two-piano team.
See MacDowell

Georgi Sviridov (1915–   ) USSR
See Glinka

Felix Swinstead (1880–1959) Great Britain
See Songs, English

Theodor Szántó (1877–1934) Hungary
See Bach, J. S.

T

Gino Tagliapetra (1887–1954) Italy
See Bach, J. S.

Alexandre Tansman (1897–1988) Poland
See Strauss, Johann Jr.

Otto Taubmann (1859–1929) Germany
See Sibelius

Carl Tausig (1841–1871) Germany, born Poland
Tausig was one of Liszt's favorite students. He inherited his special talent for piano transcription from his father, Aloys Tausig, who studied with Thalberg.
Ungarishe Zigeunerweisen (Musica Obscura) 23 pp. An excellent paraphrase of gypsy tunes. Requires dazzling pianism. D.
See also Bach, J. S.; Moniuszko; Scarlatti; Schubert; Strauss, Johann Jr.; Wagner; Weber

Colin Taylor (–   ) Great Britain
See Liszt; Paganini

Peter I. Tchaikowsky (1840–1893) Russia
Andante Cantabile, from *Quartet* Op. 11, trans. by Karl Klindworth, (Musica Obscura) 6 pp. The beautiful melodies in this movement are carefully preserved in this highly effective transcription. Much *portato* usage. M-D.
Capriccio Italien Op. 45, originally for orchestra, arr. for duet by the composer (Jurgenson; LC) 41 pp. Tchaikowsky had a fine sense of what would "work" on the piano, and this version is extremely effective. M-D to D.
Chinese Dance, arr. for duet by Joseph Strimer (BMC 1953; LC) 5 pp. Delightful and in good taste. Int. to M-D.
Concerto in b-Flat, Op. 23, first movement, trans. by Percy Grainger. In *Concert Transcriptions of Favorite Concertos* (GS 1947; IU). Mainly an arrangement of the primary themes and episodes. M-D.
Dance of the Sugar Plum Fairy, arr. for duet by Joseph Stimer (BMC 1953; LC) 5 pp. Delightful and in good taste. Int. to M-D.
Excerpts from Sleeping Beauty, arr. for 2 pianos by Celius Dougherty (CF 1960; LC) 16 pp. Pas de Quatre; Fée d'argent; Oiseau bleu. Tasteful. M-D.
Lullaby, Op. 16, trans. by Sergei Rachmaninoff, in *Rachmaninoff—A Commemorative Collection* (Belwin-Mills) 4 min. Much syncopation, fabulous sonorities. This was Rachmaninoff's last work, completed on August 12, 1941. M-D.

Marche Militaire, originally for military band, arr. for duet by the composer (Nov 1894; LC) 15 pp. The trio is the most effective part. M-D.

Nutcracker Suite, Op. 71a, arr. for duet by Stepán Esipoff (Schott 1686, 1687; LC). Vol. I: Ouverture; Marche; Danse de la Fée-Dragée; Danse russe (Trepak). Vol. II: Danse arabe; Danse chinoise; Danse des mirlitons; Valse des fleurs. Excellent arrangements that work and sound well. Requires two first-rate pianists. M-D.

Paraphrase on Tchaikowsky's Flower Waltz from the *Nutcracker,* Op. 71, trans. by Percy Grainger (Forsyth 1905). Includes such Graingerisms as "harped" for *arpeggiando,* "louden lots" for *crescendo molto,* and "excel to presto," which is what Grainger did all his life! This pianistic show piece is a "recomposition" of a very familiar work. M-D.

Paraphrase de Concert from Tchaikowsky's "Eugen Onegin," trans. by Paul Pabst (Rahter) 11½ min. This is Pabst's most admired piece, and it is more than twice as long as Liszt's version. It appears to be modeled after Liszt's Waltz from *Faust.* Pabst's version concerns itself mainly with the well-known Waltz from Act II, with a reference to the opera's Prelude by way of introduction. The contrasting middle section cites Lensky's Act I declaration of love for Olga, which in turn encapsulates a fragment of Onegin's aria from the same act. A brilliant coda based on the Waltz concludes the work. D.

Polonaise from opera "Eugen Onegin," trans. by Franz Liszt, G.429 1880 (Paragon; in Collection *Piano Transcriptions from French and Italian Operas,* Dover). Transcribed by Liszt just months after the opera's premiere. Mainly a transcription of the glittering ball scene that opens Act III. "In his paraphrase Liszt follows Tchaikowsky in contrasting the brilliantly orchestrated outer sections with the more sensual, subdued tone of the middle portion" (Charles Suttoni, "Liszt's Operatic Fantasies and Transcriptions," *Journal of the American Liszt Society* VIII [December 1980]:12).
See: Barrie Jones, "Liszt and Eugen Onegin: Some Reflections on a Transcription," *The Liszt Society Journal* (Centenary Issue 1986):81–86.

Scherzo à la russe, Op. 1/1 1867, trans. for 2 pianos by Soulima Stravinsky (CFP 1988) 24 pp. The original solo piano piece seems to want orchestrating or transcribing. This transcription makes it much more exciting for both performers and listeners. M-D.

The Sleeping Beauty, ballet, Op. 66, trans. for duet by Sergei Rachmaninoff 1890 (Robert Forberg/P. Jürgenson) 53 pp. Includes five movements from the ballet. Rachmaninoff wrote this duet version under the supervision of Alexander Siloti, who made the first solo-piano transcription of the same five movements. M-D.

Symphonie Pathétique No. 6, Op. 74, arr. by the composer for duet (Forberg 1893?; LC) 97 pp. Very accurate when compared with the original. Remarkably effective. D.

Valse, from *Serenade for Strings,* Op. 48, trans, by Mario Castelnuovo-Tedesco for duet (Delkas 1945; LC) 13 pp. A graceful transcription of a charming piece. M-D.

Waltz, from *The Sleeping Beauty* ballet, trans. for duet by Ralph Berkowitz (EV 1941; LC) 11 pp. Delightful; fits the medium well. M-D.

Waltz from "Eugen Onegin," trans. for 2 pianos by Ralph Berkowitz (EV 1944; LC) 12 pp. Straightforward transcribing, usable. M-D.

See also Songs, Russian

Fritz Teichmann (–   ) Germany
See Grieg

Georg Philipp Telemann (1681–1767) Germany

Concerto No. 14 in g, trans. by J. S. Bach, BWV 985. Based on a violin concerto by Telemann. In J. S. Bach, *Complete Keyboard Transcriptions of Concertos by Baroque Composers* (Dover 1987). See Bach, J. S.

Fantasia on Themes by G. P. Telemann, arr. for 2 pianos by Victor Babin (EV 1950; LC) 16 pp. Babin imitates a style of composition suitable to the thematic material; the work is commendably free of harmonic anachronisms. M-D.

Fantasia in G Minor, in a setting for 2 pianos by Sherman Storr (Alacran Press, 695 Wrelton Dr., San Diego, CA 92109) 10 pp. Contains a preamble. Needs much *staccato* and *leggiero* touch to bring off. M-D.

Sigismond Thalberg (1812–1871) Austria, born Switzerland

Thalberg was one of the great piano titans of the nineteenth century. He concertized for approximately thirty years, and most of the prominent pianists of the time performed his works. Even though he was given the name of "old arpeggio" (because of his way of treating melodies between the thumbs with arpeggios accompanying in both hands), Thalberg was greatly admired by amateurs and professionals alike. His method of sustaining the melody by the pedal, while both hands roamed from one end of the keyboard to the other, was so unusual that audiences would stand up to see how it was accomplished. Thalberg capitalized on the popularity of opera during this time and drew crowds with his opera fantasies, paraphrases, and reminiscences. Liszt and Thalberg were the most accomplished composers of this genre, and these fantasies, etc., became works of art as well as vehicles for virtuosic display. Ernest Legouvé said: "Thalberg began slowly, quietly, calmly, but with a calm that thrilled. Under those notes so seemingly tranquil one felt the coming storm. Little by little the movement quickened, the expression became more accentuated, and by a series of gradual crescendos he held one breathless until a final explosion swept the audience with an emotion indescribable . . ." (quoted in James Huneker, *Franz Liszt* [New York: Charles Scribner's Sons, 1911]). Probably Thalberg's biggest problem as a composer was that even his finest operatic fantasies have little dramatic connection with the original opera and have a sameness from work to work. Thalberg was considered Liszt's only serious rival as a keyboard wizard. Except for two operas, Thalberg's entire output was for his own instrument, the piano—mostly fantasies, variations, "souvenirs," or caprices on operatic themes.

See Bellini; Benedict; Bishop; Donizetti; Hérold; Mozart; Meyerbeer; Pergolesi; Rossini; Schubert; Weber

See: Daniel L. Hitchcock, "Sigismund Thalberg—1812–1871," PQ 77 (Fall 1971):12–16.

Eric Thiman (1900–1975) Great Britain
See Haydn

Theodore Thomas (1835–1905) USA, born Germany
See Gounod

Virgil Thomson (1896–1989) USA

Thomson is the Peter Pan among American composers. As a debunker of artistic pomposity, he is the American counterpart of Erik Satie.

Synthetic Waltzes 1925, originally for piano duet, rev. for 2 pianos by the composer (EV 1948; AMC) 18 pp., 6 min. One of Thomson's most successful spoofs. A chain of waltzes in one continuous movement, in different keys, in a quirkish diatonic and eclectic Romantic style, kind of a Strauss pot-pourri. The waltzes are synthetic (exactly as the title says), funny, and good. They would add spice to a program. M-D.

Walking Song 1952, arr. for 2 pianos by Arthur Gold and Robert Fizdale (GS; LC) 7 pp. From music for the film *Tuesday in September*. Folk-song influence, "walking tempo," jaunty and casual, glissando, highly effective, quiet. Int.

Jon Thorarinsson (1917–   ) Iceland
See Hindemith

Michael Tippett (1905–   ) Great Britain
See Handel

Hans Tornieporth (–   ) Germany
See Strauss, Johann Jr.

Vlastimir Trajkovic (1947–   ) Yugoslavia

Duo, originally for piano and orchestra, arr. for 2 pianos by the composer (ESC 1979). A study in sudden contrasts, much use of pedal, many atonal histrionics, ends on an octotonic F spread over three octaves. Given the proper performers this could produce a powerful effect. Moderately avant-garde. D.

Joan Trimble (1915–   ) Great Britain
See Delius; Weinberger

U

Hermann Uhticke (–) Germany
See Hindemith

V

Leonard Van Camp (–   ) USA
See Brahms

Felix Van Dyck (–   )
See Beethoven

Camil Van Hulse (1897–   ) USA, born Belgium
See Clementi

Ralph Vaughan Williams (1872–1958) Great Britain
Fantasia on Greensleeves, originally for orchestra, arr. by Hubert Foss for duet
(OUP 1942) 8 pp. Lends itself well to this medium. More pianistic than
some of Vaughan Williams's original piano writing. Int. to M-D.

Jacob M. Velt (–   )
See Moszkowski

Giuseppe Verdi (1813–1901) Italy
Aida (Sacred Dance and Finale Duet), paraphrase by Franz Liszt, G.436 c.1879
(Paragon 1975; LC) 24 pp. One of Liszt's most effective works in this
medium; kind of a rhapsody on some of the most important themes from
Acts I and IV. Ends quietly, as does the opera. D.
Concert Paraphrase on the Quartet from Verdi's "Rigoletto," trans. by Franz
Liszt, G.434 1859 (Dover; Br&H; UE) 7 min. Based entirely on the famous
Act III quartet, *Bella figlia dell' amore.* Makes no attempt at either dramatic
summation or character study, but does simulate various orchestral effects.
M-D to D.
Rigoletto—Fantaisie Caprice, by Richard Hoffman (GS 1864; LC) 15 pp.
Flamboyant and virtuosic. D.
Rigoletto: Paraphrase, by Franz Liszt, G.434 1859 (Schott; Ric; GS; LC) 15 pp.
Preludio; Andante. A program staple for more than half a century. Eminent-
ly impressive. Based on the famous quartet from Act III. Climaxes high-
lighted with flashing cadenzas. The entire scene is summarized with pianistic sorcery of the greatest elegance, wit, and ingenuity. D.
Ernani: Paraphrase, by Franz Liszt G.431a (Paragon; LC). Brilliant setting
of a small section of the opera. Extended range, many octaves and
runs. D.

Miserere du Trovatore, paraphrase de concert, Op. 52, arr. by Louis M. Gottschalk (TP 1909; GS 1907; LC) 11 pp. Virtuosic; fluent octave technique required. D.

————. Trans. by Franz Liszt G.433. In collection *Franz Liszt—Piano Transcriptions from French and Italian Operas* (Dover). Based on scene from Act IV. Multi-voiced texture. M-D.

Réminiscences de S. Boccanegra, trans. by Franz Liszt G.438 (Musica Obscura) 18 pp. Fully half of this opera fantasy is original composition, though generated by melodic ideas from the opera. Liszt recomposes some of Verdi's harmonic detail and phrase structure. This piece is extravagantly successful. M-D to D.

Salve Maria de Jerusalem from the opera *I Lombardi,* trans. by Franz Liszt G.431 (Schott; LC) 7 pp. Many tremolo chords under melody, fluent left-hand figuration, coda diminishes to *ppp* at end. M-D to D.

Renaud de Vilbac (1829–1884) France
See Clementi

Heitor Villa-Lobos (1887–1959) Brazil

Amazonas (Brazilian Indian Poem) 1917, originally for orchestra, arr. by the composer (ESC 6675 1953) 24 pp. Sensual dance of the Joven Indian contains many glissandi, syncopated chords, bitonal writing, and tremolo full chords between alternating hands. Requires large span. D.

Moreninha (The Little Paper Doll), from *A Prole do Bebê* No. 1, arr. for 2 pianos by Arthur Whittemore and Jack Lowe (AMP 1943; LC) 8 pp. Clever and colorful. M-D.

The Little Train of the Caipira, from *Bachianas Brasileiras* No. 2, trans. for duet by Henry Levine (Franco Columbo, 1963; LC) 9 pp. A clever and attractive transcription; train whistle in small notes is optional throughout; measures numbered. Int. to M-D.

Antonio Vivaldi (ca. 1675–1741) Italy

Concerto No. 1 in D, Op. 3/9, trans. by J. S. Bach BWV 972.
Concerto No. 2 in G, Op. 7, Bk. 2, No. 2, trans. by J. S. Bach BWV 973.
Concerto No. 4 in g, Op. 4/6, trans. by J. S. Bach BWV 975.
Concerto No. 5 in C, Op. 3/12, trans. by J. S. Bach BWV 976.
Concerto No. 7 in F, Op. 3/3, trans. by J. S. Bach BWV 978.
Concerto No. 9 in G, Op. 4/1, trans. by J. S. Bach BWV 980.

These works are each based on a different violin concerto by Vivaldi. They are all in the collection J. S. Bach, *Complete Keyboard Transcriptions of Concertos by Baroque Composers* (Dover 1987). See Bach, J. S.

Max Vogrich (1852–1916) USA, born Transylvania
See Schubert

Otto Vrieslander (1880–1950) Switzerland, born Germany
See Bach, J. S.; Mozart

W

Richard Wagner (1813–1883) Germany

Am stillen Herd (By silent hearth), from *Die Meistersinger*, trans. by Franz Liszt G.448 (Br&H; CFP; UE). Liszt makes textural additions in the form of left-hand countermelodies during the first interlude, which comes to a thundering climax. He also adds some extensions but preserves the essence of the original aria. M-D.

Ballade, from the *Flying Dutchman*, trans. by Franz Liszt G.441 (Br&H; CFP; UE). Introduction derived from motives of the opera material; chordal support in first stanza; variation treatment of second stanza; closing has unusual modulations that help increase tension. Dramatic and grandoise. M-D.

Complete Piano Transcriptions from Wagner's operas, trans. by Franz Liszt (Dover 1981) 176 pp. Reprint of the Russian edition, published in association with the American Liszt Society. Contains all of Liszt's piano arrangements of Wagner's works, some of which are not available elsewhere. Many are really original pieces on familiar themes. Since Liszt was close to Wagner, one might expect some special insights in his arrangements of the music dramas, but except for the fantasy on themes from *Rienzi*, Liszt's Wagner is very conservative. Liszt was using his name and his skill to help present Wagner's work to a public that could only rarely hear the original. But even when he is playing it comparatively straight, Liszt, like any good artist, translates into the medium at hand. Neat little pianistic touches are everywhere, not to show off the pianist but to enhance the music and make it work. M-D to D.

See: Charles Suttoni, "Liszt's Operatic Fantasies and Transcriptions," JALS 8 (December 1980):3–14.

Elsa's Bridal Procession, from *Lohengrin*, Act II, Scene 4, trans. by Franz Liszt G.446/2. In *Twenty Transcriptions by Liszt* (OD). Well laid out for piano. Light and capricious, contains a few *ossias*, disappears into *ppp*. M-D.

The Entrance of the Guests to the Wartburg, from *Tannhäuser*, trans. by Franz Liszt for 2 pianos, G.445/1 (Kunkel 1898; LC) 23 pp. In Act II of the opera, the guests have come to attend the song contest, the grand prize of which will be Elizabeth's hand in marriage. Liszt cannot resist the interpolation midway of an exciting variant of his own invention. The work builds to a grand climax of pianistic fireworks. D. Trans. by Liszt for solo piano, G.455 (Br&H; LC).

Eine Faust-Ouverture, originally for orchestra, trans. for duet by the composer (Br&H; LC) 19 pp. Contains some tremolo; parts complement each other. M-D.

Festival and Bridal Song, from *Lohengrin,* trans. by Franz Liszt G.446. In Liszt, *Complete Piano Transcriptions from Wagner's Operas* (Dover). *Festival* is dazzling; it sets the mood for the wedding festivities of Lohengrin and Elsa and leads directly into the bridal chorus. *Festival* begins with a fanfare-like explosion of color, with the vigorous and rhythmic main theme heard against a shimmering background. Liszt adds an eight-bar introduction. M-D to D.

Isolde's Death, from *Tristan und Isolde,* trans. by Franz Liszt G.447 (Durand; LC) 10 pp. Highly emotional and chromatic; tremolo in left hand; fast full repeated chords in descending scales; *ppp* closing. Liszt faced a challenge here because the piano is mainly a percussive instrument, but the *Liebestod* contains no percussive elements and is loaded with surging *crescendos* on sustained chords. Therefore the *fortissimos* must seem like an overwhelming flood of sound and not like hammerblows. Liszt's transcription is so subtle that Wagner's rich, erotic masterpiece receives its due magic in superb pianistic fashion. M-D to D.

————. Trans. by Carl Tausig (Musica Obscura 1914) 19 pp. Includes vocal text. Much use of arpeggios, tremolos, and multiple textured layers of sonorities. D.

Isolde's Love Death, trans. for the left hand by Paul Wittgenstin, in collection *School for the Left Hand,* vol. 3: *Transcriptions* (UE 12329). Difficult but surprisingly effective in this version. D.

Meditation, from *Die Meistersinger,* Introduction to Act III, arr. by Carl Tausig, rev. and fingered by Clarence Adler (GS 1924; LC) 4 pp. Dotted lines indicate voice leading. M-D.

Die Meistersinger von Nürnberg—Vorspiel, trans. by Zoltán Kocsis (EMB). This piece poses very divergent problems for the transcriber, but Kocsis exploits many of the possibilities in Lisztian style and is very successful in creating an orchestral illusion. D.

O Thou Sublime, Sweet Evening Star, from *Tannhäuser,* Act III, Scene 2, trans. by Franz Liszt G.444 (1849). In *Twenty Transcriptions by Franz Liszt* (OD). Recitative and aria setting of text, followed by interlude and postlude. Beautifully set. M-D.

Parsifal. Solemn March to the Holy Grail 1882, trans. by Franz Liszt G.450. In *Complete Piano Transcriptions from Wagner's Operas* (Dover; Tagliapietra—Ric; LC). This unjustly neglected piece is based mainly on the ostinato bass and theme of the Holy Grail March from the end of Act I. These are intermingled with a great deal of improvisation as well as other themes from the opera. To give an impression of the bells used in the opera, Liszt makes very effective use of the pedal. M-D.

Quintet, from *Meistersinger,* trans. for the left hand by Paul Wittgenstein, in

School for the Left Hand, vol. 3: *Transcriptions* (UE 12329). Fluid writing, carefully fingered and pedaled, effective. M-D.

Siegfried Idyl 1870, originally for chamber orchestra, trans. by Heinrich Esser (Musica Obscura) 20 pp. Wagner wrote this piece as a present for his wife, Cosima, in commemoration of the birth of their son Siegfried. Contains the major themes from the then recently completed opera *Siegfried* together with an old German lullaby, "Schlaf, Kindchen." M-D.

Spinning Song (Spinnerlied), from *The Flying Dutchman* 1860, trans. by Franz Liszt G.440 (Br&H; CFP; UE; in collection *Twenty Transcriptions of Franz Liszt,* OD). Constant use of 16ths gives effect of spinning; recitative-like short part in mid-section; much *staccato* and *scherzando* usage. Every stanza allots a different form of accompaniment to the simple folksy tune; the Dutchman's horn call is heard between the stanzas. An excellent recital piece because of its charming finger display. M-D.

The Ride of the Walküre, trans. by Carl Tausig (Schott 073) 13 pp. Full of trills, arpeggios, and many fast alternating hand patterns. Virtuosic. D.

The Ride of the Valkyries, trans. by Ernest Hutcheson (TP 1920; LC) 16 pp. Olga Samaroff recorded this transcription for R.C.A. Victor. D.

Transcriptions sur les Opéras de Richard Wagner, trans. by Franz Liszt (Durand 1920; LC) 102 pp. *Rienzi:* "Santo spirito Cavaliere." *Flying Dutchman:* "Choeur des Fileuses." *Tannhäuser:* "Marche"; "Romance de L'Étoile"; "Pilgrim's Chorus." *Lohengrin:* "Elsa's Dream and Supplication"; "Religious March"; "Choeur des Fiancailles." *Tristan und Isolde:* "Isolde's Death."

Valhalla, from *Der Ring des Nibelungen,* trans. by Franz Liszt, G.449 1880, (Schott; CFP). This piano "tone poem" is based on motives from the four operas of the cycle. The motives, the Valhalla motive in particular, are pianistically ornamented. An exceptionally difficult and rich-sounding piano score of the opera. D.

Vorspiel (Introduction) to *Lohengrin,* trans. for duet by the composer (GS 1897; LC) 7 pp. A usable version. M-D.

Wedding March from *Lohengrin,* arr. by Ernst Pauer (GS) 7 pp. Serviceable; numerous arpeggios used for harmonic filler. M-D.

Chester Wallis (–)
See Sibelius

William Walton (1902–1983) Great Britain
Façade, second suite for orchestra, arr. for duet by the composer (OUP 1938; LC) 36. This version is delightful. M-D.

————. Arr. for 2 pianos by Herbert Merrill (OUP). More color and excitement in this version than in the duet. M-D to D.

Two Pieces from Henry V, music from the film, arr. for duet by the composer (OUP 1972; LC) 5 pp. Passacaglia—Death of Falstaff; Touch her soft lips and part. Lovely. Int.

David Ward-Steinman (1936–   ) USA
See Songs, American; Songs, French

Peter Warlock (1894–1930) Great Britain
Capriol—A Suite based on dance tunes from Arbeau's Orchésographie (1588),
    arr. for 2 pianos by Maurice Jacobson (Curwen 1947; LC) 26 pp., 9 min.
    Basse-Dance; Pavane; Tordion; Bransles; Pieds-en-l'air; Mattachins (Sword
    Dance). Archaic sounds, charming, wide dynamic range. M-D.
See also Delius

Vernon Warner (–   ) Great Britain
See Arensky

Donald Waxman (1925–   ) USA
See Bach, J. S.

Charles Webb (1933–   ) USA
See Bach, J. S.

Carl Maria von Weber (1786–1826) Germany
Choeur-Barcarolle, from *Oberon*, trans. by Charles Alkan (Musica Obscura).
    Rocking motion heightened by arpeggiated chords. Beautiful melody is
    featured. M-D.
Duett über Luetzows Wilde Jagd von Carl M. von Weber, Op. 108, trans. by
    Ferdinand Hiller (Schott 20450; LC; Oberlin Conservatory Library) 15 pp.
    A *Vivace* chromatic scalar introduction leads to the first main section,
    Allegro energico. Four other sections follow, each exploiting contrasting
    moods and figurations. Dated but fun to play. Int. to M-D.
Freischütz Studies, Op. 127, trans. by Stephen Heller (Br&H c.1872). Four
    etudes based on partial themes from the opera. Each etude is actually an
    original study with the motive as its basis. The first and fourth are based on
    motives from the scene in the Wolf's Glen. Heller integrated characteristics
    of the opera fantasy with familiar figures in the opera into original composi-
    tions. M-D.
    See: Charles Suttoni, "Piano and Opera," pp. 241–42.
Fantaisie on themes from Der Freischütz of Weber, trans. by Sigismond Thal-
    berg, Op. 57/2 (Br&H; SBTS) 15 pp. Themes are not developed but are
    arranged in logical order. M-D to D.
Invitation to the Dance, Op. 65, Contrapuntal arrangement by Leopold Godow-
    sky (Schlesinger 1905; LC). Intricate, tricky, and only for the most de-
    termined pianist. D.
————. Trans. by Carl Tausig (Musica Obscura) 20 pp. Brilliant and effusive
    writing until last ten bars; then ends *ppp*. D.
————. *Contrapuntal Paraphrase* for 2 pianos, trans. by Leopold Godowsky
    with an optional accompaniment of a third piano (CF 1922) 74 pp. Danger-
    ous unless played by the most experienced virtuosos. Melodious tunes are

contrapuntally developed. At one place three previously stated themes are combined above a conventional waltz accompaniment. D.

Momento Capriccioso, Op. 12, concert arrangement by Leopold Godowsky (Musica Obscura) 14 pp. Requires the fleetest fingers and much stamina. D.

Perpetuum Mobile, Rondo from *Sonata,* Op. 24, trans. by Leopold Godowsky (Musica Obscura) 17 pp. Concert arrangement. D.

Rondo, Finale from *Sonata* I, Op. 24, arr. by Johannes Brahms 1869 (Br&H; Ric; Simrock). Consists of an inversion of the parts for right and left hands; contains some awkward moments. M-D.

Scherzo du Trio, Op. 63, trans. by Charles Alkan (Musica Obscura) 4 pp. Fast double thirds and sixths; requires a good octave technique. M-D.

Anton von Webern (1883–1945) Austria
See Schoenberg

Jaromir Weinberger (1896–1967) Czechoslavakia
Polka, from *Schwanda, The Bagpiper,* arr. for duet by Joan Trimble (Br&H 1939; LC) 7 pp. A scintillating arrangement. Int. to M-D.

June Weybright (–   ) USA
See Kreisler

August Heinrich von Weyrauch (1788–?) Germany
See Liszt

Maurice Whitney (1909–   ) USA
See Gershwin

Arthur Whittemore (–   ) USA
See Morgenstern; Villa Lobos

Paul Wittgenstein (1887–1961) Austria
Wittgenstein lost his right arm in World War I and decided to continue his concert career. He developed a remarkable technique for the left hand alone and commissioned numerous works for this medium. His own arrangements for left hand are well known.
See Bach, J. S.; Grieg; Haydn; Henselt; Mendelssohn; Meyerbeer; Mozart; Puccini; Schubert; Schumann, R.; Wagner

Z

Harold Zabrack (1929–   ) USA

Scherzo (Hommage à Prokofieff), originally for solo piano, arr. for 2 pianos by the composer (Bo&H). Rhythmic motives alternate between instruments, an exciting display piece. M-D.

Michael (von) Zadora (1882–1946) USA
See Chopin

Count Géza Zichy (1849–1924) Hungary
Zichy studied with Liszt and Volkmann. At the age of fourteen he lost his right arm in a hunting accident. He developed his left-hand technique to the point of virtuosity and made arrangements and composed pieces for the left hand.

Valse d'Adèle for Left Hand, trans. by Franz Liszt for 2 hands, G.456 1877 (Ric). Contains both the original piece and Liszt's transcription. Provides an interesting comparison and quickly lets the performer see the scope of Liszt's transcription ability. M-D.
See also Bach, J. S.

Bernd A. Zimmermann (1918–1970) Germany
Zimmermann combined influences from many different fields in his compositions and used the collage technique.

Monologue (Hommage à Claude Debussy) 1960–64, originally for 2 pianos and orchestra, reduction for 2 pianos by the composer (Schott 5427) 17 min. Seven serial sections. Despite its title, this piece is a dialogue, not only between the pianists but also between fragments of music, old and new. Integrates collage techniques and fragments from *Jeux* of Debussy, the Bach chorale prelude *Wachet auf, ruft uns die Stimme,* Mozart, and Gregorian chant. Fragmentation; extreme eclecticism. M-D to D.

Domenico Zipoli (1688–1726) Italy

Pastorale in C, originally for organ or harpsichord, trans. by Béla Bartók (CF 1930; LC) 5 pp. Opening *Andantino* leads to an *Allegro;* opening idea and mood return. Effective and highly pianistic. M-D.

Toccata 1716, originally for organ arr. by Alberto Ginastera (Bo&H 19950 1973) 10 pp. In the Busoni transcription style; many octaves, fast-moving chords, full resources of the instrument used, enormous climactic ending. M-D to D.

Bibliography

Ash, Philip R. "Technique of Piano Transcribing, 1800–1954." DMA diss., University of Rochester, Eastman School of Music, 1955.

Bach, Carl Philip Emanuel. *Essays on the True Art of Playing Keyboard Instruments* (1758). Trans. and ed. by William J. Mitchell. New York, 1949.

Bellak, Richard Charles. "Compositional Technique in the Transcriptions of Franz Liszt." Diss., University of Pennsylvania, 1976.

Berlioz, Hector. *Memoirs* (1870). Trans. by Rachel and Eleanor Holmes. Annotated by Ernest Newman. New York, 1932.

Bie, Oskar. *Das Klavier und seine Meister*. Munich, 1898. Trans. by E. E. Kellett and E. W. Naylor as *A History of the Pianoforte and Pianoforte Players*. London, 1899.

Briskier, Arthur. *A New Approach to Piano Transcriptions and Interpretation of Johann Sebastian Bach's Music*. New York, 1958. This is more or less a reprint of his article "Piano Transcriptions of J. S. Bach," MR 15/3 (August 1954):191–202.

Busoni, Ferruccio. *The Essence of Music and Other Papers* (1907–22). Trans. by Rosamond Ley. New York, 1957.

Brown, Maurice J. E. *Chopin: An Index of His Works in Chronological Order*. London, 1960; reprint, 1972.

Chopin, Fryderyk. *Selected correspondence*. Trans. and ed. by Arthur Hedley. London, 1962.

Closson, Ernest. *History of the Piano*. Trans. by Delano Ames. London, 1947.

Cory, William M. "Franz Liszt's 'Symphonies de Beethoven': Partitions de Piano." Diss., University of Texas, 1981.

Crockett, Barbara. "Liszt's Opera Transcriptions for Piano." Diss., University of Illinois, 1968.

Czerny, Carl. *Complete Theoretical and Practical Piano-Forte School,* Op. 500. Trans. by J. A. Hamilton. 3 vols. London, 1839.

———. "Recollections from My Life" (1842). Trans. by Ernest Sanders. *The Musical Quarterly,* XLII (1956):302–17.

Dale, Kathleen. "The Three C's; Pioneers of Pianoforte Playing." *The Music Review* VI (1945):138–48.

———. *Nineteenth Century Piano Music*. London, 1954.

Dannreuther, Edward. *The Romantic Period. The Oxford History of Music,* vol. VI. Oxford, 1905.

Dent, Edward J. *Ferruccio Busoni: A Biography*. Oxford, 1933. Reprint, 1966.

Dorgan, Peter P. "Franz Liszt and His Verdi Opera Transcriptions." Diss., Ohio State University, 1982.

Edwards, Robert L. "A Study of Selected Song Transcriptions of Franz Liszt." Diss., University of Oregon, 1982.

Einstein, Alfred. *Gluck.* Trans. by Eric Blom. London, 1936.

──────. *Mozart: His Character and Work.* Trans. by Arthur Mendel and Nathan Broder. New York, 1945.

Eitner, Robert. "Thalberg," in *Allgemeine Deutsche Biographie,* vol. 37. Leipzig, 1894.

Friedheim, Arthur. *Life and Liszt: The Recollections of a Concert Pianist.* Ed. by Theodore L. Bullock. New York, 1961.

Friedheim, Philip, "The Piano Transcriptions of Liszt." *Studies in Romanticism* I (1962):83–96.

Garden, Edward. *Balakirev: A Critical Study of His Life and Music.* New York, 1967.

George, James M. "Franz Liszt's Transcription of Schubert's Songs for Solo Pianoforte: A Study of Transcribing and Keyboard Techniques." Diss., University of Iowa, 1976.

Georgii, Walter. *Klaviermusik.* 3d ed. Zurich, 1956.

Gerig, Reginald. *Famous Pianists and Their Technique.* Bridgeport, CT, 1974.

Gibbs, Dan Paul. "A Background and Analysis of Selected Lieder and Opera Transcriptions of Franz Liszt." DMA diss., North Texas State University, 1980.

Gill, Dominic, ed. *The Book of the Piano.* Ithaca, 1981.

Godowsky, Leopold. "Apropos Transcriptions, Arrangements and Paraphrases," Preface to *Twelve Songs by Schubert.* New York: G. Schirmer, 1927.

Goertzen, Valerie W. "The Piano Transcriptions of Johannes Brahms." Ph.D. diss., University of Illinois at Urbana-Champaign, 1987.

Graf, Max. *Composer and Critic: Two Hundred Years of Musical Criticism.* New York, 1946; reprint, 1971.

Grout, Donald Jay. *A Short History of Opera.* 2d ed. New York, 1965.

Hagan, Dorothy Vainus. "French Musical Criticism between the Revolutions (1830–1848)." Diss., University of Illinois, 1965.

Hanks, Sarah E. "The German Unaccompanied Keyboard Concerto in the Early Eighteenth Century Including Works of Walther, Bach, and Their Contemporaries." Diss., University of Iowa, 1972. Bach's arranging techniques in BWV 596, 972, 987, and 592A are of special interest.

Hinson, Maurice. *Guide to the Pianist's Repertoire.* Bloomington, 1973. 2d, rev. and enl. ed., 1987.

──────. *Music for More than One Piano.* Bloomington, 1983.

Hoerée, Arthur. "J.-S. Bach, ses transcripteurs, ses interprètes, ses auditeurs." *Revue Musicale* 131 (December 1932):72–79.

Howard, Leslie. "The Keyboard Music" [of Percy Grainger]. *Studies in Music* XVI (1982):62–68.

Howard-Jones, Evlyn. "Arrangements and Transcriptions." ML 16/4 (October 1935): 305–11.

Hummel, Johann Nepomuk. *A Complete Theoretical and Practical Course of Instruction on the Art of Playing the Piano Forte*. 3 vols. London, n.d. [ca.1828].

Hünten, Franz. *A Complete Book of Instruction for the Pianoforte*, Op. 60. Mainz, 1835.

Jones, Howard, E. "Arrangements and Transcriptions," M&L XVI (October 1935).

Keller, Hans. "Arrangement for or Against?" MT 110 (January 1969):22–25.

Kirby, F. E. *A Short History of Keyboard Music*. New York, 1966.

Ku, Hsiao-Hung. "Liszt's Schubert 'Lieder' Transcriptions, A Study of Liszt Pianistic Idioms in the Transcriptive Procedure." Diss., North Texas State University, 1983.

Kullak, Adolph. *The Aesthetics of Pianoforte-Playing*. Trans. by Dr. Th. Baker from the 3d Ger. ed., rev. and ed. by Dr. Hans Bischoff. New York, 1893.

Kullak, Franz. *Beethoven's Piano Playing*. New York, 1901; reprint, 1973.

Lenz, Wilhelm von. *The Great Piano Virtuosos of Our Time*. Trans. by M. R. Baker. New York, 1899; reprint, 1972.

Locks, Arthur Ware. *Music and the Romantic Movement in France*. London, 1920.

Loesser, Arthur. *Men, Women and Pianos: A Social History*. New York, 1954.

Mendelssohn, Felix. *Letters of Felix Mendelssohn to Ignaz and Charlotte Moscheles*. Trans. and ed. by Felix Moscheles. London, 1888.

―――. *Letters*. Ed. by G. Seldon-Goth. New York, 1945.

Middleton, Roeboyd Hugh, Jr. "Three Perspectives of the Art of Ferruccio Busoni as Exemplified by the 'Toccata,' 'Carmen Fantasy,' and Transcription of Liszt's 'Mephisto Waltz'." DMA diss., North Texas State University, 1981.

Milinowsky, Marta. *Teresa Carreño*. New Haven, 1940.

Moldenhauer, Hans. *Duo-Pianism*. Chicago, 1950.

Molner, A. "Über Transkriptionen und Paraphrasen von Liszt," in *Liszt-Bartók: Report of the Second International Musicological Conference* (1961). Budapest, 1963. Pp. 227–32.

Moscheles, Ignaz. *Aus Moscheles Leben nach Briefen und Tagebüchern*. Hrag. von seiner Frau. 2 vols. Leipzig, 1872–73. Adapted to English by Arthur Duke Coleridge as *Life of Moscheles*. 2 vols. London, 1873.

―――. *Letters*. See Mendelssohn.

[Mozart, W. A.]. *The Letters of Mozart and His Family*. Trans. and ed. by Emily Anderson. 3 vols. London, 1936.

Musgrave, Michael. *The Music of Brahms*. London, 1985.

Nelson, Robert. *The Technique of Variation*. Berkeley, 1948.

Nettl, Paul. *Beethoven Encyclopedia*. New York, 1956.

The New Grove Dictionary of Music and Musicians. London, 1980.

Newman, William. S. *The Sonata since Beethoven*. 2d ed. New York, 1972.

————. *Beethoven on Beethoven—Playing His Piano Music His Way*. New York, 1988.

Niecke, Frederick. *Frederick Chopin as a Man and Musician*. 2d ed. 2 vols. London, 1890.

————. *Robert Schumann*. London, 1925.

Ostwald, Peter. *Schumann—The Inner Voices of a Musical Genius*. Boston, 1985.

Perkins, Marion L. "Changing Concept of Rhythm in the Romantic Era: A Study of Rhythmic Structure, Theory and Performance Practice Related to Piano Literature." Ph.D. diss., University of Southern California, 1961.

Plantinga, Leon. *Schumann as Critic*. New Haven, 1967.

————. "Clementi, Virtuosity and the 'German Manner'." *Journal of the American Musicological Society* XXV (1972):303–30.

Raabe, Peter. *Liszte Leben und Schaffen*. 2d ed. 2 vols. Tutzing, 1968.

Rawlins, Joseph T. "The Arrangement and Its Role in the Performer's Repertoire." AMT 34/4 (February 1984):26–28, 30.

Ringer, Alexander R. "Beethoven and the London Pianoforte School." *The Musical Quarterly* LVI (1970):742–58.

Rostand, Claude, *Liszt*. Trans. by John Victor. New York, 1972.

Rubinstein, Anton. *A Conversation on Music*. Trans. by Mrs. John P. Morgan. New York, 1892; reprint, 1970.

Sachs, Joel. "Hummel in England and France: A Study in the International Musical Life of the Early Nineteenth Century." Diss. Columbia University, 1968.

Saint-Saëns, Camille. *Outspoken Essays on Music*. Trans. by Fred Rockwell, London, 1922.

Salaman, Charles. "Pianists of the Past," *Blackwood's Edinburgh Magazine* CLXX (1901):307–30.

Sándor, György. "Are Transcriptions Dead?" *Music Journal* 27 (October 1969):22–23.

Slonimsky, Nicolas. *Music Since 1900*. 4th ed. New York, 1971.

Schoenberg, Arnold. *Style and Idea*. New York, 1975.

Schonberg, Harold. *The Great Pianists*. New York, 1963. 2d rev. and enl. ed., 1987.

————. *The Lives of the Great Composers*. New York, 1970.

Schumann, Robert. *Schriften über Musik und Musiker*. Ed. by Heinrich Simon. 3d ed. 3 vols. Leipzig, 1888. Trans. and ed. in part as *Music and Musicians: Essays and Criticisms,* by Fanny Raymond Ritter. 2 vols. London, n.d. [Prefaces dated 1876 and 1880].

Schwager, Myron. "Some Observations on Beethoven as an Arranger." MQ 54 (1969):80–93.

————. "A Fresh Look at Beethoven's Arrangements." M&L LIV (1973):142–60.

Searle, Humphrey. *The Music of Liszt*. 2d rev. ed. New York, 1966.

Siloti, Alexander. *My Memories of Liszt*. Auth. trans. Edinburgh, n.d.; reprint, JALS XV (June 1984).

Sitwell, Sacheverell. *Liszt*. Boston, 1934.

Smith, C. J. "Transcriptions?; or 'But is it idiomatic?' " *In Theory Only* 1 (July 1975):28–32.

Sorabji, Kaikhosru. "The Opera Fantasies of Liszt," in *Around Music*. London, 1932. Pp. 194–97.

Spink, G. W. "From Bach-Liszt to Bach-Busoni." MO 89 (July 1966):601.

Stasov, Vladimir. *Selected Essays on Music* (1847–1906). Trans. by Florence Jonas. New York, 1968.

Stevenson, Ronald. "Busoni and Mozart." *The Score* 13 (September 1955):25–38.

Suttoni, Charles. "Piano and Opera: A Study of the Piano Fantasies Written on Opera Themes in the Romantic Era." Ph.D. diss., New York University, 1973.

————. "Liszt's Operatic Fantasies and Transcriptions." JALS 8 (December 1980):3–14.

Tetley-Kardos, Richard. "Piano Transcriptions—Back for Good?" *Clavier* 25 (February 1986):18–19.

Thalberg, Sigismond. *L'Art du chant appliqué au piano*, Op. 70. Leipzig, 1853.

Tyson, Alan. *Thematic Catalogue of the Works of Muzio Clementi*. Tutzing, 1967.

Vallas, Leon. *César Franck*. Trans. by Hubert Foss. London, 1951.

Walker, Alan. "In Defense of Arrangements." *Piano Quarterly* 143 (Fall 1988):26, 28.

————, ed. *Franz Liszt: The Man and His Music*. London, 1970.

————, ed. *Robert Schumann: The Man and His Music*. London, 1972.

Wallace, Robin. *Beethoven's Critics: Aesthetic Dilemmas and Resolutions During the Composer's Lifetime*. Cambridge, 1986.

Warrack, John. *Carl Maria von Weber*. London, 1968.

Weinstock, Herbert. *Rossini: A Biography*. New York, 1968.

————. *Vincenzo Bellini: His Life and His Operas*. New York, 1971.

Weitzmann, Carl Friedrich. *A History of Pianoforte-Playing and Pianoforte Literature* (1863). Trans. by Dr. Th. Baker. New York, 1893.

Whittall, Arnold. *Romantic Music*. New York, 1987.

Wilde, David. "[Liszt's] Transcriptions for Piano," in Walker, ed., *Franz Liszt*. London, 1970. Pp. 168–201.

Index of Transcriptions for One Hand

See under:

Bach, C. P. E.

Bach, J. S.

Bellini

Chopin

Donizetti

Grieg

Haydn

Henselt

Liszt

Mendelssohn

Meyerbeer

Mozart

Puccini

Schubert

Schumann, R.

Wagner

MAURICE HINSON, Professor of Piano at The Southern Baptist Theological Seminary, appears frequently as lecturer and recitalist at piano teachers' conventions and workshops in the U.S. and abroad. He is the author of several books on piano literature, including *Guide to the Pianist's Repertoire*, now in its second edition.